The Peculiarities of
German History

The Peculiarities of German History

Bourgeois Society and Politics in Nineteenth-Century Germany

by

David Blackbourn and Geoff Eley

Oxford New York

OXFORD UNIVERSITY PRESS

Oxford University Press, Walton Street, Oxford OX2 6DP

Oxford New York
Athens Auckland Bangkok Bombay
Calcutta Cape Town Dar es Salaam Delhi
Florence Hong Kong Istanbul Karachi
Kuala Lumpur Madras Madrid Melbourne
Mexico City Nairobi Paris Singapore
Taipei Tokyo Toronto

and associated companies in
Berlin Ibadan

Oxford is a trade mark of Oxford University Press

Published in the United States by
Oxford University Press Inc., New York

First published 1984

British Library Cataloguing in Publication Data
Data available

Library of Congress Cataloging in Publication Data
Blackbourn, David, 1949- .
The peculiarities of German history.
Rev. and expanded translation of the authors' Mythen
deutscher Geschichtsschreibung.
Bibliography: p.
Includes index.
1. Germany—History—1789-1900—Historiography.
I. Eley, Geoff, 1949- . II. Title.
DD204.B5213 1984 943'07 84-10051
ISBN 0-19-873057-8

9 10 8

Printed in Great Britain
on acid-free paper by
J. W. Arrowsmith Ltd., Bristol

Preface

This book began as two independent papers which were presented before a number of audiences in Britain and Germany in the years after 1974. As we compared notes it became clearer that we were working in a similar direction. The idea of putting the two papers together took shape, and Dieter Groh suggested that we publish them in a new social history series he was then editing in the Federal Republic of Germany. The original German edition appeared in 1980 and was followed in 1983 by a Japanese edition. For the much revised and expanded English edition we have tried to take account of the intervening discussion. The Introduction (which is entirely new) and the revised versions of our two essays were written during 1982–3. The essays were separately authored and are intended to stand in their own right. The attentive reader will notice that there are differences between our two approaches, not only in style and substance, but also in content. Our common ground should nevertheless be equally obvious, and our close working relationship over many years has meant that it is sometimes difficult to remember with whom a particular idea originated. Despite differences of emphasis, we therefore hope that our two essays will be read as complementary. The Introduction was an exercise in transatlantic co-operation, drafted by one of us, redrafted by the other, and agreed by us both.

Works of this kind necessarily owe much to the previous labours of others. Our general intellectual debts are indicated in both text and footnotes. We are happy to acknowledge a more immediate debt to the many seminar audiences in Britain, the USA, and the Federal Republic of Germany which helped us to develop our ideas. Over the years we have also profited greatly from the suggestions and criticisms of colleagues and friends, amongst whom Richard Bessel, David Bien, Jane Caplan, David Crew, Dick Geary, Raymond Grew, Dieter Groh, Gareth Stedman Jones, Keith Nield, Hartmut Pogge von Strandmann, and Roman Szporluk deserve particular mention. Dieter Groh made an important contribution to an earlier version of the essays, and we also received valuable assistance with the German edition from Hartmut Pogge and Gerhard Wilke. Finally, we should like to thank the Oxford University Press, in particular Ivon Asquith, for the encouragement they have provided in the preparation of the present edition.

Ann Arbor
London
September 1983

Contents

Introduction

James Joll has written that, while all history may be contemporary history, some is more contemporary than others.[1] During the first drafting of this Introduction, the Prime Minister of Israel was likening Beirut to Berlin and Yasser Arafat to Hitler. At the same time, a domestic critic of Mr Begin described Israeli policy in the Lebanon as 'Judeo-Nazism'. That was the summer of 1982. But if the English edition of this book had been prepared at any time in recent years there would have been other echoes of the Third Reich to accompany it: neo-Nazi demonstrations in Germany or elsewhere, a recrudescence of anti-semitism, an act of genocide somewhere to which politicians or publicists applied the ready-made label 'Holocaust'. One legacy of what happened in Germany between 1933 and 1945 has been the establishment of a standard by which historical enormities are measured and outrage registered. That moral dimension is now one of the peculiarities of German history. It is something of which historians of modern Germany cannot entirely divest themselves, whether they wish to or not, whether they are German or not. The present book is not about the Holocaust or the Third Reich; it does not bear a swastika on its cover. But the original German edition of the book has come to form one part of a long-running and recently renewed debate about the recent German past, and by implication about the German present. One of the tasks this Introduction has to perform for the English reader is to explain how and why this is so.

The German edition of the book was published by Ullstein Verlag in November 1980.[2] Like the present edition it was made up of two extended and complementary essays, largely

---

[1] J. Joll, 'War Guilt 1914: A Continuing Controversy', in P. Kluke and P. Alter (eds.), *Aspekte der deutsch-britischen Beziehungen im Laufe der Jahrhunderte* (Stuttgart, 1978), p. 60.

[2] D. Blackbourn and G. Eley, *Mythen deutscher Geschichtsschreibung. Die gescheiterte bürgerliche Revolution von 1848* (Frankfurt/M., Berlin, Vienna, 1980).

written in 1979, but based on ideas which had, in the normal way of things, taken shape over a number of years. The book met a response which surprised us both in its liveliness and in its breadth. It received lengthy reviews in the quality press and in non-specialist weeklies, it was discussed in a radio broadcast, and its theme became the subject of panel discussions at a number of conferences, including the 1982 German Historical Conference in Münster.[3] This reception cannot be explained simply in terms of the particular merits or demerits of what we wrote. The book was concerned with historical and historiographical questions; the response raised issues with deeper moral and political, as well as historical, implications. This was true, above all, of the debate about the major theme of the book, in which we tried to address some critical questions to the notion of the peculiarity of German history—the idea of a German *Sonderweg* which diverged from the history of other (western) countries.

To set this idea and our own arguments in context, it may be useful to start by pointing out that this is a fairly venerable idea. It has certainly not been an invention of the period since 1945, although the predominantly negative assessment of German peculiarity has developed, for obvious reasons,

---

[3] See E. Straub, 'Woher aber kam der Nationalsozialismus? Englische Historiker über "Mythen deutscher Geschichtsschreibung" ', *Frankfurter Allgemeine Zeitung*, 9 Dec. 1980; and 'Die eingebildeten Leiden der Deutschen', ibid., 22 Jan. 1981 (*Feuilleton*); M. Stürmer, 'Wie es eigentlich nicht gewesen. Angelsächsische Revisionsversuche an der These vom deutschen Sonderweg', *Die Zeit*, 20 Feb. 1981 (*Politisches Buch*); K. Sontheimer, 'Deutschlands historischer Sonderweg', *Süddeutsche Zeitung*, 30-31 May 1981; H.-U. Wehler, ' "Deutscher Sonderweg" oder allgemeine Probleme des westlichen Kapitalismus? Zur Kritik einigen "Mythen deutscher Geschichtsschreibung" ', *Merkur*, 35.5 (1981), 478-82; H. A. Winkler, 'Der deutsche Sonderweg: Eine Nachlese', *Merkur*, 35.8 (1981), 793-804; H.-J. Puhle, 'Deutscher Sonderweg. Kontroverse um eine vermeintliche Legende', *Journal für Geschichte* 4 (1981), 44-5. The book was discussed in a broadcast on the Deutschland-Funk by Jürgen Kocka, under the title 'Der deutsche Sonderweg in der Diskussion'. We should like to thank Jürgen Kocka for making available a copy of his script. In addition to the discussion at the Münster *Historikertag* (9 Oct. 1982), chaired by Thomas Nipperdey, panels were devoted to the subject at the SSRC Research Seminar in Modern German Social History, University of East Anglia (18 July 1981), and the 1983 conference of the Western Association of German Studies, University of Wisconsin, Madison (1 Oct. 1983). For details of a colloquium at the Munich *Institut für Zeitgeschichte*, see E. Straub, 'Deutscher Sonderweg?', *Frankfurter Allgemeine Zeitung*, 2 Dec. 1981 (*Feuilleton*).

since the defeat of the Third Reich. But the idea of a peculiar pattern of German historical development in the modern period goes back much further, at least to the beginning of the nineteenth century. By and large, those who talked before 1945 about a German *Sonderweg* were more often inclined to endow this with a positive value. In the first half of the last century, for example, while the early German national movement was partly stimulated by aping France, it was also strongly informed by a sense of difference from, and superiority to, the ideas of the French Revolution. Later, after unification, there was a widespread tendency, especially among the academic and professional *Bildungsbürgertum*, to exalt the particular German combination of political, economic, military, and educational institutions: monarchy and industrial success, university and army. Complacent assumptions about the supposed importance of 'spiritual' rather than merely 'materialist' values in the new Germany were equally apparent. Where such institutions and values were praised, Germany's special superiority was very often defined *vis-à-vis* England. Treitschke was not alone in his dismissive view that the English confused soap and civilization. Notions of a positive German *Sonderweg* were given a fillip by the First World War (the 'ideas of 1914'), and they retained a powerful purchase through the years of the Weimar Republic.[4]

We discuss these ideas in more detail in the main body of the book, particularly in the second of the two essays. Some of our reviewers felt that we should have placed greater emphasis on this persistent belief in the positive virtues of Germany's separate development. Our point, however, was precisely not to take such ideas—which are fairly familiar ones—as a set of givens. In fact, the status and weight of ideas like these was one of the things we set out to probe. We would certainly not wish to deny, indeed it is difficult to imagine that anyone would try to deny, that the attitudes described had a real existence. But their resonance and the importance attached to them need to be examined critically, as do counter-currents of respect for materialism rather than 'inwardness', of attraction to English and other western patterns of development. Nor should the uniquely German

[4] See esp. B. Faulenbach, *Ideologie des deutschen Weges* (Munich, 1980).

quality of such ideas, where they did exist, be over-stressed. Certainly it is easy to exaggerate their strength and homogeneity, as well as their German-ness, and to present them as a package. It was interesting, for example, to find two reviewers using an almost identical formula to characterize this positive belief in German peculiarity. One wrote of the view among pre-1914 academics 'that the strong monarchy with its military power and bureaucracy, its educational system and its industrial success, was superior to the western parliamentary-democratic states'.[5] Another reviewer (from the same university, as it happens) spoke in a radio broadcast about the view among pre-1914 academics 'that the monarchy, with its military power and bureaucracy was superior to the western parliamentary-democratic states.' (The point about industrial success came in the previous sentence.[6]) It is precisely the problem with such arguments—this was one of our points—that they can easily harden into a formula. Some of the responses to the German edition provided better involuntary testimony of this than anything we wrote ourselves.

These would be mere debating points if they were not so important for the argument over the German *Sonderweg*. For many post-war German historians have taken over the old view of a special German development and turned it on its head. The positive view of the German *Sonderweg* was largely discredited, at least in its overt form, by the Third Reich and the total defeat of 1945. When the idea reappeared in the 1950s, and still more in the 1960s, it had negative connotations. How, it was asked, had the German catastrophe been possible? The answer was found in the fatefully aberrant pattern of German history, by western standards. Thus the German *Sonderweg* was reinstated with all the moral signs reversed. With 1933–45 understandably regarded as the awful culmination of modern German history, the roots of Nazi success were now located in the peculiar pattern of German ideological, institutional, and political development, stretching back into the previous century. Naturally we are not dealing here with a homogeneous school of historians. But it is

[5] Wehler, 'Deutscher Sonderweg', p. 478.
[6] Kocka, 'Der deutsche Sonderweg'.

possible to see how successive historiographical currents flowed with sufficient force in one direction to cut out a fairly deep bed—which is not to deny considerable turbulence at times, as well as some rather stagnant stretches. While these historians frequently disagreed with each other and were politically and methodologically distinct, they can be said to share a recognizable common concern with the pattern of German peculiarity. The explanations they have offered vary. Some noted Germany's unique position in Europe, fatefully trapped between East and West, a view which has attracted a number of British historians and has recently been restated by David Calleo in *The German Problem Reconsidered.*[7] Others, less impressed by the iron logic of geography, looked for the essence of German exceptionalism in the malign role played by the Prussian army and by militarism more generally.[8] More widespread still, especially perhaps among émigré historians, was the attempt to consider the intellectual currents already noted as evidence of the peculiar 'German mind'. Here, values which evinced or seemed to tend towards irrationalism, the glorification of martial virtues, the abject obedience of the 'subject' (*Untertan*), inwardness, and contempt for supposedly mechanical western values, were variously seen as characteristic German aberrations from enlightened western ways of thinking.[9]

Attempts to identify German peculiarity through the Prussian army or the German mind have both enjoyed considerable scholarly and popular respectability. Residual elements of both remain important in writing on German history. Neither, however, is nowadays proposed with the

[7] Published Cambridge, 1980. As Calleo's book appeared at the same time as ours, it was understandably although somewhat misleadingly coupled with it in a number of reviews.

[8] The major German example is the work of Gerhard Ritter, *Staatskunst und Kriegshandwerk*, 4 vols. (Munich, 1954-68), translated as *The Sword and the Sceptre* (Coral Gables, Florida, 1969-73). An early and outstanding work in English was G. A. Craig, *The Politics of the Prussian Army, 1640-1945* (New York, 1955).

[9] See H. Kohn, *The Mind of Germany* (London, 1961); F. Stern, *The Politics of Cultural Despair* (Berkeley, 1961); G. L. Mosse, *The Crisis of German Ideology* (London, 1966).

former assurance. The identification of militarist 'bad Germans' can all too evidently serve an apologist purpose in distracting attention from more pervasive flaws in society.[10] There is a rather different problem with Nazi pedigree-hunting in the realm of ideas, with its habitual unwillingness to specify, sometimes even to recognize as a problem, who was influenced by what ideas, when, and to what effect.[11] There has undoubtedly been some excellent and sophisticated work in recent years in both of these areas.[12] But it is probably true to say in general that our present understanding of German historical peculiarity, while incorporating valuable elements of the approaches just noted, has moved on to more sociological and structural terrain.

It has now become customary to locate the 'failure of Western-style liberal democracy to take root in Germany', as one recent American historian puts it,[13] in a fateful discrepancy between economic development on the one hand, and social values and political forms on the other. This critical reading is not, of course, original to post-war writers. Some of the most important components of it are to be found in the political writings of contemporary critics such as Max Weber, before and during the First World War. But since the 1960s especially, such an approach to the German question has enjoyed a growing academic respectability. According to this reading, the central point about Germany's passage to 'modernity' was the lack of synchronization between the

---

[10] As, e.g., in the case of Gerhard Ritter. See below, pp. 29-30, for Ritter's role in the 'Fischer Controversy' of the early 1960s.

[11] The works cited in n. 9 above are superior examples of the genre, but a depressingly long list of slack, unhistorical books on the German mind could be drawn up. In few other areas of German historical scholarship have the temptations of *basse vulgarisation* been so weakly resisted.

[12] F. Ringer, *The Decline of the Mandarins* (Cambridge, Mass., 1969), H. Glaser, *The Cultural Roots of National Socialism* (London, 1978) and the essays in K. Vondung (ed.), *Das wilhelminische Bildungsbürgertum* (Göttingen, 1976) could be mentioned on intellectual history. On militarism, see the work of Volker Berghahn, Wilhelm Deist, Michael Geyer, and Manfred Messerschmidt. There is a good review of the literature in M. Geyer, 'Die Geschichte des deutschen Militarismus von 1860-1945. Ein Bericht über die Forschungslage (1945-1975)', in H.-U. Wehler (ed.), *Die moderne deutsche Geschichte in der internationalen Forschung 1945-1975* (Göttingen, 1975), pp. 256-86.

[13] J. M. Diefendorf, *Businessmen and Politics in the Rhineland* (Princeton, 1980), p. 6.

economic, social, and political spheres. Germany did not have a bourgeois revolution of the normal kind associated with England, France, or the United States. Indeed Ralf Dahrendorf, whose importance here is considerable, wrote a very influential book which acquired its cutting edge by posing the question 'Why wasn't Germany England?'[14] Why, in effect, had economic modernization in Germany not been accompanied by modern social values and political institutions? The answer generally given was that the German bourgeoisie gained much of what it wanted not by its own efforts but via the state, from above. Bourgeois self-confidence and pride, with the accompanying civic pride and energy, were eclipsed by the power and prestige of an already existing state machine. Moreover, industrial and commercial capital in Germany never won a struggle against the landed estate owners who were so dominant in the eastern parts of Prussia. Instead they compromised, above all through the notorious 'marriage of iron and rye' between heavy industry and Junker agriculturalists. Economic dynamism was therefore purchased at a high price, and the nub of the argument is that the distortions which resulted were accompanied by a further misdevelopment: bourgeois social compromise. Late on the scene and already weakened by the failure of 1848 and Bismarck's achievement of unification from above, the German bourgeoisie supposedly capitulated to the aristocratic embrace. Rather than assert its own values, it aped instead the values of the unbroken old élite: Junker landowners, the officer corps, the Prussian bureaucracy. It underwent, in short, a process which is usually dubbed the feudalization of the bourgeoisie. From a liberal or democratic perspective, so the argument continues, this was to prove disastrous.[15] For the traditional pre-industrial élite was able to retain a significant measure of political power through the Empire and the Weimar Republic. It was they who helped Hitler into the saddle. Only the Third Reich and the total defeat of 1945 finally dislodged this stubborn élite from its anachronistic,

[14] R. Dahrendorf, *Society and Democracy in Germany* (London, 1968).
[15] For an English account, see M. Kitchen, *The Political Economy of Germany 1815–1914* (London, 1978).

but commanding, heights. In this sense, 1945 really was *Stunde Null*, or year zero. Only after 1945 did German society—at least in the west—finally come into its own, its non-western peculiarities sloughed off and its political life and social values now cast in the image of those earlier, more successful western bourgeoisies.

This broad set of views constitutes one important and valuable product of the dialogue which German society has had with itself since 1945. In more strictly scholarly terms, it represents the efforts which German historians have made since the war, in a manner unmistakably different from their counterparts after 1918, to look critically at their own national history. We return at the end of this Introduction to consider the broader issues raised by this. Yet it would be patronizing to regard such an approach as being simply understandable and honourable, although it is both of those things certainly. This view of the recent German past has also been extremely fruitful and remains compelling. It offers a view of German peculiarity which is more satisfyingly rounded than many other approaches—whether the commonplace and unreflective Anglo-Saxon view of German 'character', more subtle arguments about the German mind or German militarism, the apologist notion of the Third Reich as an accident, or the vulgar-marxist view which offers late capitalism as the key to everything. The very eclecticism of this set of views is one of its main strengths, as its proponents have not failed to point out. The German historians who espouse such views have shown themselves willing and able to put the tools of political science and sociology to use. They have, at the same time, been assiduous and successful in rediscovering earlier disregarded historians such as Eckart Kehr, whose work sheds much light on the issues under discussion. This labour of reclamation, with its challenge to the professional establishment (*Zunft*) which had rendered dissenting figures such as Kehr marginal, has been extremely important.[16] Finally, as part

---

[16] H.-U. Wehler has been the major figure here, editing an important collection of Kehr's essays under the title *Der Primat der Innenpolitik* (Berlin, 1965). He has also edited and provided introductions to the work of other neglected outsiders of the interwar years, including G. W. F. Hallgarten, Alfred Vagts, and Gustav Mayer. See H.-U. Wehler, *Historische. Sozialwissenschaft und Geschichts-*

and parcel of their writing, the historians in question have
shown a notable capacity to address themselves to, as well
as borrow from, Britain and America.

This is, indeed, a notable chapter in the Atlantic trade in
ideas during our century. Ideas such as Max Weber's, imported
and reworked by eager Americans, were re-exported to post-
war Germany as the finished goods of American social and
political science; and they have now been re-exported once
again to British and American historians in the form of
thoroughly 'western' views on the peculiarities of German
history. Those who teach or study in Britain and the New
World have good reason to observe the importance of these
views. We ourselves, students in the late 1960s at a time when
such interpretations were beginning to assume their present
imposing shape, were certainly stimulated by them, and in
some important respects guided by them too.[17] That was by
no means an uncommon experience. Above all in Germany itself, this particular form of Atlanticism has won for itself an
amply deserved respectability, even if it is not universally
accepted.

Our own arguments are not in any sense an attempt to roll
back these substantial achievements. On the contrary, as both
text and footnotes should make clear, our book could only
have been written in response to arguments that these historians have helped to establish. Still, as the oft cited Max
Weber would have been the first to agree, the voices of
epigoni do not constitute the best of tributes. Our intention
in the book which follows has been, rather, to explore some

---

schreibung (Göttingen, 1980), esp. pp. 227-97. Kehr's essays are now available
in English as *Economic Interest, Militarism, and Foreign Policy* (Berkeley, 1977),
as is his major book, first published in Germany in 1930: *Battleship Building and
Party Politics in Germany, 1894-1901* (Chicago, 1975).

[17] A number of major studies appeared in the space of a few years, including
those of Hans Rosenberg on the Great Depression (1967), Hans-Ulrich Wehler on
Bismarck and Imperialism (1969), Peter-Christian Witt on financial policy in the
Empire and Michael Stürmer's edited collection of essays on Imperial Germany
(both 1970), and Volker Berghahn on the Tirpitz Plan (1971). In addition to
Dahrendorf's book (1968), there are two other works whose impact on that
English generation is worth noting: T. Veblen, *Imperial Germany and the Indus-
trial Revolution* (Ann Arbor, 1966, first published 1915), and B. Moore, *Social
Origins of Dictatorship and Democracy* (London, 1967).

of the problems raised by the account of the peculiarities of German history presented above. At the same time we try to suggest alternative ways of looking at some of these matters. We do so in the belief that, valuable though such ideas have proved, there are respects in which they are now subject to diminishing returns.

Our starting-point is the starting-point of the arguments we are considering: the idea of a *Sonderweg*, or German historical aberration. In order to have an aberration it is clearly necessary to have a norm. One of our intentions was to probe the normative assumptions which proponents of the *Sonderweg* necessarily made about what a proper historical development looked like. And here, sometimes explicitly and often implicitly, it was 'western' and most particularly Anglo-American and French developments that were taken as a yardstick against which German history was measured and found wanting. There are, however, problems with this kind of approach. It can easily come to rest on a misleading and idealized picture of historical developments in those countries that are taken as models. One of our reviewers reinforced this point by offering some very apt examples of the way in which nineteenth-century German liberals persistently misunderstood the reality of British constitutional and political practice.[18] Something similar has persisted into the twentieth century, and it has not been confined only to the spheres of politics and the constitution. We are talking, in fact, about an idealized picture of what the 'western' pattern actually was, a picture which historians of Britain, the USA, or France themselves would usually regard as quasi-mythical. In this context we also note the curiously parallel debate in Britain about 'the peculiarities of the English', which cuts right across the grain of assumptions about any kind of Anglo-Saxon normality.

By always asking what German history was not, rather than

---

[18] W. Mommsen, in the *Bulletin* of the German Historical Institute London, 8 (1981), 22. More generally, see H. Döring, 'Skeptische Anmerkungen zur deutschen Rezeption des englischen Parlamentarismus 1917/18', in L. Albertin and W. Link (eds.), *Politische Parteien auf dem Weg zur parlamentarischen Demokratie in Deutschland* (Düsseldorf, 1981), pp. 127–46.

what it was, one also runs the risk of posing questions to which the answer is always 'No'. Of course, the point made by one reviewer is well taken: one should not always seek to formulate questions to which the answer is 'Yes'.[19] That way lies complacency. But perhaps there is the danger of a different kind of complacency in relentlessly directing attention to the sins of omission of one national history when measured against other, idealized national histories. The theoretical construct 'England' (or 'France' or 'America') can naturally be of considerable value as an ideal type. Hence the success of, for example, Ralf Dahrendorf's book. Our intention was not to suggest that such questions should be proscribed, only that they should be made explicit: ideal types lose their value when they become merely routine, self-evident assumptions. Moreover, the use of ideal types has a pragmatic justification: do they work, illuminate, turn up new questions? We suggest that as a matter of balance and richness of yield, the time has come when other sets of questions are in order. This might take the form of looking in new ways at what actually did happen in German history. It might take the form of more specific trans-national comparisons on various themes, not necessarily with Britain or America, the latter having been the main object of detailed comparisons so far undertaken by the historians we are considering. Comparisons with other European states and societies—Italy, Belgium, Scandinavia, Eastern Europe, as well as France—might also be revealing. Discussion about the role played by the state might benefit particularly from European comparisons of this sort.

Our arguments on these points in the German edition found a mixed response. Our most pungent critics argued that the ideas we were scrutinizing did not exist, or that they did exist but were perfectly understandable, or that they used to exist but had long been abandoned, or that they were in any case the ideas of political scientists and not historians. We, in turn, were taken to task, sometimes rather crossly, for having failed to attend to previous writing on the subject— except where we had, and showed ourselves to be miserably

[19] Mommsen, *Bulletin*, p. 21. Mommsen's arguments on this point were among the most stimulating made by reviewers.

unoriginal.[20] In the light of what one commentator has called this 'negative, defensive, allergic response',[21] it is probably sensible to repeat once again the point made in the original edition: we were not questioning the critical edge which arguments about the *Sonderweg* have lent to the study of modern German history; we were suggesting that this edge had become blunted. The arguments in question, we would still maintain, had threatened to become an 'open sesame'; they cropped up again and again in monographs, articles, general books, and essay collections in a form which sometimes smacked of unreflectiveness. They constituted what one American historian described in 1976 as a 'new orthodoxy'.[22] There has, indeed, been a general acknowledgement that the dangers to which we alluded were real enough. One English reviewer thought it would have to be conceded that the German historians in question had 'in four cases out of five—accept[ed] the Anglo-Saxon "model" as the norm against which to assess the German "failed development", without adequately scrutinising that model.'[23] A number of German reviewers made the same point at considerably greater length. At the German Historical Conference debate on the *Sonderweg* the subject was considered as a broad question of trans-national comparison, and comparisons with Italy and Eastern Europe in particular were broached by panel members. We hope that with the publication of the book in English this debate will broaden further.

A second series of points in our argument follows from the first. What was it, in terms of content, that was said to mark

[20] It was intriguing to find one commentator defending the use of the *Sonderweg* as an ideal type, even if it failed to accord with the facts, while others suggested that our criticism of the *Sonderweg* argument failed to accord with the facts because we were using an ideal type. The first argument came from Wolfgang Mommsen, *Bulletin,* pp. 19–26. The second came especially from three historians at the University of Bielefeld, employing strikingly similar terms but varying degrees of elegance. See Kocka, 'Der deutsche Sonderweg', Wehler, 'Deutscher Sonderweg', and Puhle, 'Deutscher Sonderweg'.
[21] Robert G. Moeller, 'Die Besonderheiten der Deutschen? Neue Beiträge zur Sonderwegsdiskussion', *Internationale Schulbuchforschung,* 4. 1 (1982), 72.
[22] James Sheehan, in a review in *Journal of Modern History*, 48. 3 (1976), 566–7.
[23] Paul Kennedy, *Journal of Modern History,* 54. 1 (1982), 176–9, quotation on p. 178.

an aberration in German history when judged by western norms? It was, above all, the failure of a proper bourgeois revolution. Bourgeoisies are supposed to rise, but the German bourgeoisie was commonly depicted as moving disastrously through modern history in the opposite direction. Retreating into mere money-making or into the private world of sensibility, aping its betters and revering the martial virtues, supine and star-struck, the German bourgeoisie appears to be a class which sold out its proper birthright. It was this set of suppositions we wanted to explore. At the simplest level, we both believed that the gaping hole where the bourgeoisie should have been was something of an illusion: the German bourgeoisie had not been quite so absent from the historical stage. Our common intention was to suggest, in rather different ways, a less abject bourgeois role in modern German history. In part this was a matter of asking what historians really meant by bourgeois revolution. If the German bourgeoisie was historically weak and immature, it was clearly worth while considering what a strong and mature bourgeoisie might look like. Yet it was clear that no one any longer, and for good reason, believed in a 'rising middle class'—except, perhaps, in Germany, where the exception still seemed to prove the rule. One of our points was therefore the need to reconsider the definition of bourgeois revolution. Substantively, we wanted to direct attention to the unfolding of an authentically bourgeois society in nineteenth-century Germany, looking especially at property rights and ideas of competition, the rule of law, the emergence of voluntary associations and public opinion, and new patterns of taste, patronage, and philanthropy. Each of our contributions also questioned a different part of the widespread idea of a 'feudalized' bourgeoisie: we suggested it might actually be more plausible to talk of an *embourgeoisement* of German society. There was, of course, undoubtedly a form of social *rapprochement* between bourgeoisie and landowning class in Germany from around the 1870s. But we wondered how far this was exceptional in European terms and what it actually signified. Richard Cobden, for example, suggested that English merchants and manufacturers desired riches 'only that they may prostrate themselves at the feet of

feudalism'.[24] Do this and many other examples from Britain,
France, and elsewhere entitle us to talk of a feudalized bourgeoisie in Europe as a whole? As one of our reviewers notes,
Arno J. Mayer's recent book on *The Persistence of the Old
Regime* suggests just that.[25] Mayer's approach is certainly not
above criticism; but however one judges its bold thesis, his
book serves as a warning against singling out the German
experience.

This part of our book was drawn on heavily in some of the
lengthier German reviews.[26] It also elicited a wide and
valuable range of questions. Some of these, it is true, seemed
in a sense to talk past our arguments. The question of employers' paternalism, for example, is an important one, and
the 'pre-industrial', feudalized roots of the phenomenon
deserve to be taken seriously (as we tried to do). But given
the very broad arguments that have so often been erected on
the assumption that this was *the* basis of paternalism, there
seemed every reason to explore alternative ways of approaching these patterns of behaviour. One of us in particular
attempted this at some length, examining the German case
itself and making comparisons with Britain. The aim was
both to suggest an alternative explanation for the patently
authoritarian attitudes and practices of certain categories of
German capitalist, and to meet the demand for a carefully
framed comparative analysis. And here the connections
between paternalism and the industrial process were considered, along lines which have recently been followed not
only by ourselves but by an impressive if disparate assort-
ment of West and East German, British, and North American
scholars. To be asked, at the end, 'what has this got to do
with the pre-industrial origins of paternalism?',[27] prompts

[24] Cited in A. Briggs, 'The Language of "Class" in Early Nineteenth-Century
England', in Briggs and J. Saville (eds.), *Essays in Labour History* (London, 1960),
p. 72, n. 4.
[25] Arno J. Mayer, *The Persistence of the Old Regime. Europe to the Great
War* (London, 1981).
[26] See, e.g., Straub, 'Woher aber kam der Nationalsozialismus?' and 'Die
eingebildeten Leiden der Deutschen'. This part of the book was also thoughtfully
discussed, although from a rather different angle of approach, by Dieter
Langewiesche, *Archiv für Sozialgeschichte*, 21 (1981), 527-32.
[27] Kocka, 'Der deutsche Sonderweg'. See also below, pp. 91-126.

the feeling that here is a question which is not looking very hard for an answer. Other questions sought to carry the argument of the book beyond the stage to which we had taken it. How far was the texture of the new bourgeois society essentially urban? To what extent did aristocratic patronage actually give way to new forms? How much weight should the voluntary associations be given, as against the more incorporated, semi-*étatiste Verbände*? Was not legal consolidation correlated more closely with national unity than with the development of bourgeois civil society? Had we not, in the end, underestimated the importance of state bureaucracy, whose existence predated that of the bourgeoisie? Some of these points were considered in the original edition, but the questions are welcome none the less. They are taken up in the present book in the appropriate places. What is certainly gratifying—and has changed even since the German edition was written in 1979—is the growth of detailed studies on subjects of this kind. An example of this is the increasing amount of work on *Alltagsgeschichte*, or the history of everyday life.[28] We have tried to take account of this and other new literature.

The key question, of course, is how all this should be related to the sphere of politics proper, to the question of power. For in this respect, surely, it is possible to speak of a failed bourgeois revolution. Here, if anywhere, the German bourgeoisie surely compromised its real interests? One way of addressing this problem is to reformulate it: to question whether one can in fact talk plausibly of a bourgeoisie anywhere which seized power and recast the state and politics after its own image. The views we were concerned with seemed to share the assumption, often implicit, that bourgeois material achievements should be expected to bring self-consciously bourgeois institutions and isms in their wake: parliamentarism, liberalism, democracy. And if they did not, something must have gone wrong. We suggested that this hardly corresponds to the reality of what happened in, say, England or France or America, or indeed anywhere else. The

---

[28] For some thoughtful general observations, see L. Niethammer, 'Anmerkungen zur Alltagsgeschichte', *Geschichtsdidaktik*, 5 (1980), 231-42.

bourgeoisie characteristically became the dominant class in European countries (which is not the same as the ruling class) through other than heroic means or open political action. Its real power—not just a superficial cultural presence—was anchored in the capitalist mode of production and in civil society, in the spheres of property relations, the rule of law, associational life, and so on. It is these, perhaps, that more truly deserve the label 'bourgeois revolution'. Approaching the problem in this way, at an oblique angle to the idea of bourgeois revolution as an episode of political sound and fury, is to shift attention away from short-term political set pieces to longer-term transformations, from the motives of historical actors to the effects of their actions. This would, among other things, help to put into perspective the argument that the failed bourgeois revolution of 1848 was a decisive event (or non-event) in recent German history. More fundamentally, it might be helpful to question the causal chain bourgeoisie–liberalism–parliamentarization–democracy, as if these went naturally and somehow logically hand in hand. We have already noted how two reviewers instinctively used the same phrase 'parliamentary-democratic western states'. Countless similar usages could be cited. Yet once break the chain between the bourgeoisie as a class and any particular form of state or political expression of interests, and a number of assumptions about bourgeois failure stand potentially open to revision. The extent to which the other links in this chain also need to be questioned is taken up below.

While aiming to broaden the notion of bourgeois revolution, however, we most emphatically did not try to present an account of German bourgeois society with the politics left out.[29] For while it is at least arguable that bourgeois revolutions should not be equated with the transfer of political power to the bourgeoisie, nor can bourgeois politics (least of all in the nineteenth century) be reduced to the primacy of

---

[29] It is rather baffling to read that we 'wanted to shift the argument away from the political' (Mommsen, *Bulletin*, p. 20), or that we 'skirt around—or only briefly cover—the constitutional and political side' (Kennedy, *Journal of Modern History*, p. 178). We had believed the opposite to be the case and were surprised by the lack of response to what we had to say about politics—Dieter Langewiesche being a major exception here.

share prices and the consolidation of the rule of law. We must clearly take into account also a forceful idea, even a rhetoric, of 'open action': of politics as a stage, political action as drama. While France might be thought the *locus classicus* of bourgeois self-understanding in this sense, it was also true in Britain, Germany, and elsewhere. It may even have been particularly important in Germany, paradoxically, where the relatively late development of the bourgeoisie served in certain ways to accentuate not only its social sense of itself but also its political self-consciousness. We are therefore talking in this book about two parallel sets of events in nineteenth-century Germany. As well as the silent bourgeois revolution in economy and society there was also a more specifically public and political set of bourgeois desiderata. As we have argued, perhaps a trifle heretically, many of these had been formally achieved by around the 1870s. Yet these two sets of achievements—the stealthier ones at the level of material and social life, the more open ones at the political level— were not equal. The former demonstrated bourgeois unity and strength, while buttressing the bourgeois claim to constitute a 'general class' in society. The latter revealed bourgeois division and weakness, while undermining bourgeois claims to represent the general interest of society. We have tried to follow through the implications of this difference in some detail, not least for the failure of political and constitutional reform in the period between unification and the First World War.

It is in this way that we seek to relate the economic and social spheres to the political, an issue which a number of reviewers rightly identified as central. This is not a simple matter, and it may be as well to outline a little more the general approach which is common to each of the essays that follow. We try to avoid the Scylla of 'base-superstructure' thinking, in which the political level simply 'reflects' economic and social developments. But we try also to avoid the Charybdis of a total dissociation between the two, which underlies much recent writing. There was certainly a lack of synchronization between bourgeois achievements at different levels. But this was not just a straightforward discrepancy whereby ersatz bourgeois success in material terms was matched by (and helped to produce) failure and capitulation to a pre-industrial power élite in the political sphere. Our arguments, following the lines set out above, depict a more general bourgeois weakness in the realm of politics. This was, in a phrase picked out and cited approvingly by one reviewer, the soft under-belly of the bourgeoisie.[30]

The bourgeoisie existed, economically and sociologically speaking as a class—as a social category of those who owned and controlled capital, together with their managerial, professional, and administrative ancillaries. This gave it a definite and powerful presence in society, one which by the end of the nineteenth century was arguably dominant. In terms of consciousness the bourgeoisie was united on subjects like property rights and the fundamental rule of law. Voluntary association and philanthropy, which reflected the local social power and patronage of the class as well as its regional and religious diversity, were also apt symbols of where its true strength lay. But when the bourgeoisie (or, more accurately, different sections of it, through specific political representatives) acted on the larger political stage, the divisions became more troublesome and evident. Bourgeois liberalism was particularly subject to political fragmentation, above all the dominant National Liberal current which emerged in the 1860s. It was faced with bourgeois critics on the left who questioned its liberal commitment and bourgeois critics on the right who questioned its nationalism. It also provoked major Catholic opposition through its support for the *Kulturkampf* and similar measures. The 'unpolitical' unity of the bourgeoisie as a class was not matched by an equivalent unity on more openly political issues.

It was also more vulnerable at the political level in its relations with subordinate social classes. Here we come back to the chain of bourgeoisie-liberalism–parliamentarization-democracy. As we have tried to argue, both the bourgeoisie's degree of liberalism and liberalism's degree of democracy depended in nineteenth-century Europe on complex social and political configurations, in which the mobilization and independent dynamism of subordinate classes like the

---

[30] Langewiesche, *Archiv für Sozialgeschichte*, p. 531.

peasantry, small property-owners, and the working class played an important, possibly even decisive, role. Without the stimulus of a popular movement that was strong enough to shift bourgeois notables to the left, the constitutionalist movements of the last century were unlikely to embrace a significant element of democracy, either in their own internal relations or in the kind of state they wanted to create. Left to their own devices liberal politicians were far more likely to opt for a limited franchise, strictly qualified by property or education, or both. Thus it is hardly surprising that, even where the German bourgeoisie was liberal, it was more interested in parliamentarization than in democracy. Even that notoriously anti-democratic instrument, the Prussian three-class franchise, was introduced by a commission which included prominent liberals who helped to design this 'bulwark of the aristocratic authoritarian state in Prussia'.[31] Similarly, the distinctive mode of bourgeois notable politics (*Honoratiorenpolitik*) which crystallized in Germany in the middle of the century was exclusive in substance, style, and personnel. Its practitioners echoed the customary bourgeois claim to represent some sort of 'general interest'; but the articulation of such a claim openly and in the political domain excited hostility. And our argument is that many aspects of anti-bourgeois hostility—fruits of the success of bourgeois material and social achievements in Germany—were displaced on to the political level. This was most obviously true of the working class, and our emphasis on the importance of the SPD and its early appearance is in line with much earlier writing. We also note a similar revolt by the peasantry and the petty bourgeoisie, whose parallel grievances were displaced in a parallel process into the political arena. The effect of these vulgar interlopers on to the political stage, together with the shrill middle-class mavericks of the nationalist associations, was to fracture the comfortable mode of politics into which political life had settled after mid-century.

These changes have often been seen as providing the raw material of manipulation—of Bonapartism, of efforts by the old élite to equip itself with a popular base by exploiting

---

[31] The phrase comes from Hans Rosenberg, *Machteliten und Wirtschaftskonjunkturen* (Göttingen, 1978), p. 96.

popular sentiment, especially of an anti-liberal kind. Our
arguments in the present book, as elsewhere, form part of a
broad historiographical trend in recent years which has
sought to question this 'manipulative' approach.[32] We suggest
that pressure from below was greater than often assumed,
and we try in particular to put into perspective the argument
that the Junker-Conservative élite was able, through the
Agrarian League (*Bund der Landwirte*), to gain a fateful new
lease of political life by co-opting popular peasant and petty-
bourgeois support. As will become apparent, we do not reject
this view out of hand. But perhaps the point of overriding importance is not that the Junkers and the old élite were prepared to act in this way, but that all the non-socialist *bürgerliche Parteien* were to some extent obliged to. Popular
ferment posed a threat as well as an opportunity. In varying
degrees the National Liberals, left liberals, and Centre Party,
as well as the Conservatives, performed political acrobatics in
order to head off and seek to harness popular discontent.
There was a similar stridency in the way in which the non-
socialist parties sought to retain their working-class constituencies. The growth of the SPD was the yardstick against
which these efforts should be considered: here, once again,
we are very much in agreement with the modern mainstream
of German historiography. More generally, it was the very
success of Germany's dynamic late-comer capitalism (which
few would dispute), together with the accompanying consolidation of a bourgeois civil society (on which we have laid
stress), that contributed to the displacement of so many
grievances directly on to the political level. It is arguably
this, rather than the malign role of a manipulative old élite,
that explains much of the unstable and febrile nature of
German political culture on the eve of the First World War.

[32] See, in general, Richard J. Evans, 'Introduction: Wilhelm II's Germany and
the Historians', in Evans (ed.), *Society and Politics in Wilhelmine Germany*
(London, 1978), pp. 11–39, and the critical arguments contained in Volker
Berghahn, 'Politik und Gesellschaft im Wilhelminischen Deutschland', *Neue
Politische Literatur*, 24 (1979), 164–95. A generally positive discussion of the
newer works can be found in Wolfgang Mock, '"Manipulation von oben" oder
Selbstorganisation an der Basis? Einige neuere Ansätze in der englischen Historiographie zur Geschichte des deutschen Kaiserreichs', *Historische Zeitschrift*, 232
(1981), 358–75.

The German political system naturally showed very marked features of authoritarian or semi-constitutional persistence. We give full weight to this, while noting certain important countervailing tendencies. It mattered that the Kaiser had powers which he used, that the Chancellor was not responsible to the Reichstag, that governments were not formed by the leaders of the majority parties, that constitutional practice in Prussia lagged so conspicuously behind that of the Reich and many of the other individual states. It is a telling fact that, to Chancellor Bülow, it even mattered whether the Kaiser approved of him wearing white trousers.[33] It is hardly surprising that historians still refer to the failure of some kind of liberal–parliamentary–democratic reform. Our point is that we should be clear what sort of reform we are talking about: what exactly is it that should have happened but somehow did not? Perhaps the lack of reformist drive should not really surprise us. All the bourgeois parties were seriously divided in ways we try to explain. These divisions can be discussed, moreover, without invoking overt manipulation from above, or stubborn pre-industrial survivals, as one of us tries to show by considering the political parties in some detail, and the other by examining the abortive liberal reformism of the commercial and export-industry organization, the *Hansabund*. As we also try to demonstrate, these divisions were reinforced, once again, by the problems the bourgeois parties experienced in dealing with a popular electorate. Nowhere was this more obvious than over the question of Prussian electoral reform.

Basic class interests of the bourgeoisie in matters such as property relations and the rule of law were largely guaranteed in Imperial Germany; while at the political level, by contrast, real differences were faithfully mirrored. Between SPD demands and the intransigence of the governing élite, the parties that 'ought' to have offered a reformist challenge were at

[33] John C. G. Röhl, 'Introduction', in Röhl and N. Sombart (eds.), *Kaiser Wilhelm II: New Interpretations* (Cambridge, 1982), p. 17. The Röhl-Sombart collection, and the book by one of its contributors, Isabel Hull, on *The Entourage of Kaiser Wilhelm II 1888–1918* (Cambridge, 1982), both explicitly suggest the need to revise our approach to the history of Imperial Germany, although the starting-point is not the same as our own.

loggerheads, each filling the idea of reform with its own content. And each faced a challenge 'from below', although they
defined it and met it rather differently. We are therefore
arguing below about the movement as well as the stasis in
Imperial politics, and in particular about the emergence of an
ambiguous and unstable new mass politics. The demagogic
process whereby popular sentiment was met and contained,
as much as the failure of reform *tout court*, was to have a significant bearing on German history after war and revolution.

Here we come to the question of the Third Reich. A number
of reviewers felt that we should have come to grips more centrally with National Socialism. And it is true that we did not
talk about this directly at all. We quite explicitly wrote a
book about nineteenth-century Germany, arguing that this
historical experience should not be reduced to the ante-room
of Nazism. We would maintain that position still. But we
tried to make it plain that we were not seeking to deny the
'continuity' of modern German history. This idea has perhaps become a little over-reverend of late, but it remains
essential. We do not, for example, believe that the advent of
Hitler was a historical accident, a *Betriebsunfall* in German
parlance. Nor do we agree with the related view of Hitler as
some kind of unprecedented political snake-charmer, sedu-
cing a German people driven to despair by the immediate
circumstances of the Versailles Treaty, inflation, and depression.[34] Such views seem to us to be too comfortable, as
well as misleading. Perhaps this is the point at which to repeat
what we said in the German edition: the question about continuity is not *whether*, but *what kind*? The present Introduction provides an opportunity to amplify this a little.

Some of the lines of continuity between what we describe
before 1914 and the Weimar Republic should already be evident. We place stress, for example, on the fragmentation of
the 'bourgeois middle',[35] on the hostility of the bourgeois

[34] The most recent general discussion of writing on the Third Reich is Pierre
Ayçoberry, *The Nazi Question. An Essay on the Interpretation of National
Socialism (1922-1975)* (New York, 1981).
[35] See L. E. Jones, ' "The Dying Middle": Weimar Germany and the Fragmentation of Bourgeois Politics', *Central European History*, 5 (1972), 23-54. For

parties to the left, on the importance of the confessional divide and its political effects in hampering a reformist bloc. One might say that the failure of the Weimar Coalition after 1923 was prefigured by the failure of a putative 'Gladstonian Coalition' before 1914, a subject we both discuss. These general problems of German politics played an obvious role in the Weimar Republic. Some were exacerbated by war and revolution, some by the post-1929 crisis, some by both. Some appeared in slightly altered form: the Communist Party (KPD), for example, inherited the SPD's mantle as the chief 'revolutionary threat'. In addition, our emphasis on the febrile nature of Wilhelmine politics, on the decline of an older and more comfortable notable style of politics, suggests other pointers to the advent of National Socialism. To take only a few features of our account, the emergence of a new radical nationalism legitimized by reference to 'people' rather than monarch, the revolt of the peasantry against urban-urbane authority, the advent of a self-conscious petty-bourgeois or *Mittelstand* movement on the political stage: all of these demonstrate affinities of both substance and style between the politics of the Weimar Republic and the politics of the Wilhelmine period. We would both argue strongly that the popular social and political roots of National Socialism must be sought in the period before war and revolution.

This emphasis on popular support does not mean that we are talking about 'the revolt of the masses'. Even shorn of its more evidently patrician overtones, such a view is clearly unsatisfactory. Nazi success cannot be explained solely in terms of the popular support it received, even if it cannot be explained fully without it. National Socialism, like other fascisms, requires explanation in terms of both its appearance and its function, in terms of its public rhetoric, but also its effects, as a focus of popular appeal, but also as a vehicle of rather narrower interests. This prompts two further questions about continuity which we would like to take up. The first concerns the 'Old Gang' and its responsibility for the Nazi

a good review of the literature on this subject covering both pre- and post-First World War periods, see J. C. Hunt, 'The Bourgeois Middle in German Politics, 1871-1933: Recent Literature', *Central European History*, 11 (1978), 83-106.

seizure of power, something which is strongly emphasized by the historians whose work we have been trying to probe, and has indeed been reiterated in some of their reviews. It is undoubtedly true that they did 'hold the stirrups for Hitler', as one of these historians suggests.[36] Who would try to deny the responsibility of Hindenburg, Papen, Schleicher, and the institutions behind them? They not only helped to make Hitler respectable; in the crucial years 1930–3 they helped into power a man they believed they could tame. But it remains to be asked whether we are really talking about the same pre-industrial élite doing the same things it had supposedly been doing before 1914. Was it, in fact, the same Old Gang? Recent work on Schleicher's *Reichswehr*, for example, suggests that it was an army of 'professionals' rather than 'Junkers': that we are dealing with an army closer to the Federal Republic's *Bundeswehr* than to the army of Schlieffen (which was itself changing in this direction).[37] Nobody, equally, could maintain that Hugenberg's German National People's Party (DNVP) was simply the linear successor of pre-war Conservatism, 'radicalized' and demagogic though the latter undoubtedly already was.

These are important issues when we consider the form that continuity took, and they prompt a further question: just why did the old élite have to call in Hitler at all? Why was their own manipulative repertoire inadequate to consolidate an authoritarian, anti-parliamentary regime, one which might indeed have fallen short of outright fascism? The answer, of course, is that National Socialism was able to exert a radical, populist anti-system appeal which the old élite itself could make only partially, and with growing implausibility, against the liberal and left-wing elements of the 'system'. Nazism attracted many away from the Old Gang, away from a party such as the DNVP as well as from the fragmented and ineffectual parties of the bourgeois middle. If we view this course of events in the light of a linear continuity between

[36] Wehler, 'Deutscher Sonderweg', p. 479.
[37] M. Geyer, 'Professionals and Junkers: German Rearmament and Politics in the Weimar Republic', in R. J. Bessel and E. J. Feuchtwanger (eds.), *Social Change and Political Development in Weimar Germany* (London, 1981), pp. 77–133.

the self-interested manipulation of the old élite before 1914 and again in the Weimar Republic, then this turn of events requires an explanation. For how do we explain this loss of support, the necessary resort to Hitler? If the pre-1914 Agrarian League became the Weimar *Reichslandbund*, if pre-1914 Conservatives became the DNVP, if the Kaiser became Hindenburg, and if—above all—the successfully manipulative Old Gang remained a successfully manipulative Old Gang, then Hitler actually appears to have been something of a break in continuity. The much vaunted continuity of élite legerdemain seems suddenly to fail, and Hitler is the joker needed to take the last trick. Of course, one could reply quite plausibly that the popular desertion of the Old Gang which required the joker to be played was nothing other than the final revenge of the peasantry and the petty bourgeoisie on their puppet masters. But this argument itself acquires greater plausibility if two additional assumptions are made: first, that the demagogy of Imperial Germany was more wide-based than to be simply that of a narrow old élite; and secondly, that this demagogy was a more convulsive (and only a partly successful) enterprise than historians often suggest. Then the denouement after 1928 seems more explicable, as the product of an irregular and convulsive, rather than linear and predictable continuity.

That is where our arguments about Wilhelmine politics may be reintroduced. We stress the difficulties that the old élite—although not it alone—experienced with pressure from below. The same is true of the shrill, middle-class nationalism of the period. The institutionalizing of such truculence within the Conservatives and the Agrarian League (although not only there) was a real enough gambit. But the élite had not called these forces into being, and it could not fully control them. The demagogy of the political Right was always akin to riding the tiger. It was not an accomplished act, to be repeated at will; it was a difficult exercise, and always a potentially dangerous one. What was true of the Wilhelmine period was still more true of the years after war and revolution. Thus the DNVP, for example, was not a simple continuation of pre-war Conservatism, but a political creature shot through with the volatile relations between socially dominant and subordinate classes, both within the party and between leaders and electorate. These arguments could be made at considerably greater length. The main point is this: if we see pre-war and post-war demagogy as an increasingly reckless process of attempted political containment, rather than as accomplished political manipulation by one particular and narrow élite, then the Nemesis of Nazism becomes more readily explicable. However necessarily brief our own arguments must remain on this point, they certainly do anything but deny the continuity across the 1914–18 divide, or make the subsequent success of National Socialism into an accident.

There is a second point about continuity which has to be made regarding the function rather than the popular appeal of National Socialism. It concerns the importance, not so much of the Old Gang, but of the new: the relationship of German capitalism to German fascism. This is not a question of 'Who financed Hitler?' Nor are we talking about any sort of automatic, law-like 'logic of monopoly capitalism', of the kind invoked by strenuously orthodox marxist-leninist historians. Capitalism has historically been able to survive and reproduce itself within varying state forms, along a continuum from parliamentary democracy to radical fascism. That was one of the points made in the German edition of the book. The question concerns, rather, the particular options open to German capital in the circumstances of the late Weimar Republic; and here the elements of continuity with the period before 1914 can be illuminating. Before the First World War, so we argue, the very success of German capitalism on the shop-floor and in the market place was responsible for the displacing of many material and social grievances into the political arena. Both the SPD, and in different ways the groundswell of peasant and petty-bourgeois political movements, were symptoms of this. The enlargement of the political nation—the importance, rather than unimportance, of public life and political conflict in Imperial Germany—confirmed the power-brokers and functionaries of capitalist interests in their desire to retreat off the political stage, away from potentially damaging public scrutiny. At the same time the political divisions of capital worked in such a way that, as we argue, the liberalizing tendencies of an organization such as the *Hansabund* were undermined.

The 1920s witnessed comparable developments, but screwed several notches higher. The political divisions of capital remained severe, pre-dating the crisis of 1929 and contributing, as David Abraham has recently shown at length, to the destabilizing of Weimar democracy.[38] Moreover, the retreat of business away from the political stage went on apace—a process which, as Charles Maier has reminded us, was by no means confined to Germany, although it was especially marked there.[39] For in Germany the new Republic was not only synonymous with revolution, inflation, and Versailles: from capital's point of view it was also synonymous with trade-union rights and welfarism, which the SPD was now in a position to defend—had to defend indeed, or try to, if it were not to see even larger working-class defections to the KPD. When, after 1928, the SPD found it increasingly difficult to defend the social gains of the Republic, its refusal to countenance dismantling those gains meant a significant narrowing of the possibilities for a democratic resolution of Weimar's economic crisis in a manner consonant with the interests of capital. At the same time, the economic rationalization of the 1920s on the basis of American loans reproduced a situation in which the ballot box was used to register protest at the shake-out this entailed —a shake-out more telescoped even than that produced by dynamic capitalist development before 1914. This political protest came partly from the petty-bourgeois men and women who went to the wall, partly from unemployed workers. Once again, therefore, the success of a highly modern capitalism created political conditions that were threatening. Before 1914 this back-lash found expression through universal suffrage; now it found expression within a parliamentary democracy. The political effects of economic rationalization were therefore critical. The Wall Street Crash brought into sharp focus a problem which pre-dated 1929 and in some ways 1914 as well, but which had been softened earlier by

[38] D. Abraham, *The Collapse of the Weimar Republic. Political Economy and Crisis* (Princeton, 1981).

[39] C. Maier, *Recasting Bourgeois Europe* (Princeton, 1975).

the non-parliamentary form of the Imperial constitution. Capital was faced after 1929 with its own divisions, with the growth of a radicalized petty bourgeoisie which the Nazis harnessed so effectively, and with the rise of the KPD which presented a red spectre more terrifying than that of the SPD before the First World War. Furthermore, in the depth of the depression the different representatives of capital were looking for a solution to the profits crisis via the dismantling of welfarism, yet without the co-operation of the SPD and Free Trade Unions, and hemmed in by the electoral popularity of both National Socialism and Communism. The attempts to square this circle led the new gang, like the old, into support, if not enthusiasm, for Hitler.

These remarks on Weimar and the advent of National Socialism are necessarily brief, and attempt mainly to follow up some lines of continuity between German history before and after the First World War. They should indicate that we believe in the importance of continuity—or continuities—in modern German history, although our continuities may not always be the ones that are often emphasized. Some observations on this subject are probably called for in a book on the German *Sonderweg*, even when it is concerned with the nineteenth century. Certainly the reception of the German edition showed how 1933 continues to preoccupy German historians, even when they do not themselves work on the Weimar Republic or the Third Reich. Here we return finally to that difficult political and moral dimension with which this Introduction began. History can never be innocent of these considerations, but in post-war Germany the public and moral implications of historical writing have been felt with particular acuteness. It is therefore appropriate to end the Introduction by discussing the broader debate of which the German edition of this book has come to be a part.

Commentators did not fail to note that there were some parallels between the renewed debate over the *Sonderweg* and the Fischer controversy twenty years earlier. This indicates the moral charge that history carries in Germany. In 1961 the Hamburg historian Fritz Fischer published a book dealing with German aims in the First World War.[40] Two features of the book in particular established it as a symbolic landmark. First, Fischer suggested lines of continuity between German aims in the two world wars. Secondly, he devoted a significant amount of space to an examination of the role played by economic interests in Wilhelmine Germany, and to the general background of economic and social instability which existed in Germany on the eve of the war. Both emphases were widely considered heterodox in 1961; and the contemporary significance of the controversy lay, in fact, in the hostility that Fischer and his relatively small number of supporters faced, both from the then Christian Democratic government and from the historical *Zunft*.[41] Indeed, the political and methodological issues raised by Fischer were always intertwined. *Zunft* historians such as Gerhard Ritter represented the doubly conservative traditions of nineteenth-century German historicism. As scholars they stressed the need for an intuitive and 'understanding' (*verstehend*) penetration of the individual mind to yield the intentions and motives of historical actors. Politically, this 'understanding'–hermeneutic approach led readily to the conclusion that what is, ought to be. To understand everything does not necessarily mean to forgive everything; but if often seemed to. By its nature, moreover, historicism was hostile to comparative history and to the application of analytical theories drawn from the social sciences to historical 'reality'.[42] Thus Gerhard Ritter angrily denied the possibility of comparisons between Bethmann Hollweg and Hitler, between German foreign policy before 1914 and in

[40] F. Fischer, *Griff nach der Weltmacht* (Düsseldorf, 1961), translated as *Germany's Aims in the First World War* (London, 1967).

[41] There is an English account of the 'Fischer controversy' in J. A. Moses, *The Politics of Illusion* (London, 1975). See also I. Geiss, *Studien über Geschichte und Geschichtswissenschaft* (Frankfurt/M., 1972), pp. 108–98, and A. Sywottek, 'Die Fischer-Kontroverse', in I. Geiss and B.-J. Wendt (eds.), *Deutschland in der Weltpolitik des 19. und 20. Jahrhunderts* (Düsseldorf, 1973), pp. 19–74.

[42] On German historicism, see G. Iggers, *The German Conception of History: The National Tradition of Historical Thought from Herder to the Present* (Middletown, 1968), and *New Directions in European Historiography* (Middletown, 1975), for opposition to it. To prevent confusion, it should be added that the term historicism as used by historians of Germany (and by historians more generally) has a quite opposite meaning from the one given to it by Karl Popper in *The Poverty of Historicism*.

the 1930s, between Bismarck's Imperial Germany and Hitler's Third Reich. The historicist approach showed a comparable lack of sympathy towards the anonymous forces they detected in economic and social history. Hence the combination of political and methodological distaste which prompted some to suggest that Fritz Fischer would be more at home in the German Democratic Republic.

In retrospect the significance of the Fischer controversy lies in the stimulus it gave to historians who were dissatisfied both with the complacency towards the German past which they diagnosed in the German educational system and society at large, and with the historical guild which they indicted for encouraging this complacency. The 'new orthodoxy' with which we are concerned was therefore given a reference point by the Fischer episode; and the 'critical school' which emerged in the 1960s and consolidated itself in the 1970s did much to develop lines of approach which were only latent in Fischer's own work.[43] It did so with considerable pedagogic zeal. If the historicists of the guild looked back to Ranke, the principal exponent of the critical school, Hans-Ulrich Wehler, has been depicted as 'Treitschke *redivivus*'.[44] This new emphasis on history as a means with which the nation could be educated about its own past was evident in particular points of interpretation, such as the stress on continuity. More generally, and perhaps more important, a methodological attack was launched on historicism in the name of an emancipated and emancipating history. It was pointed out that the *verstehend* approach had clear limits, especially in considering collective rather than individual historical subjects, and in the elucidation of unintended historical consequences. The importance of theory in history has thus been a central proposition of these historians. Indeed, a large amount of energy has been devoted to establishing the fundamentals of 'critical' history as a social science and to

[43] This stimulus was explicitly noted by the authors of the second *Festschrift* for Fischer: D. Stegmann, B.-J. Wendt, and P.-C. Witt (eds.), *Industrielle Gesellschaft und politisches System: Beiträge zur politischen Sozialgeschichte* (Bonn, 1978), pp. v–vi.

[44] Thomas Nipperdey, in his review of 'Wehlers Kaiserreich', *Geschichte und Gesellschaft*, 1 (1975), 539–60.

determining the relations between a historical social science and neighbouring social-science disciplines.[45]

We have already noted the substantive (and substantial) achievements of this new departure. They are considered in detail in the essays that follow. Here we are concerned with the broader public implications of these views, and their relevance to the *Sonderweg* debate in particular. For the inescapable fact is that some German commentators seized eagerly on the publication of our book as a stick with which to beat the influential historians of the 1960s and 1970s. In just the same way, although with more warrant, they welcomed David Calleo's *The German Problem Reconsidered* as a justification of their own views. Here, it seemed, were historians who promised to lift the curse of the German past and render critical history superfluous. Better still, they were Anglo-Saxons, which doubled the value of their testimony. One review typified this approach, with its headline 'The Imagined Troubles of the Germans'.[46] Perhaps it is not surprising, therefore, that our book met with a 'defensive, allergic response' in some quarters, for a public and pedagogic, as well as a scholarly, enterprise was at issue. The Fischer controversy had generated a certain siege mentality, and the conservative *Tendenzwende* in the historical profession since the late 1970s probably reinforced this embattled state of mind. With the revival of historical traditionalism and muted apologetics at home, and revisionist sniping from Anglo-Saxon quarters, the historians in question must have felt that they faced a war on two fronts.[47]

Where do we stand on this thorny issue? Perhaps two sets of observations are called for. The first is that in the field of history—unlike war or diplomacy—it is misleading to proceed on the assumption that my enemy's enemy is my friend.[48] In

---

[45] In addition to the writings of Iggers (n. 42 above), there is a useful introduction to the voluminous literature on this subject in J. Kocka, *Sozialgeschichte* (Göttingen, 1977).

[46] Straub, 'Die eingebildeten Leiden der Deutschen'.

[47] See the reviews of Kocka, Puhle, and Wehler. A similar point was made by Wolfgang Mommsen and Robert Moeller.

[48] See Paul Kennedy's comments in *Journal of Modern History*, pp. 177–8: 'To chastise Blackbourn and Eley for indirectly giving support to older, conservative elements of a historical school who defend the German *Sonderweg* is surely off the mark.'

this case it is methodological conservatives and apologists for the German past (by no means necessarily identical) who have misled themselves. In truth, our book offers little to either group. On the more strictly methodological issue, we do not believe that facts speak for themselves, or that history can be innocent of theory. We do share the frequently quoted view of Jürgen Habermas that history is not exhausted by 'what human actors mutually intend'.[49] On the broader issue, we do not believe that Germany's troubles are 'imagined', or that the 'critical' historians of the 1960s and 1970s have been wasting their time. We do take the view that if Hans-Ulrich Wehler had not existed, it would have been necessary to invent him. The tone and substance of the German edition should really have left little room for doubt on this score. If historians have to be assigned to camps, we are therefore—on these fundamental issues—in the camp of those whose views we have considered critically. Theirs, after all, are the views that command the most serious attention.

Differences remain, of course, and that brings us to a second set of observations. Our views on the methodological and moral implications of the current *Sonderweg* debate run parallel to our views on the *Sonderweg* model itself. Just as the latter shows signs of becoming a blunted analytical weapon, so it seems to us that insistence on this particular way of 'coming to terms with the past'[50] can breed its own complacency. Methodologically, for example, the use of social-science models of a particular kind—above all 'modernization theory'[51]—has sometimes seemed to impart an excessively present-minded flatness to the work of German historians. History does need theory, and it should indeed break down our complacency about how the present came to seem 'natural'. But if, as Jürgen Kocka has argued,[52] it is

[49] J. Habermas, *Zur Logik der Sozialwissenschaften. Materialien* (Frankfurt/M., 1970), p. 116. This particular passage from Habermas has been cited by both Jürgen Kocka and Hans-Ulrich Wehler on a number of occasions.

[50] The common, almost ritual, German term is *die Bewältigung der Vergangenheit.*

[51] Among the best West German historians, it should be said, the indebtedness to modernization theory has not been uncritical. See H.-U. Wehler, *Modernisierungstheorie und Geschichte* (Göttingen, 1975).

[52] Kocka, *Sozialgeschichte.*

to de-mystify the past in this way, it can hardly accomplish this successfully by presenting German history since the middle of the last century as if the known outcome in 1933 was inscribed in every event. That leads to a form of teleological blandness, even where the ending is an unhappy rather than happy one. It threatens to produce a mirror image of the problems faced by those who praised the positive qualities of the German *Sonderweg*. One of our intentions was to try to restore a sense of contingency—although not of accident— to modern German history. That lay behind our concern to rescue Imperial Germany from the tyranny of hindsight. More generally, it might be said that we attend more to historical texture, to the 'thisness' of historical experience, than those who represent the present embattled orthodoxy do. One of us made a rather playful allusion to this position in the German edition by adapting a celebrated Ranke dictum in his title. But what we are advocating hardly adds up to historicism in the bad old German sense. The positive virtues of historicism, with its emphasis on *verstehen* and the unique event, and of critical history, with its stress on the application of theory, are not mutually exclusive. We would prefer to take the view of Wolfgang Mommsen, who has argued persuasively about the need to combine individualizing and hermeneutic methods with systematic analysis of the social structures and processes in which history takes place.[53]

Moral and political conclusions follow from this. We are not opposed to 'coming to terms with the German past', but believe that there is more than one way of coming to terms with it. In the 1960s it was iconoclastic to argue the case for a negative German *Sonderweg*; now it threatens to close off questions as much as to open them up. Thus, for example, to assert one particular form of malign continuity between 1848

[53] This is the argument of Mommsen's inaugural lecture at Düsseldorf, *Geschichtswissenschaft jenseits des Historismus* (Düsseldorf, 1971). In his review of our book, Mommsen expressed some concern about the possible conservative implications of a new 'neo-historicism'. The nervousness is understandable, but the misgivings are surely exaggerated, if not misplaced. In fact, Mommsen's position in *Jenseits des Historismus* and in subsequent years might be said to map out one of the many areas of common ground which, as several reviewers of the German edition noted, we share with West German colleagues such as Jürgen Kocka and Hans-Ulrich Wehler. That common ground should also be evident to readers of the present edition.

and 1945 not only inhibits questions about other continuities: it also cuts off arguments about continuity across the divide between the Third Reich and what followed it. The concept of year zero had an emancipating function; now it threatens to become a barrier to understanding the links between past and present. Similarly, the buttressing of the *Sonderweg* argument with modernization theory brings problems in its wake. It may be comforting to see contemporary problems as merely residual elements of an unmodern past. But how far is it true? Within the Federal Republic of Germany there are many who have criticized 'modernity' in this sense, rather than use it as an incantation against a past which has been successfully overcome. One thinks of artists such as Josef Beuyss and the new Expressionists, of film-makers such as Hans-Jürgen Syberberg, of younger historians who have followed E. P. Thompson in trying to rescue the victims of modernization from 'the enormous condescension of posterity', of the Green movement. There are obvious intellectual and moral pitfalls here, of which sentimentality is only one; and it is natural that Germans should be especially sensitive on this score. Perhaps it is also prudent to note that we are suggesting no particular identification between our intentions and theirs—nor, of course, are their own preoccupations by any means identical. All, however, have one thing in common: they are reopening questions about the German past as a means of asking questions about the German present. And that is much easier if we accept that German history from 1848 to 1945 was not a one-way street which came to an end with the Third Reich and allowed the new post-war departure. Coming to terms with the German past, in short, makes different demands in the 1980s from those it made in the 1960s. In one respect, this means that the questions the present asks of the past will be different ones. In another sense, it means returning to the past in a different way in order to pose questions about the present. The alternative is to risk a complacency as paralysing in its own way as that which historians of the *Sonderweg* successfully challenged. Hans-Magnus Enzensberger wrote in the 1960s about the dangers of a merely ritual self-abasement in the face of the German past. As he put it, 'qui s'accuse, s'excuse'.[54] Enzensberger had in mind the apologists of the 1950s and 1960s. The sentiment is no less apt today.

[54] H. M. Enzensberger, *Deutschland, Deutschland unter anderm: Äusserungen zur Politik* (Frankfurt/M., 1968), p. 10.

The British Model and the German Road:
Rethinking the Course of German History before 1914

Geoff Eley

I
Basic Assumptions
of German Historiography

The argument of this essay is about German exceptionalism. It concerns the view (too common, almost, to need specific illustration) that German history is *different* from the rest of Western Europe, not just because Germany produced Nazism (which in itself is hardly to be contested), but because this sprang from peculiarities deeply embedded in the German past. In the nineteenth and twentieth centuries (as readers will know, the argument can also be pushed back much earlier, as in the 'Luther to Hitler' type of approach) German society is thought to have shown some distinctive traits which set it clearly apart from, say, Britain or France. 'Authoritarian', 'militarist', 'bureaucratic', 'Prussian', are the adjectives that come readily to mind. The following essay is an effort to specify the nature of the German difference, by exploring some of the concepts normally used to define it.

In the views of most German historians the 'exceptionalism' argument is linked to the supposed failure or absence of bourgeois revolution in German history and its consequences for the country's future political development. It reflects the belief that unlike the other developed industrial societies of Western Europe and North America, German political culture was until the 'new beginning' of 1945 retarded and fatally flawed. In nineteenth-century Germany, the argument runs, the forces of progress had failed to establish certain necessary traditions of liberty through the achievement of parliamentary constitutional guarantees. In German history, it is argued, liberal ideals were simply not fought for with the same degree of vigour, consistency, and success as in Britain and France, where power was wrested from aristocrats and monarchs in a process of violent political revolution. The tragedy of German history, Max Weber said, was that unlike the Stuarts or the Bourbons (and one might add the

Romanovs), a Hohenzollern had never lost his head. By failing to conquer the past (pre-industrial traditions of authoritarianism), Germany was left vulnerable to the future (the internal strains of a 'modernizing' society, the political crises of 1917-23 and 1929-33, the rise of fascism).

This view centres on the Revolution of 1848. Its origins may be traced back to contemporary discussions of the later nineteenth and early twentieth centuries. Both Marx and Weber held recognizable versions, although neither gave the argument systematic theoretical, as opposed to journalistic or polemical, form. Thus, reacting to the political backsliding of the Prussian bourgeoisie in the later stages of 1848 (as he saw it), Marx directly contrasted the German experience with the English and French Revolutions of 1648 and 1789, where (in his view) 'the bourgeoisie were the class which was genuinely to be found at the head of the movement'. By contrast,

the Prussian bourgeoisie was not the class which represented the *whole* of modern society in the face of the representatives of the old society, the monarchy and the nobility. It had sunk to the level of a type of *estate*, as clearly marked off from the people as from the Crown, happy to oppose either, irresolute against each . . . inclined from the outset to treachery against the people and compromise with the crowned representative of the old society . . . making a bargaining-counter of its own wishes, without initiative, without faith in itself, without faith in the people, without a world-historical function; an accursed old man, who found himself condemned to lead and mislead the first youthful impulses of a robust people in his own senile interests—sans teeth, sans eyes, sans taste, sans everything . . .[1]

Max Weber took up the story around the turn of the century, regretting the inability of the German bourgeoisie to become as forthrightly liberal and 'bourgeois' as its British rivals and to equip German society with the kind of political culture its 'modernizing' capitalist economy deserved. As Anthony Giddens says in his concise summary of Weber's views, the impact of capitalist development was experienced 'within the framework of a social and political order which was in important ways quite different from that characterizing the

---

[1] Quoted from 'The Bourgeoisie and the Counter-Revolution', *Neue Rheinische Zeitung*, 14 Dec. 1848, Karl Marx, *The Revolutions of 1848* (Harmondsworth, 1973), pp. 192-4.

emergence of capitalism in its "classical" form', i.e. in Britain earlier in the nineteenth century.

The Industrial Revolution in Britain took place in a society where prior developments had created a 'compromise' social order in which, as Marx once expressed it, the aristocratic landowners 'rule officially', while the bourgeoisie 'in fact *dominate* all the various spheres of civil society'. But in Germany, the liberal bourgeoisie did not engineer a 'successful' revolution. Germany achieved political unification as a consequence of Bismarck's promotion of an aggressively expansionist policy; and industrialization was effected within a social structure in which power still devolved upon traditionally established elite groups.[2]

More generally this view runs through most left-liberal and radical critiques of the German political tradition in the twentieth century, descending from the Imperial period itself, through the beginnings of a democratically inclined intellectual culture in the Weimar Republic, to the post-war analyses of the North American emigration, before being revived in the Federal Republic during the later 1960s.[3] Moreover, the idea of German exceptionalism implies equally forthright conceptions of other national histories (notably Britain, France, and increasingly the USA) and certain notions of modern political development as such.[4] A strong typification of the German 'case' for the purposes of comparison—

[2] A. Giddens, *Politics and Sociology in the Thought of Max Weber* (London, 1972), pp. 15 f.

[3] The best introduction to the *Sonderweg* syndrome in German historiography is now B. Faulenbach, *Ideologie des deutschen Weges. Die deutsche Geschichte in der Historiographie zwischen Kaiserreich und Nationalsozialismus* (Munich, 1980). See also G. Iggers, *The German Conception of History: The National Tradition of Historical Thought from Herder to the Present* (Middletown, 1968); G. Iggers, 'Beyond "Historicism"—Some Developments in West German Historiography Since the Fischer Controversy', in *New Directions in European Historiography* (Middletown, 1975), pp. 80-122; H.-U. Wehler, *Historische Sozialwissenschaft und Geschichtsschreibung* (Göttingen, 1980); H. Schleier, *Die bürgerliche deutsche Geschichtsschreibung der Weimarer Republik* (2 vols., Cologne, 1975). The best introduction to the specific East German version of the tradition is the volume edited by H. Bleiber, *Bourgeoisie und bürgerliche Umwälzung in Deutschland 1789-1871* (Berlin, 1977), especially the introductory essay by W. Schmidt, 'Zu einigen Problemen der bürgerlichen Umwälzung in der deutschen Geschichte', pp. 1-33. See also R. J. Evans's review of that volume in *Social History*, 4. 3 (1979), 535-40.

[4] In fact, West German historians have turned increasingly to comparative analyses of Germany and the United States. By far the most fruitful of these is J. Kocka, *White Collar Workers in America, 1890-1940. A Socio-Political History*

as an authoritarian syndrome of pre-industrial traditions and arrested liberalism—functions centrally in the theoretical literature on political development, particularly where this engages directly with the problem of fascism and its origins. This is common to much of western political science since its institutionalization since the late 1950s (e.g. in the discussions sponsored by the Committee on Comparative Politics), and much the same could be said of the marxist literature too. The classic representations may be found in the enormously influential works of Alexander Gerschenkron, Ralf Dahrendorf, and above all Barrington Moore.[5] In sum, this provides the basis for a general interpretation of German history between 1848 and 1945, which proposes its marked peculiarity when compared with Britain, France, or the USA (and presumably the Low Countries and Scandinavia).[6]

This deeply ingrained belief in the German *Sonderweg* hinges upon certain alleged deficiencies in the political behaviour of the bourgeoisie. It is said that the German bourgeoisie was a weak or underdeveloped bourgeoisie, which failed during the nineteenth century to constitute itself as a

in International Perspective (London, 1980). I have discussed Kocka's arguments in G. Eley, 'What Produces Fascism: Pre-Industrial Traditions or A Crisis of the Capitalist State?', *Politics and Society*, 12. 1 (1983), 53–82.

[5] A. Gerschenkron, *Economic Backwardness in Historical Perspective* (New York, 1965), and *Bread and Democracy in Germany* (Berkeley, 1943); R. Dahrendorf, *Society and Democracy in Germany* (London, 1968); B. Moore Jr., *Social Origins of Dictatorship and Democracy* (Harmondsworth, 1966), esp. chs. VII and VIII. Between 1963 and 1978 the American SSRC Committee on Comparative Politics sponsored nine collaborative volumes in the series Studies in Political Development published by Princeton University Press, which are a primary source for the interpretative syndrome discussed in this essay. For an example of marxist thinking, see N. Poulantzas, *Political Power and Social Classes* (London, 1973), esp. pp. 168–84. For a further idiosyncratic but probably influential version of the argument, originally published in 1915, see T. Veblen, *Imperial Germany and the Industrial Revolution* (Ann Arbor, 1966). Finally, it will be interesting to see how Perry Anderson deals with the question of German exceptionalism in his promised typology of bourgeois revolutions in the successor volume to *Passages from Antiquity to Feudalism* and *Lineages of the Absolutist State* (both London, 1974).

[6] Most discussions of German exceptionalism are not actually very specific about what they do mean by the 'West' in this evaluative sense, but we are probably justified in assuming that they have some notion of Anglo-French-American liberal democracy in mind. One of the purposes of this essay is to bring such assumptions out into the open.

self-conscious class-subject acting politically in its own collective interests, in direct confrontation with the established domination of a landowning aristocracy. On the contrary, so far from realizing its essential interests through a political struggle with the aristocracy, the bourgeoisie in Germany embarked on a course of compromise with the old order in 1848 and the 1860s, allowed itself to become subordinated to the pre-industrial élite, failed to achieve basic reforms in the state, and permitted its own assimilation to the existing 'aristocratic' and 'authoritarian' value system. Under the *Kaiserreich* this 'feudalization' or 'refeudalization' of the bourgeoisie was heavily institutionalized. It was assisted by manipulative techniques of 'social imperialism', anti-socialism, and 'secondary integration', at which Bismarck was the supreme master and which his epigoni sought to repeat. The Imperial state's socializing institutions also played their part in habituating the bourgeoisie to a subordinate place in German society. In short, in Germany there failed to develop that 'emancipatory will' or 'sense of citizenship' which had sustained a process of democratization in Britain or France, and which is thought to be a hallmark of politically 'modern' societies. Denied an outlet in politics, it is often said, bourgeois aspirations were directed elsewhere— either into commerce and economic enterprise (according to some), or into cultural contemplation (according to others).

In the historical literature there seems to be fairly general agreement. The German bourgeoisie's failure to seize power in 1848, to carry through its own revolution in the supposed manner of the British and the French, has been described by historians of all shades of opinion as the pivotal event—or non-event—for the entire future course of German history. For E. J. Feuchtwanger, 'the very class which should have been the buttress of liberalism and stability' (the middle class) 'became a prey to extremism' (provided reserves of support for the radical right) because it had failed to develop a sufficiently strong liberal constitutionalist backbone. Or, as Theodor Hamerow puts it, 'the penalty for the mistakes of 1848 was paid not in 1849, but in 1918, in 1933, and in 1945.'[7]

---

[7] E. J. Feuchtwanger, 'Introduction', E. J. Feuchtwanger (ed.), *Upheaval and*

Now, this way of putting the problem presumes a certain set of assumptions about historical agency—about the character of the bourgeoisie as a dynamic force for progressive social and political change (as the bearer of 'progress', in fact), about the characteristics of a 'strong' or 'fully developed' bourgeoisie (as a measure for the inadequacies of the German case), and about the possibilities for conceptualizing the bourgeoisie's historical presence as that of a collective acting subject in the first place. These assumptions, as the following critique will try to suggest, are not without their problems. But for the moment we shall simply note the implications in a more general way.

For this squeezes the rich complexity of modern German history into the confining intellectual space of a very specific problematic. Our ability to conceptualize the German past is heavily constrained, I want to argue, by the two dates of 1848 and 1933. The one initiates a process of 'misdevelopment', the other brings it to its terrible conclusion. The questions German historians bring to the past originate in a kind of reverse Whiggism. Their main interest, as Ernst Fraenkel put it in one typical formulation, is in 'why . . . Germany has found it so difficult to understand the parliamentary system of government, to come to terms with it and apply it successfully.'[8] Ralf Dahrendorf put this perhaps most explicitly of all:

Why is it that so few in Germany embraced the principle of liberal democracy? There were enemies of liberalism everywhere and still are today. There may even be or have been other countries where liberal democracy has found as little recognition as it did in Germany . . . But in this study we want to find out what it is in German society that may account for Germany's persistent failure to give a home to democracy in its liberal sense.

Shortly afterwards he says: 'I want to explain what it was in German society that continued to prevent the establishment of a democratic order.'[9] In this view the real crux of

Continuity. *A Century of German History* (London, 1973), p. 21; T. S. Hamerow, *Restoration, Revolution, Reaction. Economics and Politics in Germany 1815–1871* (Princeton, 1966), p. viii.

    [8] E. Fraenkel, 'Historical Handicaps of German Parliamentarism', T. Eschenburg (ed.), *The Road to Dictatorship, Germany 1918–1933* (London, 1964), p. 27.
    [9] Dahrendorf, *Society and Democracy*, p. 14.

Germany's 'mistaken development' by comparson with the 'healthier' trajectories of the 'West' was the failure to create a 'pluralist democracy', and the vital continuity in German history is one of 'authoritarian and anti-democratic structures in state and society.'[10] This postponed the inevitable march of progress—the ultimate necessity of Germany's 'bourgeois revolution' or its functional equivalent, which would finally 'open the road to modernity', in Dahrendorf's revealing phrase.[11]

As a view of German society focused on the period 1871–1918 this has several features which are worth noting at this early stage of the argument. *First*, as already intimated above, it is a view with a long and venerable provenance. There is a fairly continuous lineage linking its exponents in the present (the period since the Fischer Controversy between the 1960s and 1980s) with radical critics of the late nineteenth century, although for a long time (between 1933 and the late 1950s) the connection was displaced into the English-speaking world, where it was kept alive by a mixture of émigrés and British and North American enemies of Nazism. It is hard not to be impressed by the degree of correspondence between (a) the views of the present historians, (b) those of an older generation formed mainly in the 1920s and 1930s (pre-eminently represented by Hans Rosenberg and the celebrated Eckart Kehr), and (c) those of Wilhelmine radicals, both liberals and socialists, themselves.[12]

But *secondly*, the 'peculiarities of the Germans' have not always been seen as a mark of inadequacy. There is a further tradition that accepted the arguments for German exceptionalism, yet grounded them differently in a historicist

---

[10] Ibid., p. 15.

[11] K. D. Bracher, 'The Nazi Takeover', *The History of the 20th Century*, 48 (London, 1969), 1339; Dahrendorf, *Society and Democracy*, p. 398.

[12] The interwar generation included Eckart Kehr, Hans Rosenberg, Georg W. F. Hallgarten, Alfred Vagts, Gustav Mayer, and Veit Valentin. As has often been observed, they amounted to a disconnected minority of talented outsiders, who received little recognition from the academic establishment of the 1920s. The individual more recently with most responsibility for bringing their dissenting perspectives to light is Hans-Ulrich Wehler, who over a period of two decades has produced a succession of valuable editions of their works. His writings in this area (mainly introductions to the above editions) are conveniently collected in Wehler, *Historische Sozialwissenschaft*, esp. pp. 227–97.

conception of national individuality, traditional notions of great-power politics, and geopolitical ideas about Germany's relationship to *Mitteleuropa*, and emerged with a positive rather than a negative evaluation of the German *Sonderweg* through modern political history. This 'ideology of the German way', as Faulenbach calls it, was properly fashioned in the essentially National Liberal intellectual culture of the Bismarckian years, before acquiring a more brazen countenance in the time of Wilhelm II. It flourished in the heavily revisionist atmosphere of the nationalist professoriat in the 1920s and 1930s, and still found many subscribers after the Second World War.[13] In this different discourse the factor seized upon by the 'dissenters'—liberalism *manqué* and the immaturity of the bourgeoisie—is acknowledged, but reinterpreted as a distinctive German *strength*, namely Germany's freedom from the corrupting liberalism of its Franco-British rivals. The stress on 'failed bourgeois revolution' is obviously absent, except as an expression of relief that (at least until 1918-23) Germany had avoided the plebeian terror of 1793-4. Accordingly, this more affirmative conception of German peculiarity will not be considered extensively in the following critique.

Thirdly, over the past two decades there has been a surprising degree of consensus about the validity of the 'exceptionalism' perspective as outlined in this essay. Historians of very different persuasions find it possible to agree on this underlying orientation. As my early references to Marx and Weber imply, for instance, this has tended to be true of both marxists and non-marxists, and while most of my citations so far have come from the latter, many examples of the former could also be found: Georg Lukacs, Isaac Deutscher, and Nicos Poulantzas each held to an 'orthodox' version of the same argument.[14] In a modified way the same is true of

[13] By far the most comprehensive treatment of this tradition is by Faulenbach, *Ideologie des deutschen Weges*.

[14] The perspective runs through many of Georg Lukacs' works, including *The Historical Novel* (Harmondsworth, 1969), and esp. *Die Zerstörung der Vernunft* (Berlin, 1954). For a brief statement, see T. Pinkus (ed.), *Conversations with Lukacs* (London, 1974), pp. 49-51. For Deutscher, see his remarks in 'Germany and Marxism', *Marxism in Our Time* (London, 1972), p. 169: '... since the Reformation the tragedy of Germany consists in the fact that it has not

historians in the German Democratic Republic.[15] That a liberal and a marxist can share the same point of departure (and to a great extent the same framework of questions) is interesting in itself, and says something about the mutual indebtedness of each. But to stress this common perspective is not to minimize differences of detailed interpretation, let alone of a more fundamental theoretical kind. To argue that many different historians have worked with similar assumptions on this specific question of the 'failed bourgeois revolution' is not to argue that their approach to history is otherwise the same. Moreover, whereas it is safe to say that a particular grouping in German historiography—the so-called 'Kehrites' in the Federal Republic of Germany and their many admirers in Britain and North America—have become especially closely identified with the *Sonderweg* thesis as it is here described, it would be wrong to regard this essay as an attack on them in particular. Likewise, to review a tradition of interpretation and to question its assumptions is not to impugn the value of individual works or the quality of their scholarship.[16] The intention is really more general and less polemical than that. It is to reflect as rigorously as possible on a well-established tradition of explanation by uncovering its logic, identifying some weaknesses and contradictions, and indicating some of the effects.

advanced with the times, and that Germany has never fought through its own revolution. The French had their great revolution. The English carried theirs through in the seventeenth century and then experienced a long process of reform, democratization, and progress. Germany in many respects has remained fixed in the sixteenth century and at the catastrophe of the Thirty Years War. Every revolution has failed.' For Poulantzas see *Political Power and Social Classes,* pp. 168-84.

[15] See Bleiber (ed.), *Bourgeoisie und bürgerliche Umwälzung,* and for a valuable discussion of related perspectives within the West German New Left, H. Grebing, *Aktuelle Theorien über Faschismus und Konservatismus. Eine Kritik* (Stuttgart, 1974).

[16] All this should go without saying. It is necessary to make the point here only because the German publication of this essay provoked widespread misunderstanding, with a number of reviewers accusing me of conflating the widely differing views of very different people into an artificial homogeneity of opinion. There is always a danger of building straw men in this kind of exercise, it is true. But I hope that the intellectual benefits of my chosen approach in this essay (freshness of perspective, a new agenda of questions) may ultimately outweigh the disadvantages (potential unfairness to individual historians).

Fourthly, more substantively the approach is characterized by a heavy emphasis on 'pre-industrial traditions'. The *Sonderweg* thesis attributes decisive explanatory weight to 'pre-industrial continuities' which should really have been overcome—what Wehler calls the successful 'defence of traditional ruling positions by pre-industrial élites against the onslaught of new forces'.[17] In other words, the weakness of German liberalism before 1918 is explained less by what happens inside the Imperial period itself than by ideological traditions surviving from a previous epoch—not by the structures, conditions, and consequences of industrial capitalism, but by 'pre-industrial' survivals thought to have been out of phase with the 'normal' logic of industrialization. Of course, to call such survivals 'ideological' traditions is a shorthand notation which should not be allowed to mislead. Such traditions are thought to have been powerfully embodied in particular institutions (the Prussian Constitution, the army, and the civil service), particular socio-economic structures (the social relations of East Elbian large-estate agriculture and the locally based repressive paternalism of the Junkers), and particular political practices (the conservative 'stabilization strategies' of government and the right-wing parties). But even allowing for this more 'materialist' dimension of the argument, I would argue that we are still justified in stressing the 'ideological' factor, because when its exponents explain the 'failures' of the bourgeoisie (its 'feudalization', its lack of liberalism), it is to the dominance of traditional values that they repair. Ultimately the battle for 'modernity' is fought out in the hearts and minds of the bourgeoisie.

Now, deep within this argument is the belief that by some universal criteria of 'modernity' the German bourgeoisie's reluctance to struggle for further-reaching parliamentary reform after 1870-1 was an irrational denial of its own best interests, certainly in the longer run. There are various ways of illustrating this point, and many of them will be aired later in this essay. But one of the best examples concerns the well-known hostility of the big employers to trade-union recognition

---

[17] Hans-Ulrich Wehler, *Das Deutsche Kaiserreich 1871-1918* (Göttingen, 1973), p. 14.

and social reform. If we follow the argument I am trying to identify, it was a 'backward' and unusually reactionary mentality—the so-called *Herr-im-Hause* standpoint—as opposed to a particular form of capitalist rationality that prevented the acceptance of more 'modern' forms of industrial conciliation. Traditional patterns of authority stopped the big employers in heavy industry from developing an enlightened view of their own self-interest by acknowledging the 'just' demands of the working class for 'political and social equality of status'. Accordingly, here as elsewhere events simply revealed the backwardness of the power élites, 'who showed themselves neither willing nor able to introduce a timely transition to modern social and political relationships'.[18]

Fifthly, this type of argumentation also contains a particular view of fascism, which defines the latter very much by its long-term origins. Here the weakness of liberal-democratic traditions also signifies Germany's greater vulnerability to fascist or modern authoritarian politics. Thus the failure to 'modernize' the political system under the *Kaiserreich* and to build a strong enough democratic consensus during the Weimar Republic are both traced back to the critical 'defeats' of the bourgeoisie in the period 1848–71, with the resulting survival of 'pre-industrial traditions' referred to above.[19] In effect the problem of Nazism is thereby redefined as a more general problem of political backwardness, what Dahrendorf calls the 'structural syndrome' of German authoritarianism.[20] Puhle puts this particularly explicitly, explaining fascism in terms of a society 'in which the consequences of delayed state formation and delayed industrialization combined closely together with the effects of the absence of bourgeois revolution and the absence of parliamentarization to form the decisive brakes on political democratization and social emancipation.'[21] With this we are

---

[18] Ibid., pp. 140, 238.

[19] For a good example of this approach, see H. A. Winkler, 'From Social Protectionism to National Socialism. The German Small Business Movement in Comparative Perspective', *Journal of Modern History*, 48 (1976), 1–18. I have discussed the problem of fascism from this point of view in Eley, 'What Produces Fascism'. [20] Dahrendorf, *Society and Democracy*, p. 404.

[21] H.-J. Puhle, *Von der Agrarkrise zum Präfaschismus* (Wiesbaden, 1972), p. 53.

back to the starting-point of this essay: the explanation for Nazism is derived from a specific contrast with the deep histories of the 'western democracies', in which Germany's alleged absence of bourgeois revolution plays a key role.

Finally, the purpose of these remarks and the detailed exposition which follows is not to minimize the differences between Germany and other European societies and to homogenize nineteenth- and twentieth-century European history in some kind of capitalist developmental stew. My aim is not to argue that before 1914 Germany was merely one capitalist society iike any other, separated only by certain 'accidents' of previous historical development from Britain or France. I have no desire to demote the importance of specific political differences amongst societies or to explain away the patent authoritarianism of the German political system, diminishing the latter to a purely epiphenomenal significance. Nor (to go to the opposite extreme) am I advocating the practical historian's familiar nominalism, in which every society is 'peculiar' and history's comparative calling completely dissolved. My intention is certainly more positive than this and the following arguments will, I hope, fall more constructively within the given terms of intellectual debate. I am really arguing for an experimental shift of perspective. In the following pages it will certainly be argued that Imperial Germany was less 'backward' and more 'modern' —and therefore more positively comparable to say Edwardian Britain—than most historians have been prepared to admit.[22] But in general my wish is not to question the *existence* of 'authoritarian and anti-democratic structures in state and society' (Bracher). My aim is simply to ask *how else* they might be understood, with a view to generating some new and interesting questions.

---

[22] If convincing, of course, this argument has major implications for our understanding of the period after 1914 and for the origins of German fascism in particular. In effect, it redirects primary attention away from deeper historical continuities and towards the immediate fascism-producing conjunctures.

II
German Historians and the Problem of Bourgeois Revolution

Thus the assumption that Germany did not have a bourgeois revolution in the nineteenth century has structured our general understanding of the German past. It affects both the questions we ask and where we look for the answers. Fixed on the apparent subordination of the bourgeoisie under the Second Reich and the seeming archaism of the Imperial state, most historians address the following question: why was the German bourgeoisie not more liberal in the style of its Franco-British counterparts, and why was its commitment to parliamentary democratic institutions apparently so weak? Moreover, this is also thought to deliver an explanation for the victory of fascism, so that the cultural specificity of Nazism—why it happened when and where it did—is almost wholly collapsed into a description of its deeper nineteenth-century origins. The peculiarity of German history is situated in a linear continuity of 'pre-industrial traditions', which blocked the development of 'modern political institutions'.

Arguably this leads to a view of the German past that is intellectually very undemanding. For the nineteenth and twentieth centuries it delivers a closed system of interpretation, each of whose elements logically presumes the others: because Germany produced Nazism, it was an illiberal society excessively vulnerable to authoritarianism; because it failed to generate a viable liberalism, it was an imperfectly 'modern' society; because the bourgeoisie are the agents of 'modernization', Germany must have lacked a self-confident and class-conscious bourgeoisie; because the German bourgeoisie occupied a subordinate place in an aristocratically dominated society, Germany lacked a successful bourgeois revolution. Of course, this logical regression from the 'outcome' of German history—the Nazi seizure of power—to its logically presumed 'origins' in the earlier period—in what I have called an authoritarian syndrome of pre-industrial traditions and arrested liberalism—is licensed by a definite conception of comparative European political development. And that in turn is composed of both 'historical' and 'theoretical' elements—a set of ideas and images about other national histories, and a set of assumptions about how 'political modernization' should normally take place. These have been most lucidly explicated by Barrington Moore, who organizes them typologically into 'three main historical routes from the pre-industrial to the modern world': 'the bourgeois revolutions leading to capitalist democracy, the abortive bourgeois revolutions leading to fascism, and the peasant revolutions leading to communism.'[1]

It is with the second of these three routes, 'abortive bourgeois revolutions leading to fascism', that this essay is directly and critically concerned. But at the same time, the idea of failed bourgeois revolution requires some notion of bourgeois revolutions elsewhere that succeeded, and before proceeding with the German discussion it will be useful to say something about the latter too. But here we enter a paradoxical situation. For once we leave the terrain of German historiography for the wider European world, it becomes unclear exactly who still believes in the idea of bourgeois revolution as we encounter it in the orthodox marxist traditions of the Second and Third Internationals. In the 1960s non-marxist historians of the English and French Revolutions spared few efforts in trying to discredit this usage, and (it must be said) pretty much succeeded. Today, few historians outside the pages of the *Annales historiques de la Révolution Française* would call the French Revolution flatly a 'bourgeois revolution' or the Ancien Régime a 'feudal society' with a completely clear conscience. Similarly, Christopher Hill stands increasingly alone in maintaining the same definition of the English Revolution (or even in calling the Civil War a revolution at all), and to do so has developed an ever more qualified and nuanced perspective.[2] It is only recently that marxist historians

---

[1] Moore, *Social Origins*, pp. xi f., xiv.

[2] In French historiography the assault was led by Alfred Cobban, first in his inaugural lecture *The Myth of the French Revolution* (London, 1955), and then in a further series of essentially destructive lectures *The Social Interpretation of*

have begun to recover their nerve on the subject, but formal discussions are still few and far between. This makes it all the more surprising that German historians who would otherwise give short shrift to marxist approaches are still happily using the term, if only in a negative way, for something that should have happened in Germany but didn't. This paradox of non-marxist German historiography—the negative invocation of a concept whose positive uses have fallen into disrepute—should be kept in mind during the following critique.

What, then, does the idea of 'failed bourgeois revolution' imply? We are hampered in answering this question by the absence of any explicit or developed statements on the subject. There seems to be a general assumption that British or French history (1648/1789) provides the right sort of positive model. But otherwise we may search German historiography in vain for detailed specifications of what a successful bourgeois revolution would actually look like. We are dealing with unexplicated assumptions rather than clearly articulated theorization. That being the case, the concept of bourgeois revolution as German historians tend to use it has

---

the French Revolution (Cambridge, 1964). In France itself, where marxist orthodoxy descended from Georges Lefebvre to Albert Soboul, the present mood of militant scepticism began with François Furet and Denis Richet in *La Révolution française* (2 vols., Paris, 1965-6). The nature of the detailed debates are conveniently summarized in W. Doyle, *Origins of the French Revolution* (Oxford, 1980). For recent interventions, see F. Furet, *Interpreting the French Revolution* (Cambridge, 1981), and E. Fox-Genovese and E. D. Genovese, 'On the Social History of the French Revolution: New Methods, Old Ideologies', *Fruits of Merchant Capital. Slavery and Bourgeois Property in the Rise and Expansion of Capital* (New York and Oxford, 1983), pp. 213-48. In British historiography the older concepts of bourgeois revolution have fallen less by direct assault than by the slow attrition of accumulating monographs, so that by the mid-1970s a pretty solid consensus had developed against the classical marxist description. However, in some ways the analogous position to Cobban's critique was occupied by J. H. Hexter's 'The Myth of the Middle Class in Tudor England', *Reappraisals in History* (London, 1961). For general critical introductions to the literature, see L. Stone, *The Causes of the English Revolution 1529-1642* (London, 1972); R. C. Richardson, *The Debate on the English Revolution* (London, 1977); J. Morrill, *The Revolt of the Provinces. Conservatives and Radicals in the English Civil War 1630-1650* (London, 1980); J. G. A. Pocock (ed.), *Three British Revolutions: 1641, 1688, 1776* (Princeton, 1980). Finally, for examples of the older orthodox usage, see J. E. C. Hill, *The English Revolution 1640* (London, 1940); A. Soboul, *The French Revolution 1787-1799* (2 vols., London, 1975); C. Mauzariac, *Sur la Révolution français* (Paris, 1970).

to be pieced together more speculatively from the larger body of practical references in the literature as a whole. Attributing ideas to people on this sort of basis (by logical imputation) is always a hazardous enterprise, and the ideas I am about to outline may not always be found as consciously adopted formulations in individual texts, which to that extent are being 'read for their silences'.[3] The advantages of getting the conceptual issue out into the open outweigh the possible injustices of interpretation to individual authors. At any rate, what follows is deliberately an exercise in abstraction, exploring the logic of certain influential interpretations to establish the limits of their explanatory potential. The object is to tease out the dominant meanings, to see how the idea of 'failed bourgeois revolution' actually functions in the discourse of most German historians, with a view to opening up some new perspectives. In this sense there seem to be five areas of potential difficulty.

(a) Talk of Germany's 'failed bourgeois revolution' seems to imply that all 'modern industrial' societies worthy of the name must at some stage pass through a bourgeois revolution of the (attributed) British or French type. (This is particularly marked in the case of Dahrendorf.) Where such an experience fails to occur, as in Germany, we have an instance of mis-development. From this it is clear that the bourgeois revolution (as a specific body of yet to be specified change) is thought to have a functional relationship to processes of 'modernization'. But if the concept of bourgeois revolution being used is marxist (and it is hard to see what other one is available), this fits rather uneasily with the developmental couplet of industrialism and democracy, which is drawn far more from mainstream political science. Now, there is nothing wrong *per se* with drawing one's concepts eclectically from different theoretical traditions. There is a very good

---

[3] On the other hand, given the absence of explicitly theorized discussions of bourgeois revolution in the German literature, I am not sure what alternative is open. Some reviewers of the German edition accused me of constructing straw men in this way. But none took up the specific issue of bourgeois revolution in this sense, either to suggest alternative forms of definition or (so far as I know) to dispute the accuracy of the one I have attributed to the current German literature.

example of this in Barrington Moore, who uses the term bourgeois revolution as 'a necessary designation for certain violent changes that took place in English, French, and American societies on the way to becoming modern in-dustrial democracies and that historians connect with the Puritan Revolution (or the English Civil War as it is often called as well), the French Revolution, and the American Civil War.' In Moore's view such revolutions result from 'the development of a group in society with an independent economic base' (presumably the bourgeoisie, although Moore never actually says as much), 'which attacks obstacles to a democratic version of capitalism that have been inherited from the past.'[4] But while this is undoubtedly a fruitful 'borrowing' of concepts, it works only because Moore is careful to define his own use of the terms. In current German historiography this is much less the case: an unmistakable orientation towards 'modernization theory' rests simul-taneously on a notion of 'bourgeois revolution' which the latter does not really share. This rather disjointed eclecticism needs to be discussed. At the least it makes for obscurity. At the most it brings contradiction and logical inconsistency.

(b) Abstracting from the historiography at large, the following definition seems to emerge: the 'bourgeois revo-lution' signifies a set of changes forced through by the bour-geoisie itself, acting collectively in its own class interests, in direct confrontation with a feudal or 'pre-industrial' ruling class. We should be clear about what this definition implies. It encourages a stress on motivations and the social identity of the participants in revolutionary events, suggesting that the bourgeoisie would itself be at the head of the revolutionary movement in an authentic bourgeois revolution, leading the insurgent masses and seizing the helm of the state. Now aside from the empirical objections to this conception which should be clear enough from work on the English and French Revolutions (the revolutionaries were not only or even mainly

---

[4] Moore, *Social Origins*, p. xii. The industrialism-democracy couplet is seriously problematic, as I shall argue below. For an excellent critique of its role in much of post-war social and political science, see G. Therborn, 'The Rule of Capital and the Rise of Democracy', *New Left Review*, 103 (1977), 2-42.

'bourgeois', their opponents were not 'aristocratic' in the same straightforward sense, the 'bourgeoisie' was on both sides of the barricades, the conscious aims of the revolutionaries were not particularly 'revolutionary', and so on), this raises some serious theoretical problems. For one, it presumes that the bourgeoisie can be conceptualized in the first place as a corporate political actor, with a collective class interest traceable through particular events and ideas in a directly expressive way, speaking through the acts of individual politicians. Though marxist in origin, this is not perhaps a conception that many marxists would now want to defend. On the other hand, it seems to be present in much German historiography 'in a practical state'. At the very least it is not inconsistent with how German historians currently talk about the nineteenth century. Again: this is a point obviously worth discussing.

(c) Thirdly, talk of the German bourgeoisie's chronic political failings strongly implies that a 'rising' bourgeoisie (if, that is, it is to be granted the status of a fully formed class-conscious bourgeoisie) should be naturally or necessarily liberal in its political inclinations. There is often a great deal of conceptual slippage from 'bourgeois' to 'liberal' in the writings of German historians, confusing the two terms' legitimate application, with a tendential reduction of politics to class. It is hard to know whether this is any more a fault of German than of other historiographies. But it does seem that the further east we go, the stronger the coupling becomes. British historians will rarely characterize Victorian liberalism in such a way, i.e. as mainly the product of a specifically bourgeois class interest, in the sense that the bourgeoisie collectively formed the Liberal Party in its own image, consciously organized it for the pursuit of unambiguously bourgeois objectives, and brought it to governmental power by the force of its social predominance. But east of the Rhine, where liberalism apparently failed to hegemonize society and the state in quite the same institutional and ideological ways, a class-sociological explanation is automatically invoked: no liberalism, no bourgeoisie. Or, to put it the other way round: no industrialization, processes of urban-class formation and an independent public sphere, no

liberalism. For Tsarist Russia this is more persuasive, particularly if we ground the possibilities for liberal politics
more cautiously in the coalescence of a particular kind of
social formation (the concentration of industry in towns, the
emergence of a capitalist class in the strict sense with its professional, managerial, and bureaucratic allies, and the growth
of a new kind of associational culture). But for Germany,
where such a coalescence was well under way by the third
quarter of the nineteenth century and firmly consolidated by
the start of the twentieth, it makes far less sense.

To maintain the bourgeois–liberal couplet in such circumstances (viz. where a bourgeoisie in the sociological sense self-
evidently exists), German historians have recourse to cultural
and ideological explanations. In other words, the German
bourgeoisie failed to develop a sufficiently self-confident
liberalism (one which its material prosperity would have justified) because its natural processes of cultural and political
development became somehow deformed. It became re-
assimilated to the dominant value system (which was aristocratic, traditional, pre-industrial, authoritarian) before it had
had a chance to elaborate and impose its own hegemony on
Prusso-German society. It became, in a word, 're-feudalized'.
By this means the causal identity of bourgeoisie and liberalism
is kept broadly intact. In more extreme cases the commitment to this identity leads to some rather extraordinary
positions, as in Dahrendorf's claim that the absence of a
liberal polity meant that German society *ipso facto* could not
have been bourgeois or its economy capitalist in the full
meaning of the terms.[5]

This raises an important point of both history and theory—
the best way of formulating the relationship between the rise
of liberalism and the rise of the bourgeoisie—which will receive

[5] The claim is made in ch. 3 of *Society and Democracy in Germany*
('Imperial Germany and the Industrial Revolution'), pp. 33–48, which follows
Veblen's analysis very closely, to the extent of explicitly borrowing his title:
e.g. '. . . Imperial Germany developed into an industrial, but not into a capitalist
society' (p. 43); 'Imperial Germany absorbed industrialization quickly and
thoroughly. But she assimilated this process to the social and political structures
by which she was traditionally determined. There was no place in these structures
for a sizeable, politically self-confident bourgeoisie' (p. 47).

extensive treatment later in this essay. Here it is worth noting
the general reductionist trap. As Ernesto Laclau has observed
in a related context, much historical writing of this kind involves the assumption that specific ideologies have a specific
class-belonging, in the sense that they appear historically to
have been the 'natural property' of a particular class or social
group.[6] Many examples might be cited. Thus anti-semitism
figures conventionally in German historiography as the
natural property of small producers threatened by industrialization or 'modernization'; socialism as the natural
property of a class-conscious proletariat, liberalism as the
natural property of a 'rising' bourgeoisie; and authoritarianism
(to return to our immediate subject) as the natural property
of a 'feudalized' and subordinate bourgeoisie, which has
failed to constitute itself as a conscious class-subject through
the emancipatory act of a successful bourgeois revolution. In
each case the prevalence of particular ideologies is 'read off'
from the presence of particular socio-economic circumstances
and logically ascribed to a particular grouping in society.
These days, when 'economism' and 'reductionism' have become the cardinal sin of materialist analysis, it seems hardly
necessary to expatiate on the drawbacks of this approach.
But the habitual conflation of 'bourgeoisie' (an economic or
sociological category, which has been associated historically
with a varied repertoire of outlooks and cultural traits) and
'liberalism' (a specific ideology and type of politics), where
the one becomes the logical accompaniment of the other, is
clearly worth noting.

(d) In most discussions of 1848 in Germany (i.e. the
moment of the bourgeois revolution's failure) events tend to
be measured against a straightforward polarity of outcomes:
either liberal victory through the triumphant voluntarism of
an anti-monarchist revolution, *or* the armed counter-revolution
of resurgent aristocratic authoritarianism. Accordingly, the
test of success for both the bourgeois revolution and an
authentic liberalism becomes a particular abstract model of
the revolutionary process. The bourgeois revolution becomes

---

[6] E. Laclau, *Politics and Ideology in Marxist Theory* (London, 1977), pp.
81 ff.

a contest, which the bourgeoisie must either win or lose, with state power as the coveted prize. If we accept the notion of the bourgeoisie as a collective political actor outlined in (b) above, this perhaps makes some sense. But if we do not, this strict polarity of alternatives begins to look unnecessarily constricting. It is not very helpful in unscrambling the complexity of events, the shifting configuration of political forces, or the full range of possible outcomes. This can be said both of 1848 itself and of later points in the nineteenth century.

(e) The idea of Germany's failed bourgeois revolution contains one further assumption which is the most dubious of all, namely that the model of 'bourgeois revolution' attributed to Britain and France (i.e. that of a forcibly acquired liberal democracy seized by a triumphant bourgeoisie, acting politically as a class, in conscious struggle against a feudal aristocracy) actually occurred. This assumption is both basic and extremely questionable. For the thesis of the abortive bourgeois revolution (so far as we can reconstruct its specific content from the present badly under-theorized usage) presupposes a reading of the English and French experience which is effectively discredited. Of course, the simplified reduction of other national histories into ideal-typical models for the purposes of comparison has a long, not to say respectable provenance. But there is a certain poignancy in the reliance of impeccably non-marxist historians on an old shibboleth of orthodox marxism, which recent historical work has thrown into disrepute. In an oddly similar controversy concerning the 'absence' of a proper bourgeois revolution in Britain, Edward Thompson dealt this kind of thinking a devastating blow:

I am objecting to a model which concentrates attention upon one dramatic episode—*the* revolution—to which all that goes before and after must be related; and which insists on an ideal type of this Revolution against which all others must be judged. Minds which thirst for a tidy platonism very soon become impatient with actual history. The French Revolution was a fundamental moment in the history of the West, and in its rapid passage through a gamut of experiences it afforded incomparable insights and prefigurements of subsequent conflicts. But because it was a gigantic experience it was not necessarily a typical one. So far from an advanced, egalitarian, left-Jacobin phase being an intrinsic part of any fulfilled bourgeois revolution, recent research into the role of the Parisian crowd, the actual social composition of the sections and of the institutions of the Terror and of the revolutionary armies, as well as into the national emergency of war dictatorship, calls into question how far it is meaningful to characterize the Jacobinism of Year II as an authentic 'bourgeois' experience at all. And certainly the *industrial* bourgeoisie cannot be credited with being either the 'vanguard' of Jacobinism or the major social force upholding this profoundly ambiguous political movement.[7]

In other words, the social determinations of revolutionary crises (whether in France in 1789, or Germany in 1848) remain extremely complex, and the specific contribution of the bourgeoisie and its various fractions far from clear. In the abstract most German historians would be unlikely to disagree with this statement or the main thrust of the revisionist scholarship to which Thompson is referring (and which has made enormous strides in the two decades since he wrote). But this makes it all the more surprising that they continue to use the older notion of bourgeois revolution in their work. Frequently we find the same historian noting quite correctly the relative unimportance of businessmen and industrialists (as opposed to professional men and civil servants) in the ranks of mid-century German liberals, and yet arguing (in an implicitly comparative manner) as though we should have expected them to be there.[8] What in the British and French settings is treated as normal—the greater conservatism and political caution of the bourgeoisie proper when compared with the intelligentsia or the 'middle strata' more generally, and the indebtedness of radical or

---

[7] E. P. Thompson, 'The Peculiarities of the English', *The Poverty of Theory and Other Essays* (London, 1978), p. 47. Note that Thompson was originally writing in 1965. After two decades of empirical scholarship on the French Revolution his remarks have an even more compelling effect. For the context of his essay, see R. Johnson, 'Barrington Moore, Perry Anderson and English Social Development', *Working Papers in Cultural Studies*, 9 (Spring 1976), 7–28; K. Nield, 'A Symptomatic Dispute? Notes on the Relation Between Marxian Theory and Historical Practice in Britain', *Social Research*, 47. 3 (1980), 479–506.

[8] e.g. compare the empirical arguments in H. A. Winkler, *Preussischer Liberalismis und deutscher Nationalstaat. Studien zur Geschichte der Deutschen Fortschrittspartei 1861–1866* (Tübingen, 1964), with the same author's more recent 'Vom linken zum rechten Nationalismus. Der deutsche Liberalismus in der Krise von 1878/79', *Geschichte und Gesellschaft*, 4. 1 (1978), 5–28, where the discussion slides continuously from 'liberalism' to 'bourgeoisie' and back.

revolutionary movements to the mobilization of forces that were still more plebeian again—is taken in Germany as evidence of socio-political pathology. At all events, what we can say is that British and French historians have largely abandoned the more schematic notion of bourgeois revolution which German historians apparently still assume.

III
Theoretical Bearings:
The British Societal Model

How, more specifically, have these assumptions helped form our understanding of the *Kaiserreich*? At the centre is a strong concept of 'misdevelopment', implying that Germany's industrial revolution failed to produce a corresponding movement in the political sphere towards 'democratization'. On the contrary, this argument normally runs, the salient feature of the Second Reich was an induration within institutional forms no longer appropriate to the notional needs of a 'modern industrial society'. After the dramatic innovations of Bismarck's first decade (1862-71) German governments showed a stubborn attachment to the new status quo. This comprised a range of attitudes no less inimical to the liberals than to the more radical canon of Social Democracy. They included the executive's relative freedom from parliamentary controls; the jealous protection of the army's repressive capability; the ruthless closure of the civil bureaucracy to progressive influences; a restricted franchise at the level of the federal states; a hopelessly unjust tax system; and in general the labour movement's systematic exclusion from the established framework of industrial and civil legality. In this way, it is claimed, a 'pre-industrial élite' of landowners preserved the essentials of its power and reduced the chances of any genuine liberalization in German public life. The recent history of Imperial Germany has been rewritten largely as the stiffening of conservative resistance to social and political change. This was made easier by the defensive 'interest politics' inaugurated by the Great Depression between 1873 and 1896. Finally, the bourgeoisie's willingness to hitch its independent class interests to those of the 'ruling élite' was cemented by the precocious rise of Social Democracy.[1]

---

[1] This and the succeeding paragraphs are meant to be a fair and accurate

It is a key part of this view that the Imperial state should have been incapable in the long run of solving·its problems and of proving adequate to the tasks of managing a 'modern industrial society'. A great deal is made of the contrast with Great Britain in this respect (though often implicitly), where a pluralist equilibrium of competing interests supposedly provided a durable framework for the peaceful containment of conflict. In Germany, it is said, this was missing, and the resulting disjunction between economic and political development (as it is viewed) allegedly placed the state into a 'permanent structural crisis'. Hence the 'ruling strata' could only overcome the absence of a suitable democratic consensus by using artificial techniques of 'secondary integration'.

This view has many sides. Thus it is usually argued that the Empire's Constitution demanded a degree of bureaucratic coordination and plebiscitary manipulation which lay beyond the powers of any Chancellor but the ascendant Bismarck, and by 1889-90 even he was running out of manipulative resources.[2] The army and civil bureaucracy became the bastions of aristocratic privilege, and even where personnel were recruited from the ranks of the bourgeoisie they were easily socialized into the prevailing illiberal value system.[3] The naval officer corps, precisely because of its non-noble intake, provides the classic illustration of this 'feudalization' at work.[4] Moreover, the imperfect parliamentary representative institutions created by the settlement of 1867-71 were

rendition of widely accepted views. The arguments can be found at their most systematic in Wehler, *Das Deutsche Kaiserreich*.

[2] See esp. J. C. G. Roehl, *Germany Without Bismarck* (London, 1967); H. Boldt, 'Deutscher Konstitutionalismus und Bismarckreich', M. Stürmer (ed.), *Das kaiserliche Deutschland. Politik und Gesellschaft* (Düsseldorf, 1970), pp. 119-42; M. Stürmer, *Regierung und Reichstag im Bismarckstaat 1871-1880. Cäsarismus und Parlamentarismus* (Düsseldorf, 1974).

[3] Apart from the relevant sections of Wehler's *Das Deutsche Kaiserreich*, see above all three essays by Eckart Kehr in E. Kehr, *Economic Interest, Militarism, and Foreign Policy. Essays on German History* (Berkeley, 1977): 'The Genesis of the Royal Prussian Reserve Officer' (pp. 97-108); 'The Social System of Reaction in Prussia under the Puttkamer Ministry' (pp. 109-31); and 'The Genesis of the Prussian Bureaucracy and the *Rechtsstaat*' (pp. 141-63).

[4] See H. H. Herwig, *The German Naval Officer Corps. A Social and Political History 1890-1918* (Oxford, 1973). For a different perspective, much closer in some ways to my own, see J. Steinberg, 'The Kaiser's Navy and German Society', *Past and Present*, 28 (1964), 102-10.

quickly frozen in their potential development. A necessary mediation of sectional conflict was thereby removed and private economic interests consequently channelled their demands via the pressure groups directly at the high government bureaucracy. The net result was a disastrous interruption of any real progress towards parliamentary institutions on the British model. The liberal-democratic tradition, as Fraenkel, Dahrendorf, Bracher, Wehler, and countless other voices have maintained, was still-born, thus easing the polarization of left and right and prefiguring the later emergence of a German fascism.

By this means the full course of German history in the nineteenth and twentieth centuries is reduced to a historic absence and its effects, the failure of the German bourgeoisie to generate a combative political liberalism on the model of its counterpart in Britain. Emerging from the shadows of the nationalist reaction against the French Revolution with its inauspicious romantic and nationalist overtones, German liberalism was formed by a succession of political defeats: 1848, 1864-71, 1878-9. As we have seen, to explain the apparently poor staying-power of the German liberals historians have argued (by a simple and highly questionable equation of political opinions and social class) that the German bourgeoisie was somehow lacking in political self-confidence, that its 'weakness and lack of political maturity' were crucial determinants in Germany's failure to develop an indigenous liberal-democratic tradition of any vitality.[5]

Here the to-ing and fro-ing between social and political categories—the conceptual slippage from liberalism to bourgeoisie referred to above—is powerfully represented. As the concept of bourgeois revolution is given an unambiguously political content (viz. the achievement of parliamentary democracy), there is no difficulty in making its failure the principal reason for the weakness of liberalism; and as the bourgeoisie itself is thought to be the leading political force in the bourgeois revolution, the weakness of liberalism is converted easily enough into a weakness of the bourgeoisie. At root Germany's 'misdevelopment' was the 'misdevelopment

---

[5] G. A. Ritter, 'Einleitung', Ritter (ed.), *Historisches Lesebuch 1871-1914* (Frankfurt, 1967), p. 12.

of the German bourgeoisie', its 'inability to develop an independent class consciousness' of its own.[6] Duped by Bismarck and frightened by the rise of labour, the bourgeoisie
allowed itself to become incorporated—socially, politically,
ideologically—within the dominant aristocratic bloc of
German society and failed to achieve a significant redistri-
bution of power and status in its own favour. This explains
the disastrous persistence of authoritarian modes of political
behaviour, it is said, part and parcel of which was the failure
to create those institutions (parliamentary ones) most suited
to the ordered resolution of conflicts. In the absence of adequate mechanisms for moderating antagonisms, and saddled
with a political system which actively legitimized the arbitrary
exercise of bureaucratic and military power, the German
middle classes fell an easy prey to the attractions of proto-
fascist ideas.[7]

Two observations might be made about the intellectual
origins of this approach. On the one hand, it rests heavily on
the accumulated wisdom of the social sciences as this appeared
in the middle 1960s. This is perhaps especially true of some
basic concepts of orthodox political science, as these were
classically represented, for instance, in the *Studies in Political
Development* sponsored by the American SSRC Committee
on Comparative Politics (seven thematic and collaborative
volumes between 1963 and 1971, followed by two additional
ones with a more 'historical' bent in 1975 and 1978), in
Gabriel Almond's and Sydney Verba's *The Civic Culture*
(Princeton, 1963), or in Gabriel Almond's and G. Bingham
Powell's *Comparative Politics: A Developmental Approach*
(Boston, 1966).[8] Here the key concepts included 'partici-
pation', 'citizenship', 'civic' or 'political culture', and above

---

[6] D. Stegmann, 'Zwischen Repression und Manipulation: Konservative
Machteliten und Arbeiter- und Angestelltenbewegung 1910-1918', *Archiv für
Sozialgeschichte*, XII (1972), 351; W. Sombart, *Die deutsche Volkswirtschaft im
19. Jahrhundert* (2nd edn., Berlin, 1909), p. 508.

[7] Again, I have tried hard not to caricature or misrepresent these views, but
to present them in the most persuasive possible form.

[8] The two historical volumes in the *Studies in Political Development* series
(probably the most interesting from our point of view) were: C. Tilly (ed.), *The
Formation of National States in Western Europe* (Princeton, 1975), and R. Grew
(ed.), *Crises of Political Development in Europe and the United States* (Princeton,
1978). One of the most striking features of this theoretical tradition (which

all 'modernization'. On the other hand, as I have already mentioned several times, the German discussion derives a good deal of its meaning from a comparison with Western Europe, and on closer inspection the latter depends heavily on a particular interpretation of British history since the Industrial Revolution. Now, in fact, I want to suggest that these two influences are subtly but inextricably intertwined, because the reading of British history in question was actually constitutive for the development of some important strains of the social sciences after Parsons, particularly those reflected in the work of Neil Smelser and Reinhard Bendix.[9] This is not to say that a conscious reflection on British history was the only or even the major formal influence on the latter, or that the British experience was incorporated

probably reached its climax in the mid-1960s) was the self-confident willingness to generalize 'scientifically' about the nature of politics and political systems. But with this went a curiously naïve belief in the solidity and permanence of the currently existing historical knowledge. There was little sense of the continuously regenerative potential of historical research—that it might subvert as well as confirm existing theoretical wisdom. There is consequently an air of contrition to the final volumes in the series, with their self-conscious return to 'history'. There is a valuable critical discussion of the tradition in D. Kavanagh, *Political Culture* (London, 1972). Of course, these discussions were cognate to similar explorations of 'modernization theory' within sociology, particularly as these affected developmental theorizing about the Third World. And here the main trend since the late 1960s has been towards a fairly destructive criticism. For the best and more constructive critiques, see D. C. Tipps, 'Modernization Theory and the Comparative Study of Societies: A Critical Perspective', *Comparative Studies in Society and History*, 15 (1973), 199-266; A. D. Smith, *The Concept of Social Change. A Critique of the Functionalist Theory of Social Change* (London, 1973); J. G. Taylor, *From Modernization to Modes of Production. A Critique of Sociologies of Development and Underdevelopment* (London, 1979). For the most cogent and persuasive of recent defences: R. Grew, 'Modernization and its Discontents', *American Behavioral Scientist*, 21 (1977), 289-312, and idem, 'More on Modernization', *Journal of Social History*, 14 (1981), 179-87. In retrospect Barrington Moore appears to be both summit and supersession of this post-war tradition—in his book's self-confident commitment to grand comparative theory, but also in its recourse to a more detailed European history.

    [9] See the following in particular: N. Smelser, *Social Change in the Industrial Revolution* (Chicago, 1959); R. Bendix, *Work and Authority in Industry* (New York, 1963); idem, *Nation Building and Citizenship* (New York, 1964). For fascinating insights into the intellectual and political pre-history of post-war social science, see R. Bendix, 'Wie ich zu einem amerikanischen Soziologen wurde', M. R. Lepsius (ed.), *Soziologie in Deutschland und Österreich 1918-1945. Materialien zur Entwicklung, Emigration und Wirkungsgeschichte* (Kölner Zeitschrift für Soziologie und Sozialpsychologie, Sonderheft 23), (Opladen, 1981), pp. 347-68.

into an absolute model in some crude or simple-minded way. But for theories of political development (that specific complex of problems concerning the relationship between the rise of capitalism and the growth of political freedoms) the British past delivered the basic materials from which the most influential models were then constructed.[10]

Of course, the contribution of the German intellectual emigration of the 1930s to this tradition was considerable, and the abstract idealization of British historical experience owed much to the revulsion of an entire generation of progressive intellectuals (many of them of Central European extraction and many of them Jewish) against brands of radical authoritarian politics of which they had direct and painful experience.[11] Appropriately enough, one of the

[10] The late-1970s resurgence of classical liberal doctrines concerning the relationship between economic and political freedoms has produced some valuable discussions of this question. See the following: B. Jessop, 'Capitalism and Democracy: The Best Possible Political Shell?', G. Littlejohn, B. Smart, J. Wakeford, N. Yuval-Davis (eds.), *Power and the State* (London, 1978), pp. 10–51; A. Gamble, 'The Free Economy and the Strong State', *The Socialist Register 1979* (London, 1979), pp. 1–25; Therborn, 'The Rule of Capital'; A. O. Hirschman, *The Passions and the Interests: Political Arguments for Capitalism before its Triumph* (Princeton, 1977). Some of the most interesting such discussions have focused on Latin America, some of them with direct reference to the European experience. See G. Therborn, 'The Travail of Latin American Democracy', *New Left Review*, 113–14 (1979), 71–109; A. Boron, 'Latin America: Between Hobbes and Friedman', *New Left Review*, 130 (1981), 45–66; D. Collier (ed.), *The New Authoritarianism in Latin America* (Princeton, 1979), esp. the contributions of A. O. Hirschman, 'The Turn to Authoritarianism in Latin America and the Search for its Economic Determinants', pp. 61–98; J. Serra, 'Three Mistaken Theses Regarding the Connection between Industrialization and Authoritarian Regimes', pp. 99–163; G. O'Donnell, 'Tensions in the Bureaucratic-Authoritarian State and the Question of Democracy', pp. 285–318; J. R. Kurth, 'Industrial Change and Political Change: A European Perspective', pp. 319–62.

[11] There is now a sizeable literature on the Central European emigration to the USA. See in particular: H. Pross, *Die deutsche Akademische Emigration nach den Vereinigten Staaten 1933–1941* (Berlin, 1955); D. Fleming and B. Bailyn (eds.), *The Intellectual Migration. Europe and America, 1930–1960* (Cambridge, Mass., 1969); R. Boyers (ed.), *The Legacy of the German Refugee Intellectuals* (New York, 1972); L. Fermi, *Illustrious Immigrants. The Intellectual Migration from Europe, 1930–1941* (Chicago and London, 1971); J. Radkau, *Die deutsche Emigration in den USA, ihr Einfluss auf die amerikanische Europapolitik 1933–1945* (Düsseldorf, 1971); H. S. Hughes, *The Sea Change. The Migration of Social Thought 1930–1965* (New York, 1975); M. Jay, *The Dialectical Imagination: A History of the Frankfurt School and the Institute of Social Research 1923–1950* (Boston, 1973). The best and most systematic introductions to this whole problem may now be found in Lepsius (ed.), *Soziologie in Deutschland und Österreich,*

forms taken by the post-sixties renaissance of German historical scholarship has been the deliberate and increasingly systematic recovery of this older critical tradition, which in practice (since few of the younger émigrés of the 1930s returned to Germany after 1945) has meant a powerful intellectual alliance with the established mainstream of North American social and political science, as the latter was encountered during the 1960s.[12] But despite the self-consciousness of some recent attempts to appropriate the methods and concepts of a non-marxist social science (most notably in the work of Hans-Ulrich Wehler and Jürgen Kocka), these have usually entered the discourse of German historians by a kind of intellectual osmosis, so that the formal derivation of certain concepts and patterns of interpretation no longer remains clear.[13] Often the indebtedness of Anglo-American social science can be coarsened into an uncritical adoption of basic assumptions, as in much of the older labour history with its stress on the natural incorporation of working-class movements under advanced capitalism (what Gerhard A. Ritter calls 'the integration of the working population into

and in various of the contributions to W. Lepenies (ed.), *Geschichte der Soziologie. Studien zur kognitiven, sozialen und historischen Identität einer Disziplin* (4 vols., Frankfurt, 1981).

[12] A number of the intellectually ascendant generation of West German historians have spent significant periods in the USA (as opposed to, say Britain or France) at such places as the Institute for Advanced Study in Princeton, with obvious consequences for their mature intellectual make-up. For representative insights into this aspect of the latter, see J. Kocka, 'Theory and Social History: Recent Developments in West Germany', *Social Research*, 47 (1980), 426–57; H.-U. Wehler, *Modernisierungstheorie und Geschichte* (Göttingen, 1975); and the essays most recently collected in Wehler, *Historische Sozialwissenschaft*. The transatlantic connections are many and particular. It is no secret, for instance, that Wehler's work in the mid-1960s on US imperialism under William Appleman Williams vitally formed his views on Bismarck's imperialism in the same period and the organizing conceptual framework of social imperialism. See H.-U. Wehler, *Der Aufstieg des amerikanischen Imperialismus* (Göttingen, 1974).

[13] I am not claiming that this is some damning peculiarity of German historical discourse, and in fact the advocacy of a 'social-scientific history' is probably more systematic and self-conscious in the Federal Republic than anywhere else except the US itself, certainly more than in Britain. An unreflected assimilation of concepts is probably the normal form of the relationship between history and the social sciences. For an excellent discussion of these matters, see G. S. Jones, 'From Historical Sociology to Theoretical History', *British Journal of Sociology*, 27 (1976), 295–305.

the totality of the political, economic, and cultural life of the nation'), held back in the German case by the unnatural resistance of intransigents on the right and left and the inflexible structures of the *Kaiserstaat*. [14]

Likewise, the implicit reliance on a particular model of British historical development is seldom based on much critical or independent analysis or on any direct acquaintance with the British past, whether through primary research or a reading of the most recent secondary literature. There are naturally some honourable exceptions, but on the whole an intensive engagement with the specifics of British social and political development has not been high on the agenda of German historical inquiry. [15] This is important. It means that the British societal model, constructed in the 1950s from historical materials which have been long since superseded in the thinking of British social historians themselves, has been

---

[14] G. A. Ritter, *Die Arbeiterbewegung im Wilhelminischen Reich. Die Sozialdemokratische Partei und die Freien Gewerkschaften 1890–1900* (Berlin, 1959), p. 150. For critical discussions of German labour history and the literature on the SPD, see G. Eley and K. Nield, 'Why Does Social History Ignore Politics?', *Social History*, 5. 2 (1980), pp. 249–72; G. Eley, 'Joining the Sundered. Social History and the History of Socialism: the SPD in Imperial Germany', *Radical History Review* (forthcoming, 1984).

[15] A major exception is the early writings of Gerhard A. Ritter on the British political system. See Ritter (ed.), *Das britische Regierungssystem. Quellenbuch* (Opladen, 1958); Ritter, *Deutscher und britischer Parlamentarismus* (Tübingen, 1962); and several of the essays collected in Ritter, *Arbeiterbewegung, Parteien und Parlamentarismus* (Göttingen, 1976). In the original German version of this essay some offence was taken at my description of these writings as 'naïve and formalistic by comparison with current political history in Britain itself'. I concede that this judgement may seem a little abrupt. But it would be hard to claim that Ritter's work (or for that matter most of the British work on the nineteenth and twentieth centuries produced before the mid-1960s) really stands up to the standards established over the past twenty years. Full references would overburden these footnotes. But a historiographical essay of this kind would begin with the seminal work of H. J. Hanham, and would proceed through John Vincent on the Liberals, F. B. Smith and Maurice Cowling on the 1867 Reform Act, Paul Smith on Disraelian Conservatism, and Neil Blewitt on the franchise, to the vast literatures on the origins of the welfare state and the New Liberalism. Lately, under the beneficial influence of the German Historical Institute and its Director Wolfgang J. Mommsen, West German historians have developed more of an active interest in the Modern British field. Mommsen himself, Karl Rohe, Gustav Schmidt, Bernd-Jürgen Wendt, Wolfgang Mock, Hans Medick, Lutz Niethammer, and Günther Lottes have been producing particularly important work in this respect. By the start of the 1980s the main exponents of 'social scientific history' in the Federal Republic had apparently shown little interest in this tendency.

accessible to German historians principally through the medium of American sociology, which has been no less impervious to the challenge of more recent historiography. To this extent the model is present in German historiography only in a highly submerged way, a second-hand interpretation of British history disguised as a theory.[16]

What is the British model? There are perhaps two major aspects. One is a particular view of legal and constitutional development which stresses the evolutionary character of the British parliamentary tradition. In its early stages this can be traced through the writings of the great classical thinkers, including Mill, Bagehot, Dicey, Maitland, and Stubbs. It continues, in a less nakedly affirmative and complacent vein, in most conventional histories of Victorian and Edwardian politics. More subtly, it can probably be found in recent studies of government and social administration, notably displaced into a concern with 'the growth of the modern administrative state'.[17] In a different form it surfaces through the older tradition of British labour history, coming again from Mill (as Young points out) with his concern for 'proletarian competence for full citizenship', and flowing into Fabianism, the Webbs, and the Hammonds, and to a lesser extent Tawney and Cole. This version stressed 'the protestant virtues of working people, their docility, respectability, and basic loyalty to national institutions. Their actions are seen in a teleological schema leading to full parliamentary citizenship—and the welfare state.'[18] Trans-

---

[16] For the above discussion and much of what follows I was originally influenced (in the mid-1970s) by the argument in N. Young, 'Prometheans or Troglodytes? The English Working Class and the Dialectics of Incorporation', *Berkeley Journal of Sociology*, XII (1967), 1–43.

[17] This is particularly true of administrative histories and work on social policy, but more interestingly the same concern is present in much nineteenth-century British social history too. See the collection of essays on reforming pressure groups, esp. the more general one by Brian Harrison, P. Hollis (ed.), *Pressure From Without in Early-Victorian England* (London, 1974), and the same author's new synthetic account of Modern British history, B. Harrison, *Peaceable Kingdom. Stability and Change in Modern Britain* (Oxford, 1983). For stricter administrative perspectives, see G. Sutherland (ed.), *Studies in the Growth of Nineteenth Century Government* (London, 1972); V. Cromwell, (ed.), *Revolution or Evolution. British Government in the Nineteenth Century* (London, 1977).

[18] Young, 'Prometheans or Troglodytes', pp. 28 f.

muted through the vocabulary of British and American sociology this reappears as T. H. Marshall's model of 'citizenship' and the related theories of Bendix, Almond, Pye, and Verba.[19]

The second aspect of the British societal model has a purer sociological origin in the classic distinction between 'community' and 'society'. It postulates the internal break-up of traditional communities and their eventual reintegration within a new national framework under the auspices of higher-level loyalties. When added to the argument about parliamentary evolution, this produces a view of British history in which the British bourgeoisie is endowed with a kind of superior political intelligence. Having restructured its relations with the old 'pre-industrial ruling stratum' between 1640 and 1832, redefined the function of the Church, and established certain civil rights under the law, it then proceeded to integrate the new working class into the socio-political order. In this way British history becomes the privileged site of fundamental evolutionary processes of social and political 'modernization'. To use Marshall's schema, class conflicts were contained by the successive negotiation of three levels of equality in a way which proved exceptionally flexible and effective—legal, political, and finally social.

This gives West German historians an admirable model against which their own history can be measured and found wanting. Of course, the foregoing exposition rests on a process of abstraction from a whole body of historiography, and it is always difficult to attribute general positions of this kind in their coherent entirety to individual authors. In addition, the exact terms of the external British comparison can often be obscured by a tendency to accept the sociological categories at face value without examining the historical knowledge or evidence on which they are ultimately based. But one extremely systematic and highly influential example of the full

---

[19] T. H. Marshall, *Citizenship and Social Class and Other Essays* (Cambridge, 1950); Bendix, *Nation Building and Citizenship*; Almond and Verba, *Civic Culture*; L. Pye and S. Verba (eds.), *Political Culture and Political Development* (Princeton, 1965). For the late-Victorian and Edwardian context, see S. Collini, 'Political Theory and the "Science of Society" in Victorian Britain', *Historical Journal*, 23. 1 (1980), 203-31.

theoretical and comparative procedure may be found in the
essays of Rainer Lepsius.[20] Here the basic thesis is once
again affirmed: that the root of German 'misdevelopment'
('Germany's special position in the history of democratization') was the 'unusually protracted retardation of
democratization as against industrialization'.[21] But the
persistence of crucial 'elements of a pre-industrial social
order' is situated by Lepsius in the context of an argument
about the inadequate integration of competing and mutually
exclusive political subcultures in the life of the state.

In Lepsius's influential opinion, the German party system
remained tightly imprisoned within a field of conflict already
established before the foundation of the Reich, which stayed
extremely resistant to 'modern' political concerns like the
'achievement of democratic institutions' or the 'realization of
claims on social equality'. Political loyalties remained 'fixed'
on regional, local, confessional, and other particularist interests, rather than moving with the times and facilitating the
new citizenry's integration within a participant political
culture. The result was the abnormal persistence of a series
of self-sealing, culturally autonomous 'social-moral milieus',
each with its own characteristic party organization. Lepsius
finds four major examples of these: a conservative one, which
was 'Protestant, agrarian, regionally closed, and wedded to
traditional paternalistic precepts'; that of the Catholic Centre;
that of the *Mittelstand*; and that of the Socialists.[22] Together,
he argues, their existence lent a striking stability and continuity to the entire period between 1871 and 1933. Increasingly each became entrenched behind a wall of defensive
preoccupations, cemented by a carefully nurtured subcultural

---

[20] M. R. Lepsius, 'Demokratie in Deutschland als historisch-soziologisches
Problem', Th. W. Adorno (ed.), *Spätkapitalismus oder Industriegesellschaft*
(Stuttgart, 1968), pp. 197–213; Lepsius, 'Parteiensystem und Sozialstruktur:
zum Problem der Demokratisierung der deutschen Gesellschaft', G. A. Ritter
(ed.), *Die deutsche Parteien vor 1918* (Cologne, 1973), pp. 56–80. Lepsius's
influence is doubly symptomatic. His own footnotes read like a detailed guide
to the theoretical literature on citizenship and political development, while his
own writings are recurrently and appropriately cited by the recent historians of
the *Kaiserreich*. To this extent his essays are the point of entry for North American
social-science perspectives into West German historiography.

[21] Lepsius, 'Parteiensystem und Sozialstruktur', p. 56.

[22] Ibid., pp. 64 ff.

solidarity. Even the rise of the SPD with its 4.2 million voters in 1912 failed to alter this situation. The labour movement itself formed a highly organized defensive subculture, and its growing popular strength merely deepened the attachment of the others to 'pre-industrial conceptions of value'. This created 'a moral frontier between the bourgeois-confessional communities of sentiment and the labour movement', which denied the 'structural conditions of industrial society' and prevented Germany's gradual democratization.[23]

The political implications of all this are drawn out especially explicitly by Dahrendorf. In fact, without necessarily being directly inspirational, Dahrendorf's statement of the argument is paradigmatic for the subsequent empirical historiography. He argues that German society

did not become bourgeois, but remained quasi-feudal. Industrialization in Germany failed to produce a self-confident bourgeoisie with its own political aspirations. In so far as a bourgeoisie emerged at all, it remained relatively small and, what is more, unsure of itself and dependent in its social and political standards. As a result, German society lacked the stratum that in England and America, and to a lesser extent even in France, had been the moving force of a development in the direction of greater modernity and liberalism.[24]

Thus we have an answer to the German question. Fascism succeeded because of the persistence of illiberal, authoritarian structures in state and society; these structures endured because the German bourgeoisie, unlike its British and French counterparts, was incapable of sweeping them away in a process of successful bourgeois revolution or of transcending the cultural autonomies of Lepsius's 'traditional social-moral milieus'; this incapacity developed because in Germany the bourgeoisie never formed itself into an independent class capable of destroying feudalism and of building a society that was capitalist and liberal in the full sense of these two terms. The problem of fascism is here subsumed in a deeper and larger argument, that the main theme of German history is the failure to create a 'modern society', the failure to traverse 'the long hard road to modernity'. For 'neither in the sense

[23] Ibid., p. 73.
[24] Dahrendorf, *Society and Democracy*, p. 52. The argument can scarcely be put more clearly than this.

of a society of citizens nor in that of one dominated by a confident bourgeoisie did a modern society emerge.'[25] If only the German bourgeoisie had been as large, as strong, as self-confident, and as successful as its Franco-British counterparts, the so-called 'constitution of liberty' (Hayek) could have been established, the authoritarian tradition broken, and a basis for blocking or pre-empting the rise of Nazism developed. In this way the missing bourgeois revolution has been made to bear an immense weight of historical interpretation. The historic absence has become so large as to fill the entire stage of German history between 1848 and 1945.

[25] Ibid., p. 397. Again, it is useful to have the meaning of 'modernization' so candidly stated.

IV
Bourgeoisie—Liberalism—Democracy: Some Necessary Distinctions

This is essentially to define the existence or non-existence of a class (the bourgeoisie) by the forms of public consciousness it displays (liberalism or not-liberalism). The maturity or even the very existence of the modern bourgeoisie as a class is held to be constituted at the level of one particular political creed. Because the German bourgeoisie failed to exhibit some heroic attachment to liberal democratic principles in their pure form, *ipso facto* it could not have been fully formed as a class, and on the contrary allowed itself to become culturally subordinated within a traditional, authoritarian, and aristocratic value system. As already suggested above, this actually assumes a simple and uncomplicated relationship between formal ideological preferences and class location, and ascribes to the bourgeoisie as a class the set of values (liberalism) which according to the textbook it should have held. From this it becomes a short step to reading off a set of political responses which the bourgeoisie should be expected to display during its passage through a succession of historical conjunctures.

A number of implicit correlations are being assumed, I want to argue, which deserve to be carefully unscrambled. Most obviously, 'liberalism' is being identified with the class consciousness of the bourgeoisie. In fact, one of the first priorities is to break this identity between liberalism as a political movement and an unmediated and unitary notion of the bourgeoisie's interests as a class. For two separate questions are being confused in this common formula. On the one hand, we may speak legitimately of 'liberalism as the pioneer of modern industrial society', if this is linked chronologically to the golden age of competitive capitalism in the middle third of the nineteenth century.[1] Here 'liberalism

[1] W. J. Mommsen, 'Der deutsche Liberalismus zwischen "klassenloser

75

implied the dismantling of internal and sometimes external obstacles to competitive private enterprise, a free market in land as in all other commodities, the judicial equality of citizens before the law, the separation of Church and State, an appropriate body of commercial law, an emphasis on talent rather than birth, and some commitment to representative government.' It was the programmatic articulation for a complex of legal, constitutional, and ideological changes that provided the conditions of development for the capitalist mode of production in a crucial phase of its consolidation. Or, to put this more cautiously, it was a programmatic description of the kind of society in which the capitalist mode of production (and hence the bourgeoisie in a strict economic sense) could become dominant.[2]

But on the other hand, liberalism also signified a specific political tradition, which—in Germany no less than anywhere else—is not reducible to immediately reflected social or economic interests. Clearly, at a time when the existing state authorities seemed to be holding back the progress of 'bourgeois emancipation' in the above sense, as in Germany between the 1840s and 1860s, liberal *politics* became easily linked to the legislative programme of the *capitalist* bourgeoisie. But liberal aims were always more than this, and the liberal parties something more than the political voice of German capital. The prominence in liberal parliamentary representation of intellectuals and professional men as opposed to businessmen is now a commonplace of historical discussion, and much could also be said about the bourgeoisie's regional diversity and internal differentiation. None of these points is exactly new, although German historians could certainly benefit from far greater precision in their formulations of the liberalism–bourgeoisie relationship. By comparison the popular character of mid-century liberalism is a fact whose

---

Bürgergesellschaft" und "Organisiertem Kapitalismus". Zu einigen neueren Liberalismusinterpretationen', *Geschichte und Gessellschaft*, 4. 1 (1978), 80.

[2] G. S. Jones, 'Society and Politics at the Beginning of the World Economy', *Cambridge Journal of Economics*, 1 (1977), 84. The most recent and imaginative general treatment of this problem is E. J. Hobsbawm, *The Age of Capital 1848–1875* (London, 1975), the book reviewed by Gareth Stedman Jones.

implications are far less remarked. Political liberalism was always rooted in larger social coalitions, which extended downwards towards the petty bourgeoisie, artisanate, peasantry, and working class, though the degree of real integration of these subaltern groups clearly varied considerably, both within Germany and from country to country.

This is very much to the point. As a political movement liberalism was necessarily composed of quite disparate social and economic forces—small producers, shopkeepers, tradesmen, and wage-earners, as well as the *grande bourgeoisie* and its auxiliaries. How these different interests became condensed into a particular political formula or coalition varied richly and could not be legislated theoretically ahead of the historical situations which may or may not have produced them. To the extent that we can generalize, the strength, unity, and revolutionary potential of these popular coalitions varied with the complexity and level of development of the social formation.

For the uneven progress of industrialization produced a whole spectrum of differing forms of class confrontation. In general, the more industrial capitalism developed, the stronger was the economic power of the *grande bourgeoisie* in relation to the masses of small producers and dealers from which it had sprung, and the greater the distance between their respective aims. Conversely, the less developed the bourgeoisie, the smaller the gulf between 'bourgeois' and 'petit bourgeois', and the greater the preponderance and cohesion of the popular movement.[3]

Exactly which groups liberalism may have represented in a particular region or country at a particular time depended very much on the balance of political forces in the particular historical conjuncture, as well as on the fundamental (and uneven) movements of the economy. In view of this complexity—the several levels of contingency in the formation of liberal politics—it is doubtful whether liberalism can reasonably be regarded—however shorthand or convenient the formulation—as straightforwardly 'bourgeois' at all.[4]

[3] Jones, 'Society and Politics', p. 87.
[4] This is quite apart from the deeper theoretical objections to this way of linking politics to class. It is ironic to find avowedly non-marxist historians slipping into a reductionism which has usually been attacked as 'vulgar-marxist' (often by the same individuals). Winkler for one slides imperceptibly between

Moreover, the type of liberalism implicitly ascribed to the German bourgeoisie deserves further elucidation. I have already discussed the strategic importance for German historiography of a 'British model', and there can be no question that mid-century German liberals also formed their ideas by explicit reference to British precedents.[5] But this employment of an external standard for the maturity or backwardness of German liberalism is suspect in a number of ways. In general it is unclear why national versions of particular political movements or traditions should be expected to conform to any ideal pattern in this sort of way. Arguably the tendency to characterize liberalism by an abstract model of universal principle (e.g. liberalism as democratic capitalism and bourgeois emancipation, or liberalism as the realization of civil freedoms, parliamentary representation, and pluralist democracy) is beyond a certain point profoundly unhistorical, because it fails to observe the unpredictable dynamics of uneven and combined development in the global context of European history—i.e. a necessary diversity in liberal movements' national conditions of existence.

In the case of the Anglo-German comparison the procedure is doubly mistaken. On the one hand, criteria of advanced

the categories of 'liberalism' and 'bourgeoisie'. See his 'Vom linken zum rechten Nationalismus', where the subectivities of nineteenth-century liberals themselves (for whom the identity of citizenship, property, and intelligence made the bourgeois–liberal couplet axiomatic) are allowed to prescribe the terms of analysis. The very best work is not immune to this tendency: e.g. M. Walker, *German Home Towns. Community, State, and General Estate, 1648-1871* (Ithaca and London, 1971), 4. 283 ff.; L. Krieger, *The German Idea of Freedom* (Boston, 1957), pp. 291 ff.; J. J. Sheehan, *German Liberalism in the Nineteenth Century* (Chicago, 1978). A similar point has been remarked by Gustav Schmidt in a number of essays. See G. Schmidt, 'Die Nationalliberalen—eine regierungsfähige Partei? Zur Problematik der inneren Reichsgründung 1870-1878', Ritter (ed.), *Die deutsche Parteien*, pp. 208 ff., and G. Schmidt, 'Politischer Liberalismus, "Landed Interests" und Organisierte Arbeiterschaft, 1850-1880. Ein deutsch-englischer Vergleich', H.-U. Wehler (ed.), *Sozialgeschichte Heute* (Göttingen, 1974), pp. 266 ff. The best way out of this problem will be through investigating the particular configurations of social and political forces in which liberalism was locally based. For an excellent example of such a study, see G. Zang (ed.), *Provinzialisierung einer Region. Regionale Unterentwicklung und liberale Politik in der Stadt und im Kreis Konstanz im 19. Jahrhundert. Untersuchungen zur Entstehung der bürgerlichen Gesellschaft in der Provinz* (Frankfurt, 1978).

[5] See, e.g., C. E. McClelland, *The German Historians and England* (Cambridge, 1971).

liberal democracy are being imported from the mid-twentieth century which are entirely inappropriate for this earlier context (e.g. mature representative institutions, or highly specialized notions of civil rights guaranteed under law by the state).[6] But secondly, this also rests on a surprisingly unrealistic notion of how far representative government had actually proceeded in mid-Victorian Britain. It both exaggerates the extent of 'democratization', given the expressly limited extensions of the franchise in 1832 and 1867 (and for that matter in 1884), and understates the repressive capability of the British state, particularly in the period 1790-1822— 'the English potential for a reactionary or bureaucratic adaptation', as Richard Johnson has called it.[7] This returns to the twin co-ordinates of most German historiography as outlined earlier in this essay: a pronounced deference to the conceptual vocabulary of the non-Marxist social sciences, and an idealized conception of the British historical experience. But there is no reason why we should directly associate liberalism—as a specific political model of constitutional government—with the natural interests of a rising bourgeoisie or the triumph of capital in Britain any more than in Germany. The harmonious synchrony of 'industrialization' and 'democratization' implicitly attributed to the British experience is a matter of received dogma (and British self-congratulation) as opposed to concrete historical knowledge.

Besides, the conceptual elision of 'liberal' into 'bourgeois' is further compounded by the still riskier equation of

[6] This can be true even of the best work in the field. Thus James Sheehan tries to explain 'why liberals were unable to fight free of the coils of the state and realize the promise of a participant nation, willing and able to define and achieve its own political destiny'. See J. J. Sheehan, 'Partei, Volk, and Staat: Some Reflections on the Relationship between Liberal Thought and Action in Vormärz', Wehler (ed.), *Sozialgeschichte Heute*, p. 170. Yet the conception of 'a participant nation' in this sense is heavily over-determined by the Anglo-American experience of the mature twentieth century, and it is not clear why the terms of this ideal should be thought an appropriate yardstick for the liberalism of mid-nineteenth-century Germany.

[7] Johnson, 'Barrington Moore, Perry Anderson and English Social Development', p. 17. For the very restricted character of the British franchise, see H. J. Hanham, *The Reformed Electoral System in Great Britain 1832-1914* (London, 1971); D. G. Wright, *Democracy and Reform 1815-1885* (London, 1970), esp. pp. 103-10, 140f.; N. Blewett, 'The Franchise in the United Kingdom 1885-1918', *Past and Present*, 32 (1965), 27-65; Therborn, 'The Rule of Capital'.

'liberalism' and 'democracy'. If we take a strict formal definition of the legal-constitutional conditions of democracy—
e.g. popular representation on the basis of free, universal,
secret, adult, and equal suffrage, buttressed by legal freedoms of speech, assembly, association and press—it is difficult to see how such a correlation can realistically be made,
given the consistent attachment of nineteenth-century
liberals to restricted and exclusivist systems of political
representation.[8] This point deserves to be formulated very
strongly: by any formal criteria of democratization, the
'bourgeois revolution' had little to do with the establishment
of 'bourgeois democracy' in any immediate or causal sense,
whether in Britain, Germany, or anywhere else.[9] In all cases
the democratic departures and their consolidation came
much later than the political upheavals normally regarded as
bourgeois revolutions.

They invariably arrived under conditions of national
mobilization, frequently during wartime or after military
defeat, and in any event through complex popular struggles
against rather than for significant bourgeois interests. The
urban artisanate and petty bourgeoisie, the independent
peasantry, and then the industrial proletariat were normally
the main bearers of specifically democratic traditions in the
nineteenth and early twentieth centuries. In other words, the

---

[8] This formal definition is the one used by Therborn in 'The Rule of Capital',
an extremely useful survey of democratization in seventeen OECD states. Therborn
distinguishes four types of exclusion from the franchise: by class, race, sex, and
opinion (as in the proscription of Socialist or Communist Parties). His definition
of democracy is more satisfactory than the typically vague and idiosyncratic one
of Barrington Moore: 'a long and certainly incomplete struggle to do three closely
related things: 1) to check arbitrary rulers, 2) to replace arbitrary rulers with
just and rational ones, and 3) to obtain a share for the underlying population in
the making of rules.' See Moore, *Social Origins*, p. 414.

[9] Nor, as Therborn points out, has 'democratization' followed naturally or
smoothly on processes of 'modernization' (e.g. by Lipset's criteria of wealth,
literacy, and urbanization). By 1914 'only three peripheral capitalist states could
have been characterized as democracies: Australia, New Zealand . . . and Norway.
If we disregard sexism and include male democracies, then two more examples
could be cited: France and Switzerland.' See Therborn, 'The Rule of Capital',
p. 19. In this context see S. M. Lipset, 'Some Social Requisites of Democracy:
Economic Development and Political Legitimacy', *American Political Science
Review*, 53 (1959), 69-105, a work distinguished by its cavalier misuse of historical evidence.

possibilities for democratic politics resulted from the contradictions of 'modernization' rather than its triumph, not as a condition of the bourgeoisie's success, but from the new antagonisms it created. As Stedman Jones says, while the bourgeoisie rode the wave of industrialization it confronted 'an increasingly desperate and disunited mass of small producers and semi-proletarians', and it was from the materials of this pauperization that the mid-nineteenth-century radical democracy was constructed. It was then later, as 'the emerging contours of liberal capitalist society' became more sharply visible, that the leading role passed to the working class proper.[10] In both cases 'democratization' was the object of a struggle in which the 'bourgeoisie' as such more commonly resisted democratic gains than helped them along.[11]

In the end the implied causal chain—bourgeoisie = liberalism = democracy—rests on a fundamental misconception concerning the nature of bourgeois revolutions. As noted earlier in this essay, German historians tend to conceive bourgeois revolutions as the conscious achievement of an acting class-subject, in which power is forcibly wrested from a previously existing aristocratic-monarchical state and reconstituted in explicitly liberal-democratic terms. This logically necessitates ascribing to the bourgeoisie a corporate political consciousness of a unified and liberal democratic kind. Yet there are enormous conceptual and empirical difficulties with such an approach. It takes little account of differences within the

---

[10] Jones, 'Society and Politics', pp. 87f.

[11] See also Johnson's comments in 'Barrington Moore, Perry Anderson and English Social Development', p. 17: 'Against the familiar stereotypes one should insist that the new working-class presence was *determining*. It made not only itself, but contributed to the making of nineteenth century society and, not least, to "bourgeois" (or aristocratic) freedoms. It is arguable that it was not so much middle-class agitation nor the amateur culture of aristocracy that made England "relatively free", but a plebeian agitation and culture, or, more accurately still, the friction of all three. If space allowed this could be demonstrated in several critical areas: in the actual achievement of parliamentary *democracy* (as opposed to a wholly propertied parliamentary system); in the liberty of the press and of the public meeting, both freedoms being won or maintained by *popular exercise*; and, not least, in the stemming of the very real impulse to a bureaucratic state, signalled in the popular defeat of the full Chadwickian programme of poor law reform. Certainly in the early nineteenth century working class movements seem to have been the main bearers of the notions of natural and civil rights.'

simple category of 'bourgeois' between different kinds of capitalist, professional, and administrative groups, the intellectuals, and the petty bourgeoisie, and fails to specify why each of them should have been attracted to liberal values in the extended political sense. If we take a strict definition of the bourgeoisie as the owners and controllers of the means of production in the capitalist mode, this theoretical weakness becomes most striking of all, because the *grande bourgeoisie* was a reluctant participant in the upheavals of 1848 and was unambiguously committed to extremely moderate goals in the political sphere, which certainly fell far short of anything resembling liberal democracy. Besides, how do we reconcile this view of bourgeois revolution with the universal prominence of non-bourgeois groups (small producers and traders, peasants, proletarians, students) in the actual revolutionary movements between 1789 and 1848? If we keep to the conventional usage we are left with an uncomfortable paradox, in which the insurgent people pursue democratic aims against the bitter resistance of the very class—the bourgeoisie proper—in whose interests the revolution is supposed to occur. Much more than this, in fact, because the insurgency of the masses was actually directed against the very process of advancing liberal capitalism which the bourgeois revolution is supposed to promote.

We can only make sense of this paradox by carefully separating the content of the popular revolutionary struggles in 1848 (or 1789) from the actual changes they ultimately helped to confirm, or at least failed to obstruct. This leads to other distinctions—between the social and occupational backgrounds of the revolutionaries and the social relations of domination and exploitation that constrained their actions; between intention and effect; and between how the revolution was 'made' and how its experience was eventually assimilated. Abstractly this means distinguishing between two levels of determination and significance—between the revolution as a specific crisis of the state, involving widespread popular mobilization and a reconstitution of political relationships, and on the other hand the deeper processes of structural change, involving the increasing predominance of the capitalist mode of production, the potential obsolescence of many existing practices and institutions, and the uneven transformation of social relations. How these two levels became articulated together in the revolutionary conjuncture of a 1789 or 1848—change at the level of the state, change in the social formation—is a matter for detailed historical investigation. The precise nature of the contradictions which the development of capitalism in Germany created (or the process of 'modernization', depending on one's point of view) and how these were handled by the old absolutist states—i.e. the relation between the economic and the political —cannot be laid down in advance by dogmatic assumptions concerning the relationship of 'bourgeois revolution' to 'liberal democracy', whatever their provenance, marxist, sociological, or some combination of the two.

At the very least this requires a rethinking of terms. Perhaps the concept of bourgeois revolution should be dissociated from the necessary introduction of specific constitutional and liberal-democratic forms of rule, and instead should be related more generally to the conditions of bourgeois predominance in society. In other words, the concept could be freed from its present dependence on the notion of forcibly acquired political liberalism and could be redefined more flexibly to mean the 'inauguration of the bourgeois epoch'—i.e. 'the successful installation of a legal and political framework for the unfettered development of industrial capitalism'. As Stedman Jones goes on, 'the triumph of the bourgeoisie should be seen as the global victory of a particular form of property relations and a particular form of control over the means of production, rather than as the conscious triumph of a class subject which possessed a distinct and coherent view of the world.'[12] That being the case, the *national modalities* of bourgeois revolution could be expected to vary considerably, with widely differing consequences, and should certainly not be identified with either the British or French examples, each of which possess their own singularity. Likewise, a considerable diversity of political regimes and forms of the state are compatible with the development and consolidation of capitalist production and

[12] Jones, 'Society and Politics', pp. 87 f.

social relations. In other words, the German pattern of 'revolution from above' in 1848-71 was just as capable of securing bourgeois predominance as the different experience of Britain or France, and if that is so perhaps qualifies just as readily for the title of bourgeois revolution. In some ways this was more closely linked to the realization of specifically bourgeois interests than elsewhere, because in Britain and France the latter was complicated by the unruly interventions of the subordinate classes ('plebeians', *menu peuple*). Arguably, the greater progress of democratic forms in those two countries owed far more to these intrusive popular conflicts than to the spontaneous liberalism of a 'rising bourgeoisie'.[13]

There is a case for treating German unification, the Italian *Risorgimento*, and the Meiji Restoration in Japan as directly comparable experiences. Each might be described as a 'bourgeois revolution from above', in the specific sense that in a concentrated space of time and through a radical process of political innovation it delivered the legal and political conditions for a society in which the capitalist mode of production could be dominant. This was achieved by often quite far-sighted and visionary interventions by the existing states (or at least by the radical pragmatism of 'modernizing' tendencies within them), but without the social turbulence and insurrectionary extravagance which marked the earlier Franco-British patterns. Of course, in neither Germany nor Italy (the Japanese case is more difficult to judge) was the action of the state wholly autonomous or unrelated to wider processes of social change, although the latter might easily be imposed from the outside, as in the Napoleonic occupations

---

[13] Though in other respects (and especially at an earlier stage in the development of this essay, say in the mid-1970s) my thinking owed a great deal to a reading of Nicos Poulantzas, it should be said that at the level of historical comparison he remains squarely within the framework discussed in this essay. This is especially true of the normative elevation of the British and French experiences into *authentic* bourgeois revolutions and the concomitant definition of the German (and Italian) experiences as aberrant, leading in the long run to the emergence of an 'exceptional state' under Nazism (and Fascism). In the end he buys into the same teleology of bourgeois revolution, in which the latter is functionally tied to the development of a liberal-democratic polity in capitalist societies. Aside from N. Poulantzas, *Fascism and Dictatorship* (London, 1974), and the relevant parts of *Political Power and Social Classes*, see also N. Poulantzas, 'Marxist Political Theory in Great Britain', *New Left Review*, 43 (1967), 64ff.

of Germany and parts of Italy, or the threatening incursion of western influences into Japan. In this sense Bismarck's radical solution to the German question, under circumstances of a constitutional confrontation with a resurgent German liberalism, is the classic instance of successful revolution from above, substituting military unification and direct political negotiation with the opposition for the more confusing and volatile scenario of the English and French Revolutions. In some ways—the sharpness of the rupture with the past, the definitive character of the legal settlement, the commanding strength of capital in the new national economy—German unification was more specifically 'bourgeois' in its content and more resoundingly 'bourgeois' in its effects than either the English or the French Revolution had been, precisely because significant popular interventions failed to occur.[14]

To make sense, 'revolution from above' requires the overall European context, in both its spatial and its temporal dimensions. In other words, we need something like the classical marxist concept of 'uneven and combined development'. On the one hand, German and Italian unifications occupied a distinct temporality when compared with the earlier sequence of the Dutch, British, American, and French Revolutions. Where the latter occurred before the global victory of capitalist relations on a European, let alone a world, scale—the former actively presupposed the triumph of capitalism; where the earlier revolutions were driven forward by broad coalitions of large and small property-owners, the later ones lost this popular impetus to an intervening process of social differentiation, which (as Stedman Jones argues) set the bourgeoisie proper against the mass of pauperized small producers and the infant working class. The growth of an independent popular radicalism, which by the 1860s was already separately organized into nascent socialist parties, constrained the

[14] There is some evidence in the reactions of Marx and Engels to German unification that they shared a similar view of revolution of above, which Engels tried to express theoretically in the concept of 'Bonapartism'. For the main references see K. Marx and F. Engels, *Selected Works in Three Volumes* (Moscow, 1969), I. 604-7, 649f., and K. Marx and F. Engels, *Werke* (41 vols., Berlin, 1957-68), 31. 208f., 226f.; 34. 335; 36. 54. See also F. Engels, *The Role of Force in History*, ed. E. Wangermann (London, 1968).

oppositional potential of the German bourgeoisie, whose political imagination was in any case somewhat chastened by the spectacle of terror, barricades, and popular insurrection west of the Rhine. This tension between the modernizing aspirations of the progressive bourgeoisie and its fears of popular mobilization opened the necessary space for a 'Bismarckian' solution. The latter implemented most features of the liberal programme (national economic integration, freedom of trade, standardization of currency, weights and measures, and commercial practice, codification of the law, and so on), while stifling the pressure for a full parliamentary constitution.

But if the violent political history of the English and French Revolutions cautioned the German bourgeoisie, the impressive developmental progress of British society had precisely the opposite effect. In the triumph of Britain's industrial prosperity the German bourgeoisie saw its own future reflected. Of course, the further to the east in Europe, the greater the discrepancy between the developmental aspiration and society's real capacity for emulation. None the less, from the early nineteenth century the western experience was being systematically appropriated as an imitative programme well in advance of the indigenous social development necessary to sustain it. There is an essential political precocity to these efforts of the more backward societies of Central, Southern, and Eastern Europe to bridge the developmental gap. Rather than rationalizing an accumulation of existing change, revolutionary programmes become an attempt to anticipate the desirable future.[15]

In general, like the stress on outcomes and effects as opposed to the intentions of the revolutionary actors, the idea of revolution from above takes us away from the familiar imagery of heroic exploits and dramatic events. Instead, it leads to a stress on much longer processes of structural change, in which what would normally be regarded as *the* revolution becomes just a particularly dramatic and violent

---

[15] My thinking in this part of the essay owes much to Tom Nairn's writings on nationalism. See T. Nairn, *The Break-Up of Britain. Crisis and Neo-Nationalism* (London, 1977), esp. pp. 92ff., 329ff.

episode, as much a symptom as a cause. There is much support for this approach in the marxist tradition, from Marx's own reference to 'an era of social revolution' in the famous 1859 Preface, and the debates on the transition from feudalism to capitalism, to the GDR historians' stress on the entire period of German history between 1789 and 1871 as an epoch of 'bourgeois upheaval' (*bürgerliche Umwälzung*), in which the Prussian reform era, the 1848 revolutions, and the decade of unification form the nodal points.[16] In British history Edward Thompson has referred to the entire period between the fifteenth and early nineteenth centuries and to the individual moments of political change within it as the 'pieces of that great arch which in fact, in the epochal sense, make up the bourgeois revolution.'[17] In *The Age of Capital* Eric Hobsbawm takes a similar approach, stressing the bourgeoisie's overall cultural predominance rather than its collective political domination of the state, with implicit recourse to Gramsci's idea of hegemony.[18]

[16] The context of Marx's statement is as follows: 'The mode of production of material life conditions the general process of social, political and intellectual life. It is not the consciousness of men that determines their existence, but their social existence that determines their consciousness. At a certain stage of development, the material productive forces of society come into conflict with the existing relations of production or—this merely expresses the same thing in legal terms— with the property relations within the framework of which they have operated hitherto. From forms of development of the productive forces these relations turn into their fetters. Then begins an era of social revolution.' See 'Preface' to *A Contribution to the Critique of Political Economy*, K. Marx, *Early Writings* (Harmondsworth, 1975), pp. 425 f. The best introduction to marxist discussions of the transition from feudalism to capitalism is through R. Hilton (ed.), *The Transition from Feudalism to Capitalism* (London, 1976). For the views of GDR historians, see Bleiber (ed.), *Bourgeoisie und bürgerliche Umwälzung*.

[17] Thompson, 'Peculiarities', p. 47.

[18] See also Hobsbawm's writings on the transition and on the general crisis of the seventeenth century, where the conception of societal transformation is classical in the 1859 Preface sense: E. J. Hobsbawm, 'The Crisis of the Seventeenth Century', T. Aston (ed.), *Crisis in Europe 1560–1660* (London, 1965), pp. 5–58; E. J. Hobsbawn, 'The Seventeenth Century in the Development of Capitalism', *Science and Society*, XXIV. 2 (1960), 97–112; E. J. Hobsbawm, 'From Feudalism to Capitalism', Hilton (ed.), *Transition*, pp. 159–64; Communist Party History Group (ed.), *Feudalism, Capitalism and the Absolutist State. Reviews of Perry Anderson by Eric Hobsbawm and Douglas Bourn* (Our History Pamphlet no. 66), London, 1976, pp. 3–13; E. J. Hobsbawm, 'Gesellschaftskrise 1789–1848', R. Urbach (ed.), *Wien und Europa zwischen den Revolutionen (1789–1848)* (Vienna-Munich, 1977); E. J. Hobsbawm, 'Introduction', K. Marx, *Pre-Capitalist Economic Formations*, ed. Hobsbawm (London, 1964), pp. 9–65.

Despite the attractions of this approach, it is perhaps unclear how far it means withdrawing from the view that the bourgeois revolution represents primarily a moment of violent or convulsive political change, and there is something of this same syndrome in Gramsci's own idea of 'passive revolution'.[19] Of course, the fundamental difficulty of relating specific political events like the English or the French Revolution to the longer-run processes of social change that are thought to precede, inform, and largely determine them still remains. And to the extent that the stress on 'bourgeois revolution in the epochal sense' involves a retreat from the problem of causality, it amounts to an important weakness.

We are now in a position to recapitulate the main tendency of my argument. In a nutshell, liberal-democratic institutions have rarely been established in any pure form as the direct result of violent political convulsions (revolutions) in which the 'bourgeoisie' as such played the leading role. More often they resulted from an extremely protracted history of political conflict, in which specifically democratic achievements were more commonly precipitated by the intervention of non-bourgeois subaltern groups. Both the British parliamentary and French republican traditions originated in complex and extended conflicts of this type. At the same time, the various fractions of the bourgeoisie were perfectly capable of sustaining or accommodating to non-parliamentary forms of rule, whether monarchical, dictatorial, or some other type of repressive authoritarianism, without somehow 'betraying' the bourgeoisie's liberal tasks or alienating its 'true' destiny as a class.

Now, once we accept that the bourgeoisie need not announce a corporate presence on the political stage of a consciously liberal-democratic kind, and once we accept that the characteristic features of bourgeois consciousness in an emergent capitalist society are instead the fragmented

---

[19] For Gramsci's thinking in this respect, see A. S. Sassoon, *Gramsci's Politics* (London, 1980), pp. 204-17; C. Buci-Glucksmann, 'State, Transition and Passive Revolution', C. Mouffe (ed.), *Gramsci and Marxist Theory* (London, 1979), pp. 207-36; P. Ginsborg, 'Gramsci and the Era of Bourgeois Revolution in Italy', J. A. Davis (ed.), *Gramsci and Italy's Passive Revolution* (London, 1979), pp. 31-66, together with Davis's own 'Introduction' to the same volume, pp. 11-30.

individualist pursuit of other less political virtues (competition, merit, secularism, law and order, and so on)—then the
conventional notion of bourgeois revolution as a necessary
stage of forcibly acquired, spontaneously generated liberality,
through which any 'modern' society must eventually pass,
makes far less sense. It may be far more useful (following
Stedman Jones) to see the revolutionary nexus of the bourgeois epoch in that concentrated body of change needed to
establish 'the appropriate legal and political framework for
the unhampered reproduction of capitalist relations of production'.[20] That being the case, the exact political modalities
of the transition may vary greatly from country to country,
and may only be determined through careful historical
analysis.

Why is all this so important? Because the belief that there
was no bourgeois revolution (in the orthodox sense) in
Germany between 1848 and 1871 has led historians to argue
that in the next fifty years the bourgeoisie could only have
participated in the political system as the junior partner of
an aristocratic élite whose political dominance remained
essentially intact. By controlling the socializing institutions
and by the massive application of manipulative, repressive,
and authoritarian techniques of rule, the East Elbian nobility
were able to obstruct that higher order of rationality that
allegedly characterized the political system of Britain. This
ensured the 'stabilization of the system' in the short term, it
is said, but the artificial nature of the 'secondary integration'
which this involved left the *Kaiserreich* structurally prone to
periodic political crises. The cracks in the body politic could
only be papered over by further diversionary emphasis on
foreign policy (army, navy, colonies, the Slav peril, the arms
race, the clash of world empires, and so on), and in the end
this 'social-imperialist' mechanism led to the ultimate gamble
of all in July 1914. But yet again: this assumes that the
development of a mature capitalist society could only take
place on a stable basis within one particular framework of
political institutions, the ones we associate with the advanced
capitalist countries of Western Europe and North America

[20] Jones, 'Society and Politics', p. 86.

after 1945. What I want to suggest (reverting to my proposed redefinition of bourgeois revolution) is that the evidence of German society between 1871 and 1914 lends support to an alternative case, that the orderly reproduction of capitalist productive relations could be guaranteed within a form of state which fell considerably short of pure representative democracy. We should be clear about what this statement means. It is not that the specific forms of German political development had no consequences. It is simply that the received ideas of 'failed bourgeois revolution' and 'liberal capitulation' provide a poor means for understanding them. Rather than asking why the German bourgeoisie failed to act in an approved liberal way, we should ask ourselves why we should ever expect it to be liberal in the first place.

V
Backward State/Modern Economy: Unscrambling the German Couplet

As stated at the beginning of this essay, my remarks are meant to pinpoint a pivotal notion of German historiography, whether marxist or non-marxist. This concerns the belief that the long-term peculiarity of German history—its ability to generate a fascist response to the world economic crisis after 1929—is to be explained by the twin factors of failed revolution and absent liberalism in the nineteenth century. It is the argument of this essay that this lament for the lost liberalism of the German bourgeoisie is profoundly unhistorical. On the one hand, the German past is presented in classic idealist form as the competition of hostile principles, liberalism and authoritarianism, one 'good' the other 'bad'. Accordingly, an external measure of abstract liberalism is applied to the outcome of specific events in the German past, so that the 1848 Revolution is judged by the extent to which certain ultimate goals (in the teleological sense) are realized or glimpsed, whether to do with German unity, constitutional development, or the social movement.[1]

But at the same time, the nineteenth-century victory of authoritarianism is thought to be merely the temporary and abnormal interruption of an inevitable 'process of democratization' which necessarily 'accompanies economic growth'. In Germany a 'truly realistic' appreciation of what a lasting

---

[1] This point is also made by R. Wirtz, 'Zur Logik plebejischer und bürgerlicher Aufstandsbewegungen—Die gescheiterte Revolution von 1848', *Sozialwissenschaftliche Informationen für Unterricht und Studium* (SOWI), 8 (1979), 84. The approach being criticized is particularly evident in M. Stürmer, '1848 in der deutschen Geschichte', Wehler (ed.), *Sozialgeschichte Heute*, pp. 228-42, where the events of 1848 are judged essentially through a grid provided by three fundamental questions of the nineteenth century (as Stürmer sees them)—the national, constitutional, and social questions (corresponding perhaps to Marshall's three kinds of equality)—all of which are thought in a strongly teleological sense to have a final long-term resolution, principally in the period after 1945.

and consistent 'modernization' would require was precluded by a kind of bourgeois false consciousness resulting from a powerful combination of factors: anxieties produced by the irregularities of economic growth and the fears of social instability, but also the manipulation of those fears by the political managers of the 'old élite' (Bismarck, Bülow, Tirpitz). It is hard not to be impressed by the powerful teleology running through this conception. 'Modernization' in this discourse is indissolubly linked to present-day forms of 'pluralist democracy'. Furthermore, it is built in to the structures of economic growth and in the long run irresistable. To explain why German history diverges from the 'model', historians have not surprisingly been thrown back on to a vocabulary of 'wrong turnings', 'failures', 'blockages', and 'mistaken development'.[2]

There are perhaps two theoretical-cum-methodological points arising from this discussion. The first concerns the stress on 'values' and ideology. The explanation for why German history failed to run its proper liberal course is usually resolved in the sphere of consciousness. Recent historians have focused overwhelmingly on finding a set of institutional and other factors which allegedly inhibited the formation of an 'emancipatory' will on the part of the bourgeoisie: education, militarism, bureaucratic supervision of civilian life, patriotically inclined recreational clubs, the multiplicity of nationalist pressure groups, the social prestige of the aristocracy and monarchy, and so on. The continuity of authoritarian values so described is certainly connected to the survival of a particular power bloc in Imperial society— the alliance of heavy industrial and agrarian interests so familiar from recent historiography. But its resilience is made dependent on a combination of ideological mechanisms which warped the 'true' perceptions of the bourgeoisie and hindered the establishment of the 'constitution of liberty' on the model of the 'West'. This leads to a *primacy of 'pre-*

---

[2] Wehler's *Modernisierungstheorie und Geschichte* leaves this mode of analysis largely intact. See also H.-U. Wehler, 'Industrial Growth and Early German Imperialism', R. Owen and B. Sutcliffe (eds.), *Studies in the Theory of Imperialism* (London, 1972), pp. 71-92, where the framework is particularly powerfully present.

industrial traditions' in the explanatory repertoire of German historians—ideological continuities or survivals from a previous epoch which 'ought' to have been superseded in the course of socio-economic development. As suggested earlier in this essay, such views are predicated on a particular set of sociological orthodoxies and a related model of British societal change, refracted in particular through the historical essays of that expert 'generalizer' Rainer Lepsius.[3] In particular, it is worth mentioning the superficial, but enormously influential, essays of Talcot Parsons from the 1940s ('Democracy and Social Structure in Pre-Nazi Germany' and 'Some Sociological Aspects of Fascist Movements'), and a certain left-liberal critique going back to the political writings of Theodor Barth, Friedrich Naumann, and Max Weber in the Imperial period itself.[4] Dahrendorf puts it like this: 'The social basis of German authoritarianism, thus of the resistance of German society to modernity and liberalism, consisted in a structural syndrome that held people to the social ties in which they had found themselves without their doing and that prevented them from full participation.'[5]

But secondly, this also involves a particular understanding of power and of the relations between the political, the economic, and the social. As argued in some detail, the assertion of a German *Sonderweg* for the period of the *Kaiserreich* takes the form of two strong theses: the idea of ' "the inherited" deep discrepancies between the social structure and the political system' (Bracher), and the related assumption that the existence of 'any modern society attempting to be

---

[3] One reviewer of the German edition took this phrase to be an attack on Lepsius, presumably by seeing it as an expression of sarcasm. In fact, the intention was the opposite. Though not without a trace of playful but essentially admiring irony, it was meant as a positive commendation. Though some of my German reviewers clearly find this hard to grasp, critique can be friendly, and criticism and admiration can go together.

[4] See T. Parsons, *Essays in Social Theory* (Glencoe, 1964), pp. 104–41. For some further thoughts on the intellectual provenance of these interpretations, see two of my earlier essays: G. Eley, 'The Wilhelmine Right: How It Changed', R. J. Evans (ed.), *Society and Politics in Wilhelmine Germany* (London, 1978), pp. 112–35; G. Eley, 'Capitalism and the Wilhelmine State: Industrial Growth and Political Backwardness in Recent German Historiography, 1890–1918', *Historical Journal*, 21 (1978), 737–50.

[5] Dahrendorf, *Society and Democracy*, p. 404.

equal to the demands of constant social change' logically entails a particular constitutional framework of liberal parliamentarism (Wehler).[6] Both theses require certain conclusions regarding the 'backwardness' of German political culture and the archaism of the Imperial state, so that the latter becomes the institutional expression of the 'pre-industrial traditions' and ideological survivals mentioned above. In other words, a radical disjunction is being postulated between 'wealth' and 'power', between the 'modern' basis of the industrial-capitalist economy and the 'traditional' political arrangements which the bourgeoisie proved incapable of sweeping away. Furthermore, the stability of the system could only be assured by the development of more 'modern' institutional arrangements for containing social conflict. In the most explicit statements of the argument such containment could only be achieved by 'welfare-statist' and parliamentary-democratic replacements for 'the rule of an authoritarian leadership and of privileged social groups centring around the pre-industrial élites of the aristocracy.'[7] Otherwise the inescapable dictates of power legitimation in the developed industrial economy could be satisfied only by artificial forms of 'secondary integration', which Wehler has characterized theoretically as 'social imperialism', in which the tensions are diverted outwards into an expansionist drive for imperialist accumulation. In this case the unreformed *Kaiserstaat* was incapable of reproducing itself other than by an escalating procession of crises, culminating in the miscalculated risk of July 1914.[8]

Now it seems to me that German historians are mixing up two distinct problems in this discussion, which require careful analytical separation. Basically we have to distinguish between the state's relationship to fundamental economic processes and its relation to political conflicts and processes of

[6] K. D. Bracher, *Deutschland zwischen Demokratie und Diktatur* (Munich, 1964), p. 155; Wehler, 'Industrial Growth', p. 84.

[7] Wehler, 'Industrial Growth', p. 78.

[8] In Wehler's case this is linked explicitly to Jürgen Habermas's theory of legitimation. See esp. Wehler, *Bismarck*, p. 500. For Habermas's more recent views, see J. Habermas, *Legitimationsprobleme im Spätkapitalismus* Frankfurt, 1973); J. Habermas, 'Conservatism and Capitalist Crisis', *New Left Review*, 115 (1979), 73-86.

representation. This involves a further theoretical distinction between the *dominance* of the capitalist mode of production and its processes of reproduction in a given social formation and its simultaneous *coexistence* with other modes of production and forms of social relations, because the state had to cope with different types of problems in each case, namely meeting the complex needs of capital accumulation and maintaining cohesion in the social formation as a whole.[9] It is only by blurring these distinctions, I would argue, that German historians have jumbled the categories of 'bourgeois', 'liberal', and 'democratic' together, so that liberal democracy and the predominance of capitalist relations come to

[9] It should be clear that this presupposes a particular Marxist approach to the theory of the state, which should be sharply distinguished from the simple thesis of state-monopoly capitalism (*stamokap*, in the accepted abbreviation) and similar instrumentalist views. This statement of the marxist-theoretical status of the concepts employed in this essay is important, because the leading non-marxist exponents of the arguments being criticized continue to identify the *stamokap* thesis as the only possible marxist approach. By contrast the approach adopted here seeks to combine elements from two other marxist discussions, those associated with Nicos Poulantzas and those of the so-called state-derivation theorists, while maintaining a sense of their respective limitations. It owes most to the thoughts of Gramsci and the recent work of Bob Jessop. Regrettably (and rather surprisingly given their forthright condemnations of my own 'lumping' tendencies, lamentable failure to draw distinctions amongst intellectual positions, propensity for straw men, and so on), the German reviewers of this essay's earlier version largely ignored this explicit theoretical demarcation and accused me of trotting out the same old 'dogmatic' garbage—'a crude *stamokap* line', as one of them put it. Yet for anyone familiar with recent marxist discussions or recent theories of the state the difference should be clear enough. The unwillingness of certain critics to acknowledge it I can only put down to intellectual parochialism and a failure to see beyond certain German ideological fronts, or to tactics of debate and a cynical effort to delegitimize my own position. Either way the interests of fruitful debate are scarcely furthered. For the best guidance to my particular theoretical orientation, see G. Therborn, *What Does the Ruling Class Do When it Rules? State Apparatuses and State Power under Feudalism, Capitalism and Socialism* (London, 1978); Centre for Contemporary Cultural Studies (ed.), *On Ideology* (London, 1978); N. Abercrombie, *Class, Structure and Knowledge* (London, 1980); N. Abercrombie, S. Hill, and B. Turner, *The Dominant Ideology Thesis* (London, 1980); J. Urry, *The Anatomy of Capitalist Societies: The Economy, Civil Society and the State* (London, 1981); A. S. Sassoon (ed.), *Approaches to Gramsci* (London, 1982); G. Eley, 'Reading Gramsci in English: Some Observations on the Reception of Antonio Gramsci in the English-Speaking World, 1957–1982', *European Studies Review* (forthcoming); R. Williams, *Marxism and Literature* (Oxford, 1977), esp. 55–141. Bob Jessop's various essays have now been subsumed into B. Jessop, *The Capitalist State* (London, 1982).

be regarded as the same thing, unified through the political agency of the bourgeoisie as a collective, acting class-subject.

If we accept this argumentation, the following separation of issues results. On the one hand, we have the question of the type of state that is capable of securing the general conditions of capitalist reproduction (or to put it a different way, for the development of a 'modern industrial society'), what Engels referred to as 'the organization assumed by bourgeois society to support the general external conditions of the capitalist mode of production against the encroachments of both the workers and individual capitalists.'[10] This question concerns the legal infrastructure of the capitalist economy, the measures appropriate for capital accumulation, and the forms of state intervention that regulate both the competition of individual capitals and the contradictions of capital and labour. Here it should be stated with all possible emphasis that to postulate this relationship in the abstract is not to assume the historical necessity of particular state forms functionally appropriate to particular stages in the development of capitalism.[11] Indeed, the specific political arrangements prevailing in a society at any particular time depend precisely on the unpredictable outcome of much wider political struggles, which may infuse the formal constitution of a state with a richly varying content. How effectively the state secures the conditions of capitalist reproduction, and in what precise form, is contingent on complex political determinations in a succession of different conjunctures—on 'the balance of political forces involved in

---

[10]   F. Engels, *Anti-Dühring* (Moscow, 1954), p. 386.

[11]   Recent reference to 'restrictive conditions' following Kirchheimer is also relevant here, as in J. Kocka, *Klassengesellschaft im Krieg 1914–1918* (Göttingen, 1973), p. 130. See O. Kirchheimer, 'Restriktive Bedingungen und revolutionäre Durchbrüche', Kirchheimer, *Politische Herrschaft* (Frankfurt, 1967), pp. 30ff. For similar emphases in the recent Marxist literature, see R. Murray, 'Internationalization of Capital and the Nation State', *New Left Review*, 67 (1971), 84–109; J. Holloway and S. Picciotto (eds.), *State and Capital. A Marxist Debate* (London, 1978); Jessop, 'Capitalism and Democracy', esp. pp. 20ff. The degree of correspondence between recent marxist discussions and Kocka's own emphasis on 'relative autonomy' in the state–economy and state–civil-society relationships makes his and others' polemical hostility to the professed marxism of my approach all the more ironic (and unnecessary). For my own comments on Kocka's conception of the state, see Eley, 'Capitalism and the Wilhelmine State', pp. 744–7.

the struggle for the appropriation and exercise of state power and the reconstitution of state apparatuses' in Bob Jessop's formulation, or 'the composite of all the political factors, domestic as well as foreign', as Rosa Luxemburg put it.[12] This already raises the second, rather different question. This concerns the conditions under which a liberal-democratic form of the state can develop, and it is to this question that we must now turn.

[12] Jessop, 'Capitalism and Democracy', p. 26; M. A. Waters (ed.), *Rosa Luxemburg Speaks* (New York, 1970), p. 74. For an exactly similar statement (invoking 'the shifting distribution of power in the concrete situation'), see Kocka, *Klassengesellschaft in Krieg*, p. 130.

VI
Possibilities of Reform
in Britain and Germany

As I have tried to suggest, in castigating the German bourgeoisie for its illiberalism and the German liberals for their
infirmity, German historians have normally had a special
kind of reformism in mind, one that derives from mid-
twentieth-century definitions of parliamentary democracy
and political participation, closely linked to notions of the
welfare state. From this perspective a certain vocabulary of
liberal political science—an academic rhetoric of 'democratization' and 'social emancipation'—is also inseparable.
For the West German epigoni of this tradition reformism in
this sense tends to be regarded as a moral-political postulate
of desirable development, though one which in the best
traditions of liberal political theory is made to emerge from
the objective requirements of power legitimation, conflict
resolution, and market regulation in the mature industrial
economy.[1] In its most strongly affirmative versions this finds
its place in a universal scenario of the historical process, a
liberal teleology with manichean overtones, in which societies
are confronted with 'the great alternative between authoritarian systems on the one side (e.g. Bonapartist and ultimately also fascist ones), and welfare-statist mass democracies

---

[1] Thus we find Kocka directly associating himself with 'liberal-democratic
orientations' in the constitution of his 'knowledge-guiding interests' (*erkennt-
nisleitende Interessen*), and arguing that a central historical issue for twentieth-
century specialists should be the circumstances 'under which it might be possible
to promote a welfare-statist, liberal democratic variant of organized capitalism.'
See J. Kocka, 'Organisierter Kapitalismus oder Staatsmonopolistischer Kapitalismus? Begriffliche Vorbemerkungen', H. A. Winkler (ed.), *Organisierter Kapitalismus. Voraussetzungen und Anfänge* (Göttingen, 1974), p. 29. Naturally, such an
orientation is not illegitimate. But it is hard to see how such a forthright and
openly liberal statement of intellectual partisanship can balk at the legitimacy
of other political orientations (e.g. marxist or conservative ones). And such an
explicitly drawn liberal problematic does skew the investigation in a particular
way, ensuring that certain questions get asked and others not.

on the other.'[2] This even seems to imply a voluntarist conception of reformist change, in which societies (or a certain class within them, in this case the bourgeoisie) are given the opportunity to become 'modern'. Moreover, because the authenticity of such reforms as did occur (like the Bismarckian insurance legislation) is disqualified a priori by the chosen model of 'modernization', their content is automatically transformed into its opposite—a manipulative strategem of state intervention which is not really reformism at all.[3]

We are dealing here with an essentialist assumption about the nature of modern reformism—that any social and political reforms worthy of the name should necessarily be progressive. As I have argued above, reformism in this sense tends to be viewed as the logical consequence of a bourgeois triumphalism which has successfully deposed the 'pre-industrial élites' (aristocracy, military, bureaucracy) from their command of the political system. As this failed to happen under the *Kaiserreich* (it is argued), the possibility of reform was by definition blocked. But why exactly we should associate the victory of parliamentary democracy and the welfare state with the political fortunes of the bourgeoisie in this way remains somewhat unclear. As Roy Hay aptly observes, this amounts to a revamped Whig interpretation of history,

---

[2] Wehler, *Bismarck*, p. 19. In Germany, needless to say, 'where the decision over these alternatives had fatal results, the legacy of the nineteenth-century errors (*Fehlentscheidungen*) may be traced right up to the present day.'

[3] To concede the authenticity of the Bismarckian reforms would be to concede that German society and government before 1914 was more 'modern' after all. Interpreting the Bismarckian and later social reforms has always been one of the bugbears of the 'Kehrite' historiography which has taken shape since the late 1960s. See esp. Wehler, *Das Deutsche Kaiserreich*, pp. 136ff;. where the Bismarckian reform legislation (universally regarded, incidentally, as the most 'modern' of its day, not least in Britain, the classic land of successful 'modernization') is dismissed as the manipulative accompaniment of general repression. Quite apart from anything else, this position shows a lamentable lack of comparative vision. To take a simple example, to stress the manipulative aspects and limited range of the Bismarckian reforms (e.g. in terms of the eligibility criteria) is to assume that reforms elsewhere (e.g. in Edwardian Britain) were not manipulative or similarly restrictive in their range. For a useful guide to comparative data on this subject, see now P. A. Köhler, H. F. Zachler, and M. Partington (eds.), *The Evolution of Social Insurance 1881-1981. Studies of Germany, France, Great Britain, Austria and Switzerland* (London, 1982).

clothed in the new preoccupations of the social historian:
'Social reform has been regarded as being entirely progressive.
It has been treated as the legislative result of a deeper appreciation of social problems, such as unemployment, ill-health,
old age, and an altruistic desire on the part of governments
to help the weaker members of the community.'[4] But social
and political reform, in Germany no less than in Britain or
France or the USA, resulted neither from the stirring of some
sensitive humanist conscience nor as the natural emanation of
a rising bourgeoisie and its socio-cultural dynamism. An
alternative view of reform, presently rather popular among
Wilhelmine historians, which dismisses the bourgeois reformism starting to emerge in the 1890s as the 'functional
accompaniment' of a more efficient imperialism or the sugar
coating on the bitter pill of repression, is hardly much better.
Such views exaggerate the autonomy of the ideological process by which the consciousness of the German bourgeoisie
was or could be formed, by postulating a conflict between
the 'natural' or 'rational' inclinations of the bourgeoisie as a
'modernizing agent' and the constraints exerted by the older
authoritarian system of normative integration. In effect the
battle for democratic advance is fought out in the minds of
the bourgeoisie. The weakness of the democratic tradition
becomes a reflex of the strength of the authoritarian one.

Given the centrality of the assumed British comparison—
what Titmuss called the 'placid, conventional romance of the
rise of the Welfare State',[5] for whose absence in the *Kaiserreich* German historians show such wistful regret—it is worth
considering how British historians deal with this question. In
the past the approaches briefly invoked above have certainly
been common. Explanations for the origins of welfare legislation (particularly that of the Liberal Government of 1906-
14) have often stressed the extension of political democracy
and the strengthening of humanitarian impulses, bringing
Marshall's theoretical sequence of political and social equality
easily to mind. More convincingly, British historians have also

---

[4] J. R. Hay, *The Origins of the Liberal Welfare Reforms 1906–1914* (London,
1975), p. 12.
[5] Cited ibid., p. 21.

stressed administrative reform and the growth of expertise
(e.g. through better statistical and sociological knowledge),
leading to 'a model of bureaucratic dynamics, in which the
initiative in welfare reform is seized by civil servants and
associated experts.'[6] But these approaches have been rightly
criticized for concentrating too closely on relatively confined
circles of policy-makers rather than deepening this political
explanation with some necessary attention for the larger
social and economic context. One way of doing this is to
draw more ambitiously on the systematic and comparative
discussions in the social sciences, which proceed from the
structural compulsions of economy and society rather than
the more particularized interventions of policy-makers in
government. In this vein Rimlinger suggests that at a certain
stage of industrialization social reform became 'one of the
means of investing in human capital'. Welfare legislation 'became profitable from the point of view of productivity',
because it gave an opportunity 'to develop and maintain the
capacity and the willingness to work.'[7] This is not incompatible with marxist approaches to social policy and the
sociology of education, with their stress on state intervention
and the reproduction of the labour force.[8]

But most interestingly in this respect, British historians
have tried to understand the emergence of reformist projects
within specific social settings and in relation to specific
political conjunctures. The most familiar of such cases is
probably the campaign for 'national efficiency' after the
Boer War.[9] But a strong case has also been made for evaluating

[6] J. R. Hay, review of S. D. Brandes, *American Welfare Capitalism 1880–
1940* (Chicago, 1976), *Social History*, 3. 1 (1978), 114.

[7] G. V. Rimlinger, *Welfare Policy and Industrialization in Europe, America
and Russia* (New York, 1971), pp. 9 f.

[8] For two of the most recent syntheses within this Marxist tradition of work
in Britain, see M. Sarup, *Education, State and Crisis. A Marxist Perspective*
(London, 1982), and Centre for Contemporary Cultural Studies (ed.), *Unpopular
Education. Schooling and Social Democracy in England since 1944* (London,
1981); and for a particularly interesting micro study, M. E. David, 'The Family-
Education Couple: Towards an Analysis of the William Tyndale Dispute',
Littlejohn *et al.* (eds.), *Power and the State*, pp. 158-95.

[9] See esp. G. R. Searle, *The Quest for National Efficiency* (Oxford, 1971);
A. Davin, 'Imperialism and Motherhood', *History Workshop Journal*, 5 (1978),
9-65; B. Semmel, *Imperialism and Social Reform* (London, 1960).

the pre-1914 welfare legislation against the experiences of the stable working class and its changing ability to reproduce its former standards of living—by reference to patterns of employment, changes in the labour process, wage levels, conditions at work, position within the world market, and so on. For instance, it has been suggested that the particular structure of industrial relations in Birmingham and the West Midlands vitally predisposed the employers there to support for social legislation after the turn of the century, quite independently of the local Chamberlainite tradition.[10] Similarly, it was arguably the specific situation of the working class in Lancashire, where the regional economy was heavily dependent on cotton, which gave impetus to the New Liberalism and 'a recognizably "modern" formulation of social policy'. As 'the centre of one of the major staple export trades—cotton textiles—that was particularly affected by unfavourable trends in world markets, which led to narrowing profit margins, declining productivity and increasing industrial strife, especially in the 1880s and 1890s', Lancashire was excessively vulnerable to the general predicament of the late-Victorian and Edwardian manufacturing economy. The difficulties of the industry threatened to damage the popular credibility of the Liberal Party and the ideals of self-help, respectability, and citizenship around which this was organized. By contrast with Germany the working-class electorate was actually rather small (the number of adult males entitled to vote grew from one- to two-thirds between the two Reform Acts of 1867 and 1884), and in this situation it became an urgent priority for Liberals to reconstitute politically the eroded distinction between the 'deserving' working

[10] 'In the Midlands the pattern of relationships which emerged from the local industrial structure was not one of opposing armies of employers and employed or even two sets of parallel peaceful interests, but one single graduated hierarchy. In certain industries such as brass-working, friendly relations could be secured; in others, bedstead-making, actual "alliances" between employers and employed emerged, based on closed shop membership, agreed price-lists, and a regular use of conciliation machinery. *The alliances were particularly strong when a whole industry felt itself threatened by foreign competition*' (my italics). See A. Briggs, 'The Social Background', A. Flanders and H. A. Clegg (eds.), *The System of Industrial Relations in Great Britain* (Oxford, 1954), p. 17. See also J. R. Hay, 'Employers and Social Policy in Britain: The Evolution of Welfare Legislation, 1905-1914', *Social History*, 2, 3 (1977), 435-55.

class and the degenerate poor by some remedial intervention. As Burgess says, 'Lancashire subsequently became a laboratory for social experimentation, a test case of Liberalism's capacity to develop new perspectives and strategies aimed at tackling the causes of social unrest and re-establishing the hegemony of capital and property in relation to the working class.'[11]

By far the most important study of this kind, which locates the production of new reformist ideologies in the context of the changing class relations of a particular urban industrial environment, is Gareth Stedman Jones's investigation of Victorian London and the problem of casual labour. Here the new liberal problematic of reform is related to a crisis of London's social and industrial development in the final quarter of the nineteenth century, with 'declining industries, the breakdown of skilled crafts into a mass of semi-skilled processes, the prevalence of home work, the decline of a work-centred culture, the growth of commuting', and a specific combination of continued small-scale production and chronic unemployment of the unskilled. The social effects of these changes—the decomposition of the old artisan radical culture, residential separation of the classes, and a perceived crisis of 'urban degeneration'—produced a concatenation of middle-class anxieties, in which new reformist ideas could flourish.[12] Linked to the employers' counter-offensive against the new unionism in the 1890s, and conjoined to a new awareness of Britain's long-term difficulties in the world economy, this proved a powerful recipe for ideological renewal and a general renegotiation of political relationships. By the later 1890s British politics had entered a definite period of innovatory speculation, and it needed

[11] K. Burgess, 'The Working Class "Response" to Social Policy: The Case of the Lancashire Cotton Districts, 1880-1914', Paper presented to the SSRC/ University of Glasgow Social Policy and Social Control Conference, 27-28 May 1978, p. 2. See also K. Burgess, *The Origins of British Industrial Relations: The Nineteenth Century Experience* (London, 1975).

[12] G. S. Jones, *Outcast London. A Study in the Relationship between Classes in Victorian Society* (Oxford, 1971). The quotation is taken from the same author's article, G. S. Jones, 'Working Class Culture and Working Class Politics in London, 1870-1900: Notes on the Remaking of a Working Class', *Journal of Social History*, 7 (1974), 489.

only the public shocks of the Boer War to condense the latter into a more coherent programme of 'national efficiency'.

In other words, the British welfare reforms of 1906-14 are best explained by a particular configuration of circumstances and events and not by a universal paradigm of 'correct' or 'healthy' development. Above all, they resulted from two things: an attempt to renovate the Liberal Party's popular credentials in the face of growing pressure from an organized labour movement both within its own ranks and without; and the widespread arguments about the British economy's declining relative efficiency compared with Germany and the USA.[13] Likewise, the absence of a comparable reformism in Imperial Germany—whether or not the British case amounted to a coherent new departure of 'progressivism'[14]—may be explained by two direct contrasts with this British situation.

On the one hand, given the fracture between liberals and labour in the 1860s (what Gustav Mayer called 'the separation of the proletarian from the bourgeois democracy')[15] German

---

[13] For the former, see the recent discussions by A. Howkins, 'Edwardian Liberalism and Industrial Unrest', *History Workshop Journal*, 4 (1977), 143-62; R. McKibbon, *The Evolution of the Labour Party 1910-1924* (Oxford, 1974); S. Macintyre, 'Socialism, the Unions and the Labour Party after 1918', *Bulletin of the Society for the Study of Labour* History, 31 (1975), 101-11; M. G. Sheppard and J. L. Halstead, 'Labour's Municipal Election Performance in Provincial England and Wales 1901-13', *Bulletin of the Society for the Study of Labour History*, 39 (1979), 39-62; P. Clarke, 'The Edwardians and the Constitution', D. Read (ed.), *Edwardian England* (London, 1982), pp. 40-55; K. O. Morgan, 'Edwardian Socialism', Read (ed.), *Edwardian England*, pp. 93-111; J. White, '1910-1914 Reconsidered', J. E. Cronin and J. Schneer (eds.), *Social Conflict and Political Order in Modern Britain* (London, 1982), pp. 73-95. For the anxiety about the British economy's relative efficiency, see the literature cited in n. 9 above.

[14] For an introduction to this controversy, see Howkins, 'Edwardian liberalism', and the book that originally provoked it, P. F. Clarke, *Lancashire and the New Liberalism* (Cambridge, 1971). Clarke continued the argument with a general article, 'The Progressive Movement in England', *Transactions of the Royal Historical Society*, 5th series, 24 (1974), 159-81, and in a second book, *Liberals and Social Democrats* (Cambridge, 1978). See also the many reviews of K. O. Morgan in the *Times Literary Supplement* over the last ten years, esp. 'The Liberal Regeneration', 22 Aug. 1975, p. 941, and the subsequent correspondence. The other book that opened the current phase of discussion of British liberalism was T. Wilson, *The Downfall of the Liberal Party 1914-1935* (London, 1968), though here the controversy was more to do with the effects of war and the timing of the liberal decline.

[15] In a classic essay originally published in 1912. See G. Mayer, 'Die Trennung der proletarischen von der bürgerlichen Demokratie in Deutschland, 1863-1870',

politics never produced anything remotely resembling a Gladstonian coalition, and on the contrary the existence of a precocious and independent Social Democratic Party imposed definite limits on how far German liberals were prepared to advance in their reformist experiments. But secondly, German industry's potential strength in the world market removed the pressing motivation of 'national efficiency', particularly as the German state had already pioneered an impressive system of insurance legislation back in the 1880s to meet precisely those needs. On the whole the large employers in heavy industry, chemicals, and electrical engineering preferred their own system of company welfare, which promised both a more stable work-force and a more tangible control over costs.[16] Naturally this did not mean that individual employers could not espouse particular political commitments to reform, or that other sectors of German industry could not develop more programmatic demands. But it was no accident that the latter were mainly in the less concentrated industries which lacked the benefits of scale and market domination, and could not afford such elaborate internal provision. Moreover, again with the British comparison in mind, the sectors that were most liberal over matters of social and political reform tended also to be the ones in most need of an extra boost from the state in the export market, whether organized in associations like the *Handelsvertragsverein* (the Association for Commercial Treaties) or more specialized initiatives like the *Werkbund*.[17]

It is extraordinary that German historians have made so

Radikalismus, Sozialismus und bürgerliche Demokratie, ed. H.-U. Wehler (Frankfurt, 1969), pp. 108-78.

[16] I have discussed this question in a general review of recent literature, which anticipates much of the argument pursued here. See Eley, 'Capitalism and the Wilhelmine State', esp. pp. 742-4. See also the excellent discussion in D. F. Crew, *Town in the Ruhr. A Social History of Bochum 1860-1914* (New York, 1979), pp. 119ff., 145ff., 31ff. The question of company based and industry-wide paternalism is taken up in detail below.

[17] See D. Stegmann, 'Linksliberale Bankiers, Kaufleute und Industrielle 1890-1900. Ein Beitrag zur Vorgeschichte des Handelsvertragsvereins', *Tradition*, 21 (1976), 4-36; H.-P. Ullmann, *Der Bund der Industriellen* (Göttingen, 1976), pp. 22ff., 165ff.; J. Campbell, *The German Werkbund. The Politics of Reform in the Applied Arts* (Princeton, 1978), pp. 9-56.

little effort to investigate attitudes to reform in the context
of particular industries and their characteristics, especially
because the resistance to reform is usually attributed so
strongly to the activity of the right-wing heavy-industrial
lobby in the CVDI.[18] But in the main the latter is presented
as ideologically or politically motivated, the product of a
'feudalized' or 'backward' consciousness, a further imprint
of the bourgeoisie's failure to emancipate itself from a subordinate past. There can be no doubt of much of the descriptive accuracy of this work. Based in heavy industry,
textiles, and a further group of protectionist interests in glass,
sugar, and chemicals, the CVDI maintained a consistent
hostility to all proposals for the conciliation of organized
labour. This meant not only opposition to trade-union recognition, welfare legislation, and reform of the Prussian suffrage.
It also meant the active pursuit of new legal restrictions on
both the unions and the SPD. For a decade after the end of
the Anti-Socialist Law in 1890 the CVDI demanded new repressive legislation, and only the impracticality of getting

[18] The *Centralverband Deutscher Industrieller* (CVDI) was the most powerful
of German capital's political representations. Originally formed in 1876 under the
impact of the Great Depression to centralize the pressure for industrial protection,
it was based primarily in the extractive, iron and steel, and heavy engineering
industries of the Rhine-Ruhr, Saar, and Silesia, textiles, and a variety of other
industries linked either to these or to large-scale agriculture (shipbuilding, sugar,
iron and steel manufactures, certain kinds of light engineering, fertilizers, and so
on). The important chemicals industry had an ambiguous relationship, and in the
1890s created its own sectoral representation. The first major counter-movement
in German industry to the CVDI developed after 1895 with the launching of the
Bund der Industriellen (BdI), which became based in the less concentrated sectors
of the light-manufacturing and consumer-goods industries and any other industries with a specific interest in breaking the systems of market regulation established by the powerfully organized and cartelized sectors in the CVDI, with the
regional accent in south and central Germany. The dichotomy of heavy industry-
light industry used by German historians to express these divisions is broadly
correct, but if used simplistically can obscure important cross-cutting alignments,
which arguably became more important on the eve of the First World War. There
is a danger of exaggerating the degree of homogeneity in the two camps and the
amount of control exercised by the big barons of heavy industry in the CVDI.
The role of the banking, insurance, and commercial sectors can also be hard to
fit into this simple dichotomous framework. Full references will be supplied
during the discussion below, esp. in n. 30. The main sources for the CVDI *per se*
are Stegmann, *Erben*, and H. Kaelble, *Industrielle Interessenpolitik in der wilhelminischen Gesellschaft. Centralverband Deutscher Industrieller 1895–1914*
(Berlin, 1967).

this through the Reichstag moderated this commitment between roughly 1899 (when the so-called *Zuchthausvorlage* —Hard Labour Bill—was defeated in the Reichstag by a centre-left coalition extending from the SPD to the Centre Party and National Liberals) and around 1910–11 (when fresh exceptional legislation again became more of a live issue).[19]

In these years—the high Wilhelmine era—the larger employers fell back on self-help, with an impressive repertoire of tactics, including shop-floor discipline, black lists of militants, agitators, union joiners, and straightforward 'trouble makers', labour exchanges, compulsory welfare schemes, centralized employers' associations, and company unions. Two things stand out about this system of company- and industry-based authority. First, it was adopted by nearly all big employers in the highly concentrated sectors, regardless of industry and regardless of particular political affiliations—left as well as right tending liberal, Siemens as well as Krupp. In some ways it was a self-consciously liberal employer in the more dynamic electro-technical sector with strong links to the left liberal politics of the time—namely Siemens—that pioneered the aggressive confrontationist techniques of company or 'yellow' unionism, in a long but successful battle with the Free Trade Union in 1905.[20] Secondly, it was startlingly successful. Given the resources, the right kind of industry-wide co-ordination, and the necessary level of political commitment, union-smashing worked. In that case it was scarcely surprising that such employers demonstrated such obdurate resistance against state-administered social and political reform. Moreover, as the most radical expression of this system, company unionism often went with larger political ambitions for an anti-socialist and

---

[19] In arguing this I am going against the grain of most existing opinion, which would strongly dispute the importance of the period I have identified between the turn of the century and 1910–11. I return to this question below.

[20] For the Siemens story, see J. Kocka, *Unternehmensverwaltung und Angestelltenschaft am Beispiel Siemens 1847–1914. Zum Verhältnis von Kapitalismus und Bürokratie in der deutschen Industrialisierung* (Stuttgart, 1969), esp. pp. 346ff.; K. Mattheier, *Die Gelben. Nationale Arbeiter zwischen Wirtschaftsfrieden und Streik* (Düsseldorf, 1973), pp. 71–6; K. Saul, *Staat, Industrie, Arbeiterbewegung im Kaiserreich. Zur Innen- und Aussenpolitik des Wilhelminischen Deutschland 1903–1914* (Düsseldorf, 1974), pp. 136ff.

anti-democratic realignment of the so-called 'bourgeois parties', an aspiration most clearly embodied in the *Reichs-verband gegen die Sozialdemokratie* (Imperial League Against Social Democracy) formed in 1904. There was little unity as to how such a political initiative might proceed, however, and it was only after 1910 that a more coherent offensive could take shape. Without abandoning their company pater-nalism, the CVDI employers returned to demands for state intervention against trade unions, and after the SPD's elec-toral landslide of 1912 this threatened to provoke a serious domestic crisis.[21]

But the usual explanation for this behaviour is far from satisfactory. As David Crew has pointed out in his study of Bochum, 'the "paternalistic" control of their work-force that heavy-industrial companies like the *Bochumer Verein* tried to exercise has usually been regarded as either an anachro-nistic hangover from the pre-industrial world or simply evi-dence of the big capitalists' inability and unwillingness to accept fully "modern" and more "rational" industrial rela-tions.'[22] As he goes on to say, this view assumes 'an intrinsic logic in the nature of industrial production that requires employers eventually to realize that it is "rational" for them "to accept labour as a valid source of input to the process of framing the structure of the work-place." '[23] In other words, we are back with the notion of German exceptionalism, where Germany's failure to obey a pattern of desirable de-velopment is attributed to 'the obstructionist influences of pre-industrial elites and ideological traditions' and to the distortions of what is thought to be the 'normal' logic of industrial organization under capitalism.[24]

[21] The best sources for this anti-Socialist activity are Stegmann, 'Zwischen Repression und Manipulation'; Saul, *Staat, Industrie, Arbeiterbewegung*; Mattheier, ·*Gelben*.

[22] Crew, *Town in the Ruhr*, p. 156. Crew's book offers a rare attempt at a materialist and social historical explanation of the big employers' resistance to reformist perspectives.

[23] Ibid. The quotation used by Crew is taken from L. Schofer, *The Formation of a Modern Labour Force. Upper Silesia 1865-1914* (Berkeley and Los Angeles, 1975), p. 157. See also Crew's review of this book, *International Working Class and Labour History Newsletter*, 11 (1977), 44-6.

[24] Here I am following the argumentation of Crew, *Town in the Ruhr*, pp. 1ff., 145-57, 221-4, and of my own previous article, 'Capitalism and the Wilhelmine State'.

But this type of argument fails to appreciate that by comparison with Britain it was precisely the most 'modern' and 'progressive' aspects of Imperial Germany's capitalist development—namely, the higher levels of concentration, the rapid investment in new plant and technology, the experimentation with more sophisticated divisions of labour—that first permitted the repressive labour relations described so exhaustively in recent works to develop. The intransigence of employers such as Krupp, *Bochumer Verein*, *Gutehoffnungshütte*, or MAN when it came to recognizing trade unions was less the 'adoption of conservative-feudal notions of value' (as Stegmann calls it), than a specific form of capitalist rationality.[25] It might just as easily be argued that some form of paternalism aimed at excluding trade unions from one's company or plant is the 'natural' or 'logical' inclination of most employers when left to themselves, particularly in this period, but becomes feasible only under specific conditions, in this case when the productive units became sufficiently large. Under small-scale competitive capitalism with high labour mobility and little co-operation amongst employers, the use of black lists and company unions was not on. Moreover, once these obstacles had gone, such devices became admirable aids for rationalizing production. This was certainly true in the Ruhr coalfield, where the introduction of a black list in 1908 was not just a means of victimizing militants, but also an aid to achieving a more stable work-force. Likewise, company housing was less an expression of some pre-industrial moral paternalism than a necessary means of attracting and keeping workers at a time of breathtaking urban growth but primitive urban amenities.[26]

In other words, only the big employers who enjoyed the maximum benefits of advanced capitalist production could actually afford to be intransigent, whether in the old heavy industries or the newer sectors of electrical engineering,

---

[25] D. Stegmann, 'Hugenberg contra Stresemann. Die Politik der Industrieverbände am Ende des Kaiserreichs', *Vierteljahreshefte für Zeitgeschichte*, XXIV (1976), 337.

[26] See also the interesting discussion in R. Hay and J. Melling, 'Public Service and Private Progress: Business Welfare in British and Australian Mining, Mid-19th to Mid-20th Centuries', Paper presented to Eighth International Congress of Economic History, Budapest, August 1982.

chemicals, machine tools, and machine building. Conversely, it was the smaller firms which lacked the advantages of size and tendential monopoly organization that gave in most easily to trade-union pressures. Smaller companies in metal-working and machine building might be every bit as concerned with controlling labour costs, but had far fewer resources for extensive paternalist programmes. But given the necessary resources it made perfect sense for Wilhelmine capitalists to refuse the 'just' demands of the working class (as Wehler calls them), and this had obvious political implications, particularly in the sphere of social reform. Big employers like Krupp had no need for a national deal with the unions when the latter were effectively excluded from their plants. They had no interest in social reform at the level of the state when they were already making adequate provision for their own workers at the level of the individual firm.

Indeed, because company paternalism was so successful, its practitioners had an active interest in opposing reform, for this would duplicate facilities and increase costs. More than this even, by recognizing trade unions it would cut the legal ground from practices like the black list, compulsory membership in company schemes, and straightforward intimidation.[27] As David Crew says,

heavy industrialists had quite compelling and logical reasons that derived both from their present and future economic interests and from the contemporary German political context (and not from their inability properly to learn the 'rules of the industrial game') to use company paternalism as a way of controlling labour costs by preventing workers from organizing and striking.[28]

In general, the more 'modern' forms of productive organization (especially the higher levels of concentration) made it much easier to contain the antagonisms between capital and labour within the individual plant or sector of industry without displacing the process into the political domain proper, where it became subject to far less predictable and

---

[27] See, e.g., Crew's discussion of the housing question in Bochum, where the Bochumer Verein successfully resisted all efforts to institute provision of municipal housing, *Town in the Ruhr*, pp. 149 ff.

[28] Ibid., pp. 156 f.

manageable determinations. Or so the big employers in those sectors thought. In fact, in the long run their intransigence simply added greater weight to those voices on the reformist left who were calling for greater regulatory control. In the end their ability to operate these private paternalist arrangements made a public solution more rather than less likely.

This becomes especially clear when we look at trade unionism. Before 1914 it was still the less concentrated industries—small and medium engineering, construction, transport, woodworking, textiles, and older crafts like printing and leather-working—that provided the bulk of trade-union membership. In these industries employers lacked the financial resources and privately organized corporate power to make the option of company paternalism work. Instead they found themselves confronted much more quickly with the alternative of calling in the assistance of the state—either in the form of fresh repressive legislation or for the purpose of reaching some sort of *modus vivendi* with the trade unions (e.g. through the recognition of collective bargaining, or through some system of government backed arbitration). By the turn of the century the consolidated organizational power of the SPD-aligned Free Trade Unions had convinced large numbers of employers in the light industrial and manufacturing sector (organized in the regionally federated *Bund der Industriellen* launched in 1895) that straightforward repression in the form of an Anti-Socialist Law no longer made sense. At the same time, the idea of a grand reformist accommodation in the style of the corporatist arrangements with the unions which materialized during the First World War (in which improved productivity and labour discipline were traded against trade-union recognition and a more interventionist state) would have been too radical a departure. Before 1914 (and especially before the 1906 Mannheim agreement, which ratified the unions' growing independence from the SPD) concessions to trade unionism seemed to mean concessions to Social Democracy, and the latter was thought to be far too radical and untamable a quantity. In the immediate term, therefore, most dealing with trade unions took place on a firm-by-firm basis, and the greater flexibility of smaller-scale industry could be measured most visibly in the spread of wage agreements. By 1913 some 50 per cent of workers in the printing trades were covered by these, 46 per cent in transportation and building trades, 29 per cent in wood-working. By contrast, only 4 per cent of workers in the chemicals industries were covered by negotiated agreements, and less than half a per cent in mining (or three agreements affecting eighty-two miners). In general the Free Trade Unions continued to make least progress in the most concentrated sections of the coal, copper, iron, steel, chemicals, and heavy machinery industries.[29]

This had far-reaching implications. For over the longer term, this uneven distribution of trade-union growth threatened to divide German industry into two camps: a more concentrated and 'organized' sector distinguished by its higher levels of tendential monopoly organization and ability to hold trade unions at bay by a mixture of company paternalism and industry wide employer co-operation; and a less 'organized' sector which lacked these 'private' advantages and was consequently thrown back on to more 'public' solutions. Moreover, once trade unions had gained a sizeable foothold in certain industries, their industrial strength was easily converted into a demand for national recognition or more extensive social and political reform. Once that happened, there was always the chance that their pressure would become mediated through the activity of sympathetic or farsighted elements within the political parties. This was the

---

[29] Belatedly there is now a plentiful literature on the history of Social Democratic trade unionism before 1914. For general accounts see G. A. Ritter and K. Tenfelde, 'Der Durchbruch der Freien Gewerkschaften Deutschlands zur Massenbewegung im letzten Viertel des 19. Jahrhunderts', Ritter, *Arbeiterbewegung, Parteien und Parlamentarismus*, pp. 55–101; K. Schönhoven, *Expansion und Konzentration. Studien zur Entwicklung der Freien Gewerkschaften im Wilhelminischen Deutschland 1890 bis 1914* (Stuttgart, 1980); K. Schönhoven, 'Gewerkschaftliches Organisationsverhalten im Wilhelminischen Deutschland', W. Conze and U. Engelhardt (eds.), *Arbeiter im Industrialisierungsprozess. Herkunft, Lage und Verhalten* (Stuttgart, 1979), pp. 403–21; H. Mommsen (ed.), *Arbeiterbewegung und industrieller Wandel. Studien zur gewerkschaftliche Organisationsproblemen im Riech und an der Ruhr* (Wuppertal, 1980). For two useful case studies: F. Boll, *Massenbewegungen in Niedersachsen 1906–1920. Eine sozialgeschichtliche Untersuchung zu den unterschiedlichen Entwicklungstypen Braunschweig und Hannover* (Bonn, 1981); M. Nolan, *Social Democracy and Society. Working-Class Radicalism in Düsseldorf, 1890–1920* (Cambridge, 1981).

recurrent nightmare of the interests organized in the CVDI—
that the growing strength of the trade unions would eventually trap government, liberals, and smaller employers into
considering some ameliorative package of social reform and
legal recognition. It seemed all the more dangerous as the
differential spread of monopoly organization created important intra-industrial conflicts in other areas as well.
Briefly, new positions of strength for the monopolies entailed simultaneous difficulties for industries which were
still fragmented, and conflicts over tariffs, cartels, and price-
fixing were the characteristic result. Thus the power of the
big companies not only obstructed reformist projects. It also
directly harmed a range of capitalist interests—and not just
small and medium capital, but even larger manufacturers,
shippers, and some banks, who wanted cheaper access to raw
materials and other supplies, greater market autonomy, and
dismantlement of the protective tariffs supported by the
CVDI and its agrarian allies.

The details of this story are now well known.[30] The *Bund
der Industriellen* formed in 1895 was the first major attempt
of small and medium manufacturers to compensate for their
corporate weakness against the larger firms grouped in the
CVDI. During the campaign against higher tariffs between
1897 and 1902 it was joined by other organizations—the
Central Office for the Preparation of Commercial Treaties in
1897, the Association for Commercial Treaties in 1900—which
drew on a wider range of more powerful interests in banking,

---

[30] The best guide to these conflicts is still H. Nussbaum, *Unternehmer gegen
Monopole* (Berlin, 1966). See also Stegmann, *Erben*; Stegmann, 'Hugenberg
contra Stresemann', pp. 329 ff.; S. Mielke, *Der Hansa-Bund für Gewerbe, Handel
und Industrie 1909-1914* (Göttingen, 1976), pp. 11 ff., 166-86; Ullmann, *Bund
der Industriellen*, pp. 165-241; Saul, *Staat, Industrie, Arbeiterbewegung*, pp.
283-394; W. Gutsche, 'Probleme des Verhältnisses zwischen Monopolkapital und
Staat in Deitschland vom Ende des 19. Jahrhunderts bis zum Vorabend des ersten
Weltkrieges', F. Klein (ed.), *Studien zum deutschen Imperialismus vor 1914*
(Berlin, 1976), pp. 33-84; C. Medalen, 'State Monopoly Capitalism in Germany:
The Hibernia Affair', *Past and Present*, 78 (1978), 82-112; H. Pogge von Strandmann, 'Widersprüche im Modernisierungsprozess Deutschlands. Der Kampf der
verarbeitenden Industrie gegen die Schwerindustrie', D. Stegmann, B.-J. Wendt,
and P.-Chr. Witt (eds.), *Industrielle Gesellschaft und politisches System. Beiträge
zur politischen Sozialgeschichte* (Bonn, 1978), pp. 225-40.

shipping, chemicals, and electrical engineering.[31] This larger grouping was held together by two separate impulses: on the one side the desire for cheaper access to the supplies controlled by the heavily cartelized CVDI affiliates; on the other a broader political hostility to the artificially protected agricultural sector. This second position was also motivated by specific economic grievances, because the preferential tariff system and fiscal privileges of the big Prussian landowners each carried distinct disadvantages for industrial and mercantile capital.

But this was easily generalized into a political attack on 'feudal' survivals, which in its turn was increasingly linked to the demand for a general strengthening of representative institutions, or at least for the political *Gleichberechtigung* (equality of status, equality of rights) of the bourgeoisie. When the agrarians sabotaged the finance reform in 1908–9 (which had promised, in certain minor but significant ways, to erode the Junkers' fiscal privileges), these tendencies began to gel. The launching of a new anti-agrarian organization, the *Hansabund* (Hanse Union), in the summer of 1909, which for a couple of years acted as the general umbrella for virtually the entirety of organized industrial and commercial opinion, seemed to offer the basis for a reformist realignment of German politics. More specifically, it was hoped that the CVDI might at last abandon its longstanding economic and political alliance with the Junkers.

However, the established political nexus between the interests of the monopolies and the apparatuses of the state (which dated originally from the 1870s, with a considerable strengthening in 1897–1902) could only be broken by a sustained political offensive operating on a much broader front. Essentially this meant popular mobilization of the subordinate classes, however limited and controlled this was intended to be. Now the *Hansabund* made notable efforts to involve both the old and the new petty bourgeoisie in its counsels, and both small businessmen and white-collar workers were important components of the anti-agrarian

---

[31] Stegmann, 'Linksliberale Bankiers'; Ullmann, *Bund der Industriellen*, pp. 164 ff.

coalition, both as a large paper membership and major addressees of the propaganda. But for some elements of the leadership the organized working class also began to enter the picture. Embryonically, a new kind of reformist departure became at least imaginable. On the eve of the war the typical plea of the less concentrated, export-oriented manufacturing interests for parity of representation on official bodies with the better-organized protectionist industries and for a reduction of agrarian privilege became increasingly linked in public discussion to the questions of trade-union recognition and social reform, with or without the SPD.

Why did this reformist departure fail to materialize in Wilhelmine politics before 1914? This is naturally an extremely complex question, whose ramifications cannot be adequately dealt with here. But briefly, there were a number of reasons, none of which had much to do with the normal explanation of 'pre-industrial traditions', 'feudal blockages', or 'failed development'. The first concerns the logic of monopoly capital or (if the terminology is preferred) the process of economic 'modernization' itself.[32] As processes of concentration

---

[32] I should make clear what my use of the phrase 'logic of monopoly capital' exactly implies. It refers to striking features of German industry's leading sectors which are a commonplace of German historiography—high levels of concentration, vertical and horizontal integration, cartelization, interpenetration of industrial and financial capital, and centralized political representation. Naturally these characteristics had definite political effects, e.g. on the relations between the leading sectors and the agencies of government. In fact, most German historians would agree that they decisively structured the system of government priorities in the realm of economic policy, and one group of West German historians devised the concept of 'organized capitalism' in the 1970s to express the importance of this kind of determination. My own phrase 'logic of monopoly capitalism' (in the sense of tendencies of development, as opposed to 'laws') is meant to express the same combination of characteristics. It has a perfectly respectable place in the marxist theoretical tradition. It is explicitly not the same as the orthodox marxist-leninist concept of *stamokap* (as my footnote 84 of the German edition should already have made clear). By using it I am not proposing a monocausal explanation of the course of German history in general (as several West German reviewers of the original German edition rather disingenuously claimed). It should be plain from the context that the phrase refers to certain very specific factors, which have explanatory force for some problems (e.g. why the most organized sectors of German industry were so reactionary on labour relations), but not necessarily for others. In view of some very explicit statements to this effect in the German edition, I cannot understand why West German reviewers still accused me of adopting the orthodox marxist-leninist position, unless it was to tar me with a dogmatic brush.

in German industry continued, so key interests in the engineering and chemicals industries became detached from any potential anti-monopoly front, and the basis for an effective opposition to the CVDI (or for pulling the CVDI into forms of anti-agrarian co-operation) became correspondingly diminished. Such processes also began to undermine the existing basis of organized interest representation. Increasingly, the crucial decisions—which then prescribed the terms of the discussion inside the interest groups (like the CVDI) and helped to determine what the important decisions would be—were taken outside the older organizational structures by more informally constituted networks of powerful firms. The effect was to enmesh even the more 'liberal' employers like the two electrical engineering giants AEG and Siemens in networks of monopoly decision-making that owed nothing to liberal reform of the state (in the direction of stronger parliamentary institutions), and arguably made the latter redundant.[33] They might still criticize agrarian privilege and echo the demand for bourgeois equality of status, but there was little interest in a more positive kind of liberalism.

This indifference was strengthened by the victories of the SPD in the 1912 elections. Under such circumstances talk of reform (however limited) seemed to play directly into the hands of a dangerously successful socialism. To the economic determinations just mentioned, therefore, we must add the influence of political ones. Moreover, the kind of reformism represented by the *Hansabund* (anti-agrarianism wedded to limited parliamentary and social-reform perspectives) lacked an adequate party-political articulation. Its natural parliamentary correlate, as was evident in the party affiliations of the *Hansabund* leadership, was a unified coalition of National Liberals and left liberal fragments. After 1907 there was definite progress in this direction, first with the coalescence of left liberals into the new Progressive People's Party, and then with the strengthening of cognate tendencies under

---

[33] See Pogge von Strandmann, 'Widersprüche'; H. Pogge von Strandmann, *Unternehmenspolitik und Unternehmensführung* (Düsseldorf, 1978); Gutsche, 'Probleme des Verhältnisses'; G. D. Feldman, 'The Large Firm in the German Industrial System: The M.A.N. 1900-1925', Stegmann, Wendt, and Witt (eds.), *Industrielle Gesellschaft und politisches System*, pp. 241-58.

Bassermann and Stresemann in the National Liberal Party.

But as the descendants of this coalescence in the Weimar Republic were to discover (the German Democratic Party and Stresemann's German People's Party), to become a viable electoral force it needed an additional opening in one of two directions, either towards the Catholic Centre Party, or (more radically) towards the socialist labour movement. Either would have prefigured our familiar counterfactual friend, the missing Gladstonian coalition of Imperial German politics. But as we know only too well, given the suppositions of Wilhelmine politics and the conflicted character of the liberal, Catholic, and socialist political traditions, neither the Centre nor the SPD could be integrated straightforwardly into that kind of reformist bloc. Still more decisively, it proved impossible to win even the National Liberals as a whole for a new reformist departure, for the divisions between the two camps of industry ran through the National Liberal Party rather than to its right. All of this left the *Hansabund* in limbo—an enterprising programme devoid of solid industrial backing and without party-political focus. After 1911-12 the anti-monopoly position was soon reduced to a rump of small and medium capitalists in the *Bund der Industriellen* and simultaneously severed from a democratic politics of rapprochement with labour. Despite the initial hopes, the anti-agrarian premises of the *Hansabund* proved an inadequate basis for a new reformism of the 'British' kind.[34]

---

[34] I have discussed this problem of the *Hansabund* and the National Liberal Party in ch. 9 of my book, G. Eley, *Reshaping the German Right. Radical Nationalism and Political Change after Bismarck* (New Haven and London, 1980), pp. 293–315.

VII
The *Realpolitik* of the Bourgeoisie and Redundancy of Liberalism

But then it all depends what we mean by 'reformism'. The whole thrust of this essay has been to argue against universal or abstract definitions of the latter, and against ones that derive from inflexible criteria of advanced liberal democracy in particular. After 1909 (when the *Hansabund* was launched) there was clearly no constitutional reform of the state. There were no formal concessions to parliamentarization. Nor was there a programme of social reform to compare with the British measures of 1906–14. But we should be prepared to think about whether these omissions really exhaust the possible forms that reformist innovations could take. Here we enter some difficult and dangerous terrain, because previous attempts to identify elements of reformism on the eve of 1914 (or even a stabilization of the existing parliamentary status quo) have lent themselves to accusations of apologetics for the *Kaiserreich*.[1] But with all due caution we may draw a number of suggestive conclusions from the available research on the years between the break-up of the Bülow bloc in 1909

[1] Why the question of apologetics for the *Kaiserreich* should matter one way or the other might not be readily apparent to the non-German specialist, and has to be explained in the historiographical context of the 'continuity' arguments alluded to in the Introduction to this volume. In this sense scepticism over German 'modernization' before 1914 possesses a similar political resonance to that concerning 'modernization' in Tsarist Russia in the same period. Both reflect an ideological vested interest in the legitimacy of the social and political order which succeeded the breaks of 1917–21, the one liberal-cum-social democratic (the Weimar Republic, and eventually the Federal Republic), the other marxist (Bolshevik Russia). Conversely, belief in the 'modernizing' capabilities of the two societies before 1914 has normally implied some degree of hostility to the revolutionary upheavals to come. Of course, there is no reason why belief/disbelief in the relative stability and capacity for growth of a political order should have to imply ideological identification of this kind. The assumption that it does (and the accusation of apologetics) tends to foreclose certain types of interpretation.

and the outbreak of war.[2] Thus it seems that the Bethmann Hollweg-Delbrück administration did undertake a qualified centrist reorientation in these years, which was only properly consummated under the special conditions of the war.[3] Moreover, much of the political confusion of the last peacetime decade actually arose out of the growing observance of a *de facto* parliamentarism.[4] The significance of constitu-

[2] It is easy to forget just how limited our knowledge of these years is, in terms of the published literature. Aside from the works of Fritz Fischer and his students, there is only Zmarzlik's older study of Bethmann Hollweg's Chancellorship, Bertram's book on the 1912 elections, Groh's work on the SPD, and a smattering of things about the Zabern Affair. See F. Fischer, *War of Illusions* (London, 1975); Stegmann, *Erben*; P.-Chr. Witt, *Die Finanzpolitik des Deutschen Reiches von 1903 bis 1913* (Lübeck, 1970); Saul, *Staat, Industrie, Arbeiterbewegung*; H.-G. Zmarzlik, *Bethmann Hollweg als Reichskanzler* (Düsseldorf, 1957); J. Bertram, *Die Wahlen zum Deutschen Reichstag vom Jahre 1912* (Düsseldorf, 1964); D. Groh, *Negative Integration und revolutionäre Attentismus* (Frankfurt, 1973); K. Stenkewitz, *Immer feste druff: Zabernaffaire 1913* (Berlin, 1962); H.-U. Wehler, 'Symbol des halbabsolutistischen Herrschaftssystems: Der Fall Zabern von 1913/14 als eine Verfassungskrise des Wilhelminischen Kaiserreichs', Wehler, *Krisenherde des Kaiserreichs 1871-1918. Studien zur deutschen Sozial- und Verfassungsgeschichte* (Göttingen, 1970), pp. 65-83; D. Schoenbaum, *Zabern 1913. Consensus Politics in Imperial Germany* (London, 1982). These references are not meant to be exhaustive, of course. There are two useful general books focusing on the years 1909-14: K. Stenkewitz, *Gegen Bajonett und Dividende* (Berlin, 1960); V. R. Berghahn, *Germany and the Approach of War in 1914* (London, 1973). The most stimulating introduction is G. Schmidt, 'Parlamentarisierung oder "Präventive Konterrevolution"? Die deutsche Innenpolitik im Spannungsfeld konservativer Sammlungsbewegungen und latenter Reformbestrebungen 1907-1914', G. A. Ritter (ed.), *Gesellschaft, Parlament und Regierung. Zur Geschichte des Parlamentarismus in Deutschland* (Düsseldorf, 1974).

[3] Again, we remain somewhat uninformed about the exact nature of Bethmann Hollweg's thinking in the immediate pre-war years. Neither Zmarzlik, *Bethmann Hollweg*, nor K. Jarausch, *The Enigmatic Chancellor. Bethmann Hollweg and the Hubris of Imperial Germany* (New Haven and London, 1973), are very helpful on the domestic side of Imperial government policy in these years. In the meantime something may be inferred on the activity of Bethmann and Delbrück in the July Crisis itself, when they moved very astutely to neutralize the potential opposition of the Social Democrats to the war. See the exhaustive account in Groh, *Negative Integration,* pp. 577-729, and the annotated documentation in J. Kuczynski, *Der Ausbruch des ersten Weltkrieges und die deutsche Sozialdemokratie. Chronik und Analyse* (Berlin, 1957), and D. Fricke and H. Radandt, 'Neue Dokumente über die Rolle Albert Südekums', *Zeitschrift für Geschichtswissenschaft*, 4. 4 (1956), 757-65. See also S. Miller, *Burgfrieden und Klassenkampf. Die deutsche Sozialdemokratie im Ersten Weltkrieg* (Düsseldorf, 1974), pp. 31-74.

[4] To argue this (that there was a limited practical stabilization of public life within the available forms of Wilhelmine constitutionalism) is not the same as arguing that the political system was well on the way to a parliamentary-democratic evolution on some uncritically derived British pattern. It is here that I part company with the work of Manfred Rauh, which is otherwise disfigured by an ill-

tional peccadilloes like the *Daily Telegraph* Affair in 1908 or the Zabern Crisis of 1913-14 lay precisely in the discrepancy between the formal constitutional relations and the manner in which the dominant parliamentary parties now expected political life to be conducted—between the latitude available to the Kaiser and how the constituted head of government was expected to behave.[5] Furthermore, while there was no question of a formal compact with the labour movement, both the *Hansabund* and the National Liberals had un-equivocally—and successfully—resisted any move for fresh exceptional laws against the unions, and in the panic after the 1912 elections this was no insignificant thing. Finally, though the government might announce a freeze on social legislation to placate the right, it seems that the Bethmann-Delbrück axis now accepted the labour movement as a political factor which would not go away.

We can take this reconsideration of reformism another step further. For the possible meanings of a 'modernizing' departure (the forms, content, and potential coalitions of support) have to depend on the precise coordinates of the national society under discussion. For example, much of the bourgeois dynamism that fed into the *Hansabund* and helped to rejuvenate the National Liberals in the period after 1907 had a technocratic as opposed to a democratic direction, concerned with strengthening the 'national character' and Germany's position in the world rather than increasing political 'participation' in a parliamentary sense. Given the similar preoccupations motivating the newfound interest in welfare reform in Britain (amongst Fabians, social Darwinists, enlightened civil servants, and New Liberals), we should per-

tempered animosity against Wehler and the Kehrites. While he delivers a valuable corrective to the prevailing views of the *Kaiserreich*'s 'backwardness' and 'instability', with some good particular analyses of constitutional change, Rauh hitches his argument to an older Whiggish teleology. See M. Rauh, *Föderalismus und Parlamentarismus im Wilhelminischen Reich* (Düsseldorf, 1972), and M. Rauh, *Die Parlamentarisierung des Deutschen Reiches* (Düsseldorf, 1977). His views are ably disputed by one of the leading Kehrites in V. R. Berghahn, 'Politik und Gesellschaft im Wilhelminischen Deutschland', *Neue Politische Literatur*, XXIV. 2 (1979), 168-73. For the older version of the 'parliamentarization' thesis, see W. Frauendienst, 'Die Demokratisierung des deutschen Konstitutionalismus in der Zeit Wilhelms II', *Zeitschrift für die gesamte Staatswissenschaft*, 113 (1957).

[5] This I take to be part of the argument in Schoenbaum, *Zabern 1913*.

haps not find this orientation so surprising. In fact, we might even argue that the nationalist pressure groups (Navy League, Defence League, Pan-Germans) were Imperial Germany's authentic movement of bourgeois emancipation—in their sociology, in their anti-clericalism and hostility to outmoded dynastic authority, in their restless opposition to traditional *Honoratiorenpolitik* (notable politics), and in their ideal of a greater Germany borne by the moral zeal of self-confident citizen-patriots. In this respect the British comparison is especially interesting, because given the two countries' differing positions in the world market the German ideology of radical nationalism was not too far removed from British obsessions with 'national efficiency' after the Boer War. Germany's continued exclusion from a global empire which the British were so anxious to defend made an aggressive imperialist commitment the functional equivalent of the new British drive for domestic regeneration.[6]

This makes the question posed above—namely, the conditions under which a liberal-democratic form of the state might develop—much easier to handle. As argued extensively above, this is a specifically *political* question. It cannot be reduced to a particular social process ('the rise of the bourgeoisie'), or to a particular economic one ('the rise of a modern industrial economy'). To do so would be to assume one-to-one correlations between social and economic structures and their appropriate political expressions or forms. The most unfortunate reductionism of this sort treats liberalism as an instrumental creed of the class interest of the bourgeoisie, and makes advanced liberal democracy into an

---

[6] I have argued this interpretation of the nationalist pressure groups more extensively in my book, Eley, *Reshaping*, esp. pp. 101–235. The argument has been condensed in G. Eley, 'Some Thoughts on the Nationalist Pressure Groups in Imperial Germany', P. Kennedy and A. Nicholls (eds.), *Nationalist and Racialist Movements in Britain and Germany before 1914* (London, 1981), pp. 40–67. My thinking on the comparative aspect is greatly indebted to Karl Rohe. See his essay in the same volume, K. Rohe, 'The British Imperialist Intelligentsia and the *Kaiserreich*', Kennedy and Nichols (eds.), *Nationalist and Racialist Movements*, pp. 130–42. It is also worth noting that in Germany radical nationalism was usually accompanied by legislative demands for a strengthening of the old and new petty bourgeoisie—again, not social reform of the classic pro-labour kind normally associated with discussions of the welfare state, but social reform none the less.

essential characteristic of a strong bourgeoisie. As argued above, liberalism was always a more complex political phenomenon than this, rooted in popular coalitions of varying complexion, whose forms of combination and degrees of unity determined the extent of the democratic component and not some spontaneous drive of the bourgeoisie for 'emancipation' (whatever that actually is).

In fact, it was only when such popular coalitions began to break up and the subordinate classes began demanding a voice of their own that liberals made any serious move towards specifically democratic reforms. And when this process produced an independent popular democratic party of some substance, like the SPD in Germany, liberals might just as easily resist demands for democratization as promote them. In Germany the different fractions of the bourgeoisie each had their own reasons for doubting the advantages of democratic change, but their common and justified assumption was that greater parliamentary powers would redound to the benefit of the SPD, by that time the largest single party. The existence of a radical workers' party publicly committed to revolutionary socialism—a factor conspicuously missing in Edwardian Britain—more than anything else forestalled the chances of a 'Gladstonian coalition'. In Britain liberalism reaped the benefits of a 'corporate' working class and a poorly developed socialism; in Germany its options were severely restricted by the risks of co-operating with a relatively more advanced and vigorously independent party of the working class. Which of these situations was the more 'modern' is an arguable and perhaps even a fruitless question.[7]

The point I am trying to stress here is that the absence of liberal democracy had very specific origins in the balance of social and political forces produced by the particular forms of Germany's capitalist development. Most obviously, I have argued that the right-wing attitudes of the CVDI industrialists can only be understood in the context of the specific capitalist rationality that permitted them to flourish, and here the developing structures of monopoly capital were far more important than the alleged persistence of some 'pre-industrial'

[7] The term 'corporate' is being used here in Gramsci's sense. See P. Anderson, 'Origins of the Present Crisis', *New Left Review*, 23 (1964), 26–54.

or 'traditional' mentality. The economic power of the big concerns enabled a closer control over the labour process and introduced a form of company paternalism which went far beyond any 'pre-industrial' habits of authority and for heavy industry in Silesia and the Ruhr amounted to an important condition of expanded reproduction. In other words, this was no intrusion from a bygone feudal era which by standards of 'modernization' ought to have been superseded, but a set of eminently 'modern' relationships generated by capitalism itself. Given the necessary resources it made perfect sense for capitalists to refuse the 'just' demands of the working class, and when presented with the opportunity British employers proved just as sensitive to this principle as their German colleagues.[8] Moreover, this argument is in some ways clinched by the experience of the United States. For anything remotely resembling the 'feudal' traditions so avidly invoked by German historians was patently absent from American society. Yet not only were 'the basic characteristics and chronology of capitalist industrial development' in Germany and the USA 'remarkably similar'.[9] Those structural characteristics (which we may summarize as higher levels of tendential monopoly organization in the sense specified above) also resulted in a similar history of employer intransigence and trade-union weakness, whose main institutional expression was a particularly ruthless variety of company paternalism. If 'pre-industrial' mentalities and authoritarian traditions are at least plausible as an explanation for this phenomenon in Germany, it clearly makes no sense for the United States. In which case perhaps we should look for our explanations elsewhere.[10]

[8] See, e.g., J. Saville, 'Trade Unions and Free Labour; The Background to the Taff Vale Decision', A. Briggs and J. Saville (eds.), *Essays in Labour History* (London, 1960), pp. 317-50; D. Smith, 'The Struggle Against Company Unionism in the South Wales Coalfields, 1926-1939', *Welsh History Review*, 6 (1973), 354-78. For the general argument as it pertains to Britain, see H. Newby, 'Paternalism and Capitalism', R. Scase (ed.), *Industrial Society: Class, Cleavage and Control* (London, 1977), pp. 59-73; Hay and Melling, 'Public Service and Private Progress'.

[9] Kocka, *White Collar Workers in America*, p. iii.

[10] North American labour history is distinguished by levels of violence, repression, and authoritarianism, which have been remarkably consistent between the 1880s and the present day, and trade unions have achieved neither the degree

However, the power of the big concerns also had its limitations. The advantages of tendential monopoly organization were a much less effective weapon in the wider political arena, where the active solidarity of the working class achieved a much more threatening expression. As the CVDI bosses discovered, the electoral success of organized labour in the form of the SPD could not be contained by company unions, black lists, company welfare, and direct ideological surveillance of workers at the point of production, and it was this political difficulty that led heavy industry in particular to join the agrarians in resisting any extension of democracy. More specifically, it was this that motivated the CVDI's core interests to renew the old protectionist alliance with the agrarians in 1897-8, to embark on a more ambitious form of propagandist anti-socialism through the Imperial League Against Social Democracy after 1903-4, to leave the *Hansabund* in 1911, and to launch the *Kartell der schaffenden Stände* with the agrarians and *Mittelstand* organizations in 1913.[11] In brief, it was the massive growth of the SPD after

of recognition under the law nor the level of popular democratic legitimacy attained by the British trade-union movement between, say, the 1906 Trades Disputes Act and the contemporary erosion of their position which began in the later 1960s. For an introduction see D. M. Gordon, R. Edwards, and M. Reich, *Segmented Work, Divided Workers. The Historical Transformation of Labour in the United States* (Cambridge, 1982), esp. pp. 112-64; D. Brody, *Workers in Industrial America. Essays on the 20th Century Struggle* (Oxford, 1980), pp. 3-81. There is an excellent conspectus of nineteenth- and twentieth-century US labour history in two articles by Mike Davis: 'Why the US Working Class is Different', *New Left Review*, 123 (1980), 3-44, and 'The Barren Marriage of American Labour and the Democratic Party', *New Left Review*, 124 (1980), 43-84. The extraordinary thing in this context is that some of my critics have invoked the North American case to argue the opposite, namely the contrast with Germany and the absence of a comparable authoritarianism on the part of big employers. If industrial capitalism in the USA showed the same structural features as in Germany, in other words, but without the same kind of repressive company paternalism, then paternalism in German industry has to be explained by cultural/ideological factors (i.e. 'pre-industrial' values and traditions) and not by the structures and conditions of capitalist production and reproduction. If the premiss (absence of employer authoritarianism in US) was true, the logic might be persuasive. But such a reading of North American labour history leaves me completely mystified.

[11] The *Kartell der schaffenden Stände* ('Cartel of the Productive Estates') was an attempt to form an extra-parliamentary front of right-wing interests at a time when the right's parliamentary strength had fallen to an all-time low. Based on a tradition of industrial-agrarian co-operation, with a much stronger involvement of both *Mittelstand* and radical nationalist organizations than before, it

1895-6 (itself a specific product of the Wilhelmine era) that forced many of the largest employers to continue a close political relationship with the big landowners. But once again: this was not necessarily the survival of some 'pre-industrial' brand of politics or an ideological rejection of 'modernity'. Quite the contrary. It was a rational calculation of political interest in a situation where greater levels of parliamentary democracy necessarily worked to the advantage of the Socialist left. In Britain in this period parliamentary forms proved an admirable means of containing socialism; in Germany they threatened to work in its favour.

Thus the leading fractions of the bourgeoisie entered the agrarian alliance not from some lack of 'self-confidence' or of 'political maturity', but because this was the best means of securing certain bourgeois interests. As I have tried to argue, this becomes clearer if we can once dissociate the idea of 'bourgeois revolution' from the achievement of some necessary level of parliamentary democracy and in the process redefine it to mean the body of change that inaugurated the bourgeois epoch—'the successful installation of a legal and political framework in which the free development of capitalist property relations is assured.'[12] For there is little sense in German historiography that the interests and aspirations of the bourgeois class may be variously realized through political forms other than those of advanced liberal democracy, or that the bourgeois revolution may follow a course other than the one conventionally derived from the French 'model' of 1789. If this argument is followed through, the problem of the industrial–agrarian alliance in Wilhelmine politics appears in a significantly new light. It was less the

---

drew consciously upon earlier attempts at coalition building in 1897-8 and 1878-9. Its political importance is disputed in the recent literature. The strong view is held by Stegmann, *Erben*, pp. 305-27, 267-92, 352-60, and Saul, *Staat, Industrie, Arbeiterbewegung*, pp. 306-81, and to my mind largely survives the sceptical criticism voiced by Kaelble, *Industrielle Interessenpolitik*, p. 204; Puhle, *Agrarkrise*, p. 58; H. A. Winkler, *Mittelstand, Demokratie und National-sozialismus* (Cologne, 1972), pp. 53f.; Wehler, *Das Deutsche Kaiserreich*, p. 104; Mielke, *Hansa-Bund*, pp. 166-80. My own view is closest to that of Schmidt, 'Parlamentarisierung oder "Präventive Konterrevolution"?', esp. pp. 274-8. See Eley, *Reshaping*, pp. 316-34.

[12] Jones, 'Society and Politics', p. 86.

absence or failure of bourgeois revolution that forced a supine bourgeoisie into a junior partnership with a 'pre-industrial power élite', than the particular form of Germany's bourgeois revolution (revolution from above under the aegis of the Prussian state through military unification of Germany) that combined with the accelerated character of Germany's capitalist development to impose a specific logic of class alliance. In practice the latter meant varying degrees of accommodation within an unreformed state structure, and to that extent existing work correctly identifies aristocratic survivals as one defining feature of the Imperial polity. But it is far from clear that this involved a process of bourgeois subordination or 'feudalization' rather than, say, one of gradual adaptation of the state to the needs of bourgeois consolidation.

VIII
Defining the State in Imperial Germany

A number of questions remain to be addressed before bringing this essay to a close. In particular: if the Imperial state was neither a 'liberal' state (as most German historians have correctly argued) nor a straightforwardly 'aristocratic' one (as I am suggesting), then what kind of state was it?[1] Formulating an answer to this question is among the least tractable of the conceptual problems dealt with in this essay. This is partly because historians rarely grapple directly with the alternative approaches available in the theoretical literature on the state, so that it is unclear how far the use of the operative terminology (like 'feudal', 'aristocratic', 'absolutist', 'archaic', 'pre-industrial', and so on) is purely pragmatic and descriptive, and how far it reflects a conscious and seriously reflected theoretical conception. In addition, the few German historians who have advanced explicitly theorized definitions of the pre-1918 state (e.g. Wehler, Kocka, to a lesser extent Stürmer) do so in a way which leaves certain important ambiguities, despite the constructive value of their efforts (which should be forthrightly and generally acknowledged).[2] What follows is therefore an

---

[1] The attentive reader will have noted that these terms ('liberal' and 'aristocratic') are not equivalents, the one referring to a type of politics, the other to a particular social class. In fact (as I have tried to argue in the main body of this essay) this conceptual non-equivalence has been precisely the problem in arriving at a satisfactory notation of the Imperial German state. We need to break the entrenched assumptions of German historiography that (a) the authoritarian aspects of the 1871 Constitution expressed the political dominance of the landowning aristocracy, and that (b) the weakness of liberalism expressed the subordination of the bourgeoisie. What I am trying to argue, obviously, is that the authoritarian state (or to put it more cautiously, a state showing marked authoritarian features) could also articulate the interests of the bourgeoisie. Under specific circumstances such a state might also correspond to the bourgeoisie's social dominance and political hegemony.

[2] In other words, by criticizing certain works I do not mean to question their value or legitimacy, least of all to suggest that they should never have been written. Quite the contrary. Without Wehler's and Kocka's pioneering insistence that historians take theoretical discussion seriously, my own discussion would scarcely be possible in the first place.

attempt to disentangle a number of formal positions from the recent historical literature, with a view to clarifying the future discussion.

In recent writing the Imperial state seems to have been given four distinct definitions, which coexist together in the work of the two most thoughtful and influential writers on the subject (Wehler and Kocka), and which are by no means mutually incompatible with one another. The first (a) attributes a dominant role to the Junkers as a 'pre-industrial' ruling group whose unbroken influence explains the political system's specific 'backwardness', as that is usually understood. This is the definition that should be most familiar to us after the preceding discussions in this essay. The twin characteristics of backwardness and aristocratic dominance are thought to have been expressed in a number of institutional ways: the executive power of the King-Kaiser, the autonomy of the military, the preferential recruitment of the officer corps and the bureaucracy from the aristocracy, the limited powers of the Reichstag, the transmuted seigneurial character of the local government east of the River Elbe, the effective immunities of the landowners from certain kinds of taxation in the same region, and of course the special qualities of the Prussian as opposed to the Reich Constitution. Now, at one level these factors amply justify an 'aristocratic' description of the state. But for that description to acquire theoretical status the state–society relation must also be addressed, and in existing discussions the relationship of the Junkers (as a social class) to the state (as an ensemble of political institutions) is left regrettably unclear. Sometimes that relationship is expressed as direct political control, which subordinated state apparatuses and their direction to Junker interests. At other times the apparatuses seem to be given equivalent autonomy and social standing in a manner reminiscent of C. Wright Mills and his theory of the 'power élite', so that 'Junkers, bureaucracy, military' appear collectively as 'pre-capitalist ruling strata'.[3] Adopting a distinction advanced by Poulantzas, we might say that such writing oscillates between two different conceptions

---

[3] See C. Wright Mills, *The Power Elite* (Oxford, 1956).

of the state—an instrumentalist one which views the state as
a passive tool available for manipulation by ruling interests,
and a 'subjectivist' one, where it appears as an originating
subject, arbitrating the conflicts of classes and social interests
and apparently autonomous of their control. There is much
theoretical uncertainty involved here, and the talk of 'pre-
industrial traditions', an 'autocratic, semi-absolutist sham-
constitutionalism', and the 'feudalization of the bourgeoisie'
even suggests notions of a state which was primarily feudal.[4]

A more sophisticated variation along these lines is (b) the
concept of 'Bonapartism' adapted from Marx and Engels by
Wehler, where the state's autonomy is constituted from the
political equilibrium of dominant socio-economic interests
(the alliance of 'iron and rye'), originally beneath the direc-
tive genius of Bismarck, but then achieving an unstable
existence of its own. This is close to Gramsci's concept of
'Caesarism', 'in which a great personality is entrusted with
the task of "arbitration" over a historical-political situation
characterized by an equilibrium of forces heading towards
catastrophe'.[5] In the *Critique of the Gotha Programme* Marx
called the resultant state 'nothing but a military despotism,
embellished with parliamentary forms, alloyed with a feudal
admixture, already influenced by the bourgeoisie, furnished
by the bureaucracy and protected by the police', and this
ultimately unsatisfactory 'agglutination of epithets' (as Perry
Anderson calls it) seems consonant with Wehler's similarly
eclectic definition. Anderson's own formula places the accent
somewhat differently, arguing that 'the German state was
now a capitalist apparatus, over-determined by its feudal
ancestry, but fundamentally homologous with a social formation which by the twentieth century was massively dominated by the capitalist mode of production.'[6] In Wehler's case
the main effect of this 'Bonapartist' definition of the state is

[4] See, e.g., Wehler's discussion in *Das Deutsche Kaiserreich*, pp. 60-3.
[5] See Q. Hoare and G. Nowell Smith (eds.), *Selections from the Prison Notebooks of Antonio Gramsci* (London, 1971), p. 219. Ultimately Gramsci's exposition is very schematic, and his notes on the subject are among the most
attenuated and least fruitful parts of his political theory in the *Notebooks*. His
description of Bismarck as an example of a 'reactionary Caesarism' certainly does
not correspond to the analysis of revolution from above advanced in this essay.
[6] Anderson, *Lineages*, pp. 277f.

certainly to acknowledge the new importance of industrial capital within the German social formation in the period after unification. But this is expressed in such a way as to leave the 'aristocratic' or 'Junkerist' definition intact. Industrial capital has arrived, but its interests are accommodated within a 'traditional' power structure of a basically unreformed kind.

At some variance with these approaches is a third definition of the state (c), stressing the changing forms of economic intervention. The ubiquitous Wehler is again at the forefront of this discussion, proposing a notion of the modern interventionist state which rests on a particular appropriation of Jürgen Habermas's theory of legitimation. Here 'political power is legitimated chiefly by a deliberate policy of state intervention which tries to correct the dysfunctions of the economy, in particular the disturbances of economic growth, in order to ensure the stability of the social system.' The new interventionist ideology (which replaces what Habermas calls the 'basic bourgeois ideology of fair exchange') is meant both to re-establish conditions favourable for economic growth and to secure the acquiescence of the wage-earning masses by suitable 'compensations'. Government increasingly has no choice but to pursue these aims as the organizing priority of its activity, for otherwise the 'ruling élites' would be unable 'to preserve the system and their own vested interests.'[7] Wehler dates the start of these processes in the Great Depression of 1873-96, but others associate them with the stronger appearance of 'organized capitalism' after that time. Kocka in particular takes that view, also advancing a fourth definition of the Imperial state in the process (d), namely its 'relative autonomy' from direct control by the dominant socio-economic interests. The capitalist state's autonomy arises logically from the needs of legitimation, because government now needs a certain latitude both for the purposes of general economic management and for satisfying certain demands of the subordinate classes. Kocka sees

---

[7] See Wehler, 'Industrial Growth', pp. 77f.; Wehler, *Bismarck*, p. 500; J. Habermas, *Technik und Wissenschaft als 'Ideologie'* (Frankfurt, 1968), esp. pp. 74–80, 83f., 92, 99.

the tendencies towards relative autonomy being strengthened by the First World War, by processes of corporative growth which have become very familiar in the literature.[8]

What can we say briefly about these various definitions of the Imperial state? Most obviously, they maintain a discrepancy between the state as a system of political domination (its constitutional 'backwardness', the Junkers' controlling power and institutional privileges, and the general importance of 'pre-industrial traditions') and its role in the economy (its 'modern' interventionist character). This dualism is a defining feature of recent German historiography. Thus Wehler's work contains both a strong view of the needs of capital deriving from the logic of industrial growth (as expressed through the concepts of interventionism, organized capitalism, and legitimation), and yet an equally powerful insistence on the ultimate efficacy of specific political traditions: 'It was not the industrial economy as such that by itself established the conditions of societal development, because the latter had to unfold in an institutional framework preformed and codetermined by political culture, the system of political domination, and the political interests of pre- and non-industrial social forces.'[9] As far as it goes this distinction registers an enormously important advance over neo-Hegelian or purely instrumentalist views of the state. The problem arises with the particular weighting of the political factors, which in this case seem to be mainly conceived as linear

---

[8] Kocka, *Klassengesellschaft im Krieg*, pp. 105–31. See also this statement by Poulantzas: 'the capitalist state has inscribed in its very structures a flexibility which concedes a certain guarantee to the economic interests of certain dominated classes, within the limits of the system.' N. Poulantzas, *Political Power and Social Classes*, p. 190. The two most important historical treatments of corporatism recently have been C. S. Maier, *Recasting Bourgeois Europe. Stabilization in France, Germany, and Italy in the Decade after World War I* (Princeton, 1975), and K. Middlemas, *Politics in Industrial Society. The Experience of the British System since 1911* (London, 1979). For an introduction to the general literature on the subject, see P. Schmitter and G. Lehmbruch (eds.), *Trends towards Corporatist Intermediation* (London and Beverly Hills, 1979); L. Panitch, 'The Development of Corporatism in Liberal Democracies', *Comparative Political Studies*, 10 (1977), 61–90; L. Panitch, 'Recent Theorizations of Corporatism: Reflections on a Growth Industry', *British Journal of Sociology*, XXXI. 2 (1980), 159–87.

[9] H.-U. Wehler, 'Der Aufstieg des Organisierten Kapitalismus und Interventionsstaates in Deutschland', Winkler (ed.), *Organisierter Kapitalismus*, p. 49.

continuities from an earlier epoch—inherited structures rather than directly generated, produced, or determined by the Bismarckian or Wilhelmine conjunctures themselves. It is more than anything else in the contradiction between these two levels of the 'social system'—a non-correspondence between the political and the economic—that the Imperial state's structural instability and ultimate collapse are thought to be inscribed, on the grounds that the inherited syndrome of 'traditional' authoritarianism consistently militated against the needs of 'modern' legitimation.

Now there is nothing wrong with this idea of disjunction or non-correspondence as such, and indeed if we take the non-reductionist, non-economistic argumentation of this essay seriously we should expect to find precisely this—i.e. situations in which there is not a tidy fit between socio-economic structures and the politico-institutional and ideo-logical forms that are thought logically best to express them. The problem with the formulation discussed above ('modern' economy, 'backward' state) is that the disjunction is thought to be irrational, dysfunctional, crisis-producing, and structurally fixed. This account of the state (most forcefully and persuasively expounded in the writings of Wehler) presents German history before 1914 as a continuous dichotomous conflict between the forces of order and the forces of emancipation ('authoritarianism' and 'liberalism'; the 'traditional' and the 'modern'; the 'past' and the 'future'), in which the forces of order consistently won out, by a combination of inflexible adherence to the social and political 'status quo' (the successful 'defence of traditional ruling positions by pre-industrial élites against the onslaught of new forces') and skilful manipulation of political technique ('secondary integration', 'social imperialism' etc.).[10]

But while the disjunctions themselves should not be disputed (the Junkers clearly did retain certain privileged access to the state apparatuses; the state did display certain formal characteristics usually described as 'feudal'; the bourgeoisie did not 'rule' in the simple sense of directly controlling the state apparatuses), there are other ways of interpreting their

---

[10]   Wehler, *Das Deutsche Kaiserreich*, p. 14.

significance. As this essay has tried to argue, both the Bismarckian state and an authoritarian mode of politics were perfectly effective in securing specifically 'bourgeois' interests, if these are strictly defined in relation to the fundamental processes of class formation and capitalist industrialization. The politico-institutional forms of the *Kaiserreich* appear dysfunctional more by the external standard of an abstract liberal democracy, than by the contemporary standard of Imperial German society and its requirements. In this sense the non-correspondence (between the political and the economic) could be conceptualized not only as a source of instability, but (as in the Perry Anderson quotation above) as a relationship of formally discontinuous but ultimately functional homology.[11]

For the sake of argument, let us accept for the moment that the 'Junkerist' argument is true and that the outwardly 'aristocratic' aspects of the Imperial Constitution directly reflected the social and political domination of a 'pre-industrial power élite'. Given the way in which this is hitched to a critique of the bourgeoisie's 'political immaturity' and the idea of failed bourgeois revolution, and the accompanying sense in which the terms 'modern', 'liberal', and 'bourgeois' are elided normatively together, we might reasonably conclude that a genuinely 'modern' state would be one in which the progressive social predominance of the bourgeoisie was formally consummated in a constitutional liberalization of the state. This would then leave us with a pleasing symmetry of social structure and political power, expressed by the paired juxtaposition of aristocratic authoritarianism on the one side, bourgeois liberalism on the other. But as we know from long years of debate about these matters (and not least from the writings of Jürgen Kocka and Hans-Ulrich Wehler), there are big problems to seeing the state as the dependent superstructure of dominant economic interests or the political expression of ruling-class power. We can go a certain distance in establishing these relationships (e.g. by analysing the recruitment of state personnel and the content of state legislation, and by exploring the limits of state intervention within

---

[11] Anderson, *Lineages*, pp. 277 f.

the constraints of the existing socio-economic system). However, at a certain point we come up against the autonomy of the state ('relative' or otherwise), both as a source of independent bureaucratic, military, or judicial initiative, and as an arena in which contending social and political forces interact.[12] As Therborn says, the state is both a relatively unified system of apparatuses (whose staff and personnel have independent effects) and 'an institution where social power is concentrated and exercised' (and therefore subject to external intervention).[13]

If this is so, then even in a fully 'bourgeois' society (in Dahrendorf's double sense of a 'society of citizens' and a society 'dominated by a confident bourgeoisie') we should not expect to find the bourgeoisie directly controlling the state in any straightforward instrumentalist sense.[14] Its status as a dominant class derives less from any capacity for 'backstage string-pulling' (though this obviously takes place), than from an ability to ensure that the sum of state interventions (or 'the societal content of the actions of the state') works predominantly in its favour. If we define the state with

---

[12] 'Relative autonomy' has been stressed by most sophisticated discussions of state theory since the late 1960s. See the literature cited above, pp. 95 n. 9, 96 n. 11. In addition the work of Paul Hirst and Barry Hindess has made an important contribution in this area. Whatever one's ultimate judgement of their influence (which it has long been fashionable to decry), their consistent stress on the need to think out the relationship between economics and politics as rigorously as possible has had a salutary effect. For two good examples, see B. Hindess, 'Class and Politics in Marxist Theory', Littlejohn *et al.* (eds.), *Power and the State*, pp. 72–97, and B. Hindess, 'Marxism and Parliamentary Democracy', A. Hunt (ed.), *Marxism and Democracy* (London, 1980), pp. 21–54. Jessop's summary statement on relative autonomy is worth quoting: '. . . "relative autonomy" is either an abstract, formal concept serving merely a diacritical function in demarcating our preferred approach from simple reductionism and/or the absolute autonomisation of different regions, or else it is a concrete, descriptive concept whose content varies across conjunctures. It cannot function as a principle of explanation in its own right but is itself an explicandum in the same way as concepts such as "state power" '. See Jessop, *Capitalist State*, pp. 226 f. The subtlety of the distinctions in Jessop's and others' recent analyses belies the crude and dismissive characterization of marxist approaches in T. Skocpol, *States and Revolutions* (Cambridge, 1979), pp. 24–33, whose reversion to an idea of the state's creative institutional independence (an 'organizational' or 'realist' perspective of complete autonomy) is far less helpful.
[13] Therborn, *What Does the Ruling Class Do . . .?* pp. 153, 132.
[14] Dahrendorf, *Society and Democracy*, p. 397.

Therborn as 'a separate institution which concentrates the supreme rule-making, rule-applying, rule-adjudicating, rule-enforcing and rule-defending functions' in a society, then the dominance of a ruling class resides in its ability 'to bring about a particular mode of intervention' of that 'special body', in order to secure the conditions in which 'the economic, political and ideological conditions of its domination' in society may be reproduced.[15] In that case (and by contrast with the feudal landowner, one might argue), the bourgeoisie 'rules' less by the direct disposal of state power than by restructuring the social, institutional, and ideological arena in which politics and government have to take place—i.e. by exercising 'hegemony' in the Gramscian and frequently misunderstood sense.[16]

To illustrate this it is worth returning to the British comparison. For there is an influential reading of the British past which is eerily reminiscent of the 'Junkerist' arguments criticized here. In this view the British bourgeoisie also failed to constitute itself as a ruling class because (like the German) it lacked the driving force and domineering consciousness necessary to challenge the primacy of the aristocratic élite. This case was eloquently argued in a sequence of now classic essays by Perry Anderson and Tom Nairn in the 1960s, where

[15] The phrases in quotation marks are taken from Therborn, *What Does the Ruling Class Do . . . ?*, pp. 145, 161. See also his summary, ibid., p. 242: 'What then does the ruling class do when it rules? Essentially, it ensures that its dominant positions in the economy, state apparatus and ideological superstructures are reproduced by the state in relation both to other modes of production present within the social formation and to the international system of social formations. These reproductive state interventions are enmeshed in the structural dynamics of the mode of reproduction, but they also have to be secured in the thick of the class struggle.'

[16] Exegeses of Gramsci are now legion. The most fruitful are the following: S. Hall, B. Lumley, G. McLennan, 'Politics and Ideology: Gramsci', Centre for Contemp. Cult. Studies (ed.), *On Ideology*, pp. 45-76; A. S. Sassoon, 'Hegemony, War of Position and Political Intervention', Sassoon (ed.), *Approaches to Gramsci*, pp. 94-115; C. Buci-Glucksmann, 'Hegemony and Consent', Sassoon (ed.), *Approaches to Gramsci*, pp. 116-26; Williams, *Marxism and Literature*, pp. 108-14; Jessop, *Capitalist State*, pp. 142-52. Urry's criticisms of 'hegemony' are extremely pertinent, but do not undermine its value. See Urry, *Anatomy of Capitalist Societies*, pp. 21-5 and in general. There is no space to develop these comments here, but for my own views see Eley and Nield, 'Why Does Social History Ignore Politics?', esp. pp. 268f., and Eley, 'Reception of Gramsci into English'.

the peculiarities of the British development were explained in the very terms which are so popular amongst historians of Germany—premature and incomplete bourgeois revolution in the seventeenth century, growing bourgeois accommodation to prevailing aristocratic norms in the eighteenth, failure to reconstitute the state in the nineteenth. In other words, the British bourgeoisie was as spineless as the German. It failed to transform society in its own image. It failed to control the state. It failed to generate its own distinctive, combative, unifying view of the world. It failed to establish its own undisputed hegemony. Instead, 'the aristocracy survived, in the face of the inevitable political and ideological feebleness of the emergent bourgeoisie, as the governors of the most dynamic capitalist system in the world.' There occurred a 'deliberate, systematized symbiosis' between landowning aristocracy and industrial bourgeoisie—rooted in social and economic interpenetration, articulated through the political compromises of 1688-1832—in which the aristocracy consistently retained the upper hand. Above all it controlled the state. It set the tone of public life. It maintained the hegemony of its 'landowning civilization'—'as a mode of living, a culture and language, a type of personality and psychology, a whole dominant ethos.'[17]

This kind of argument is by no means confined to the architects of *New Left Review* marxism. It was remorselessly pursued in Martin Wiener's recently acclaimed *English Culture and the Decline of the Industrial Spirit 1850-1980*. Here, for

---

[17] The original essays were as follows: Anderson, 'Origins of the Present Crisis'; T. Nairn, 'The English Working Class', *New Left Review*, 24 (1964), 45-57; T. Nairn, 'The British Political Elite', *New Left Review*, 23 (1964), 19-25; T. Nairn, 'The Anatomy of the Labour Party', *New Left Review*, 27 (1964), 38-65, and 28 (1964), 33-62. Edward Thompson's 'Peculiarities of the English' was a direct response to these texts, and drew an equally polemical and more acrimonious rejoinder from Perry Anderson, 'The Myths of Edward Thompson, or Socialism and Pseudo-Empiricism', *New Left Review*, 35 (1966), 2-42. For subsequent commentaries, see Poulantzas, 'Marxist Political Theory' (p. 84 n. 13 above); Johnson, 'Barrington Moore, Perry Anderson and English Social Development' (p. 60 n. 7 above); Nield, 'A Symptomatic Dispute?' (p. 60 n. 7 above). Thompson, *Poverty of Theory*, and P. Anderson, *Arguments Within English Marxism* (London, 1980), represent later instalments of this mid-sixties debate, mediated through other subsequent controversies. The quotations in my own paragraph are culled from Nairn, 'British Political Elite', pp. 21 f.

instance, is a typical statement which, *mutatis mutandis*, could easily adorn the pages of a German text:

As a rule, leaders of commerce and industry in England over the past century have accommodated themselves to an elite culture blended of pre-industrial aristocratic and religious values and more recent professional and bureaucratic values that inhibited their quest for expansion, productivity and profit.[18]

There are stronger and weaker versions of this argument. Taken to an extreme, it can look similar to Dahrendorf's arguments on Germany, where even the 'bourgeois' or 'capitalist' character of German society in the full meaning of the terms is disputed. Wiener quotes Keith Joseph to the effect that Britain 'never had a capitalist ruling class or a stable *haute bourgeoisie*', with the result that 'capitalist or bourgeois values have never shaped thought and institutions as they have in some countries.'[19] Arno Mayer has developed similar claims in the context of a broader argument about the generally 'feudal and nobilitarian' character of the European social and political order before 1914. In this view the aristocracy was far more successful at developing and maintaining a unified political consciousness than the bourgeoisie. Despite the commercialization of agriculture, the 'feudalistic spirit' of the landed nobility exercised an autonomous domination over political culture. This was no 'mere integument of upper-class traditions, customs, and mentalities', but an embodied ideology located in institutional apparatuses of enormous social power. This survived because the nobility was excellently 'positioned to monopolize strategic economic, military, bureaucratic, and cultural stations.'[20] More modestly, it has been commonly claimed (in an analysis that goes back to Marx) that the British aristocracy retained its role as the 'class in charge of the state' during the nineteenth century (expressed in the powers of the House of Lords, the heavily aristocratic complexion of most Cabinets, and the

---

[18] M. J. Wiener, *English Culture and the Decline of the Industrial Spirit 1850–1980* (Cambridge, 1981), p. 127.

[19] Ibid., p. 8.

[20] A. J. Mayer, *The Persistence of the Old Regime: Europe to the Great War* (New York, 1981), p. 9.

'limited' nature of the Constitution) as a kind of proxy for the bourgeoisie (which increasingly dominated society).[21] In this case we are back to the familiar 'German' discrepancy, between 'modern' economy and 'traditional' state.

What are we to make of this alarming convergence of arguments, between a Germany locked in the structural backwardness of its 'pre-industrial traditions' and a Britain mired in the suffocating traditionalism of its aristocratic political culture? If neither Germany (the most dynamic capitalism in late-nineteenth and early-twentieth century Europe) nor Britain (the pioneer of capitalist industrialization) possessed a triumphant bourgeoisie, then where on earth has the bourgeoisie ever 'risen'? And if we take the 'rise of the bourgeoisie' to mean the ascendancy of a unified liberal-democratic world view, expressed through the organized class consciousness of a collective class-subject and secured through control of the state, then (as the earlier part of this essay tried to suggest) the concept might as well be abandoned. But in fact the choice is not quite as stark as this. We can retain a conception of the bourgeoisie (in stricter sociological terms as owners and controllers of the means of production) and its coming to predominance in society (through the dominance of the capitalist mode, the transformation of social relations, and the emergence of a new type of class structure), without postulating the climactic necessity of a liberal-democratic polity as the appropriate expression of the bourgeoisie's fundamental economic, social, cultural, and political power. The irreducible contingency of political forms is a point to which this essay has returned again and again. And indeed, a distinctive feature of the British discussions referred to above (in their various versions) is their willingness to break with the notion of an expressive totality—with the belief, that is, that the dominance of a particular social class has a logical or lawlike requirement for one type of state and political culture over another.

Now, for our purposes the ultimate validity of the approach

---

[21] See Poulantzas, 'Marxist Political Theory', pp. 64–6, and the judgements scattered throughout K. Marx and F. Engels, *Marx and Engels on Britain* (Moscow, 1953). See also R. Gray, 'Bourgeois Hegemony in Victorian Britain', J. Bloomfield (ed.), *Class, Hegemony and Party* (London, 1977), pp. 73–93.

of Anderson, Nairn, Wiener, and Mayer to British history is relatively unimportant.[22] What matters is the willingness to concede the complexity of the state–society relationship and the finely structured compatibility between a bourgeois-dominated class structure and a variety of state forms—what Poulantzas called 'the possibility of social formations in which there are "disjunctions" between the class whose mode of production ultimately imposes its dominant political role on the one hand and the objective structures of the state on the other.'[23] Because if the 'rule' of the bourgeoisie may be exercised indirectly in the one case (within a political culture which remained outwardly heavily aristocratic), then why not in another?

In other words, if (at least in the abstract) the functional combination of 'bourgeois society–aristocratic state' seems to make sense for Britain, why when we come to Germany should we rule it automatically out of court? As I have tried to argue, there were many reasons why a stronger parliamentary state on the model of either the British or the French was unlikely to develop, whether we stress the economic, social, and religious divisions of the bourgeoisie itself, the formidable radicalism of an independent Social Democratic labour movement, or (and not least) the residual aristocratic strengths entrenched defensively in the 1871 Constitution. But 'parliamentarization' does not exhaust the possible forms of peaceful or relatively stable development for the Imperial German state as it entered the twentieth century. There is no reason (again in the abstract) to assume a priori that a modified or stabilized version of the Imperial state should be incapable of meeting the needs of the emerging capitalist social order. Once we acknowledge that the 'rule' of the bourgeoisie (as the dominant class in society) is exercised indirectly, we should also accept that in theory a wide variety of state forms is adequate to the task, from the most authoritarian (late forms of absolutism, fascism, and other

[22] The principal critiques are those of Johnson, 'Barrington Moore, Perry Anderson and English Social Development', and Nield, 'A Symptomatic Dispute?'. My own reaction to Arno Mayer's book may be found in *Journal of Modern History*, 54. 1 (1982), 95–9.

[23] Poulantzas, 'Marxist Political Theory', p. 65.

forms of dictatorship) to the most democratic (the democratic republic, forms of the welfare state, types of social-democratic corporatism), depending on the society and period in question. Once we concede this, we can also acknowledge that intermediate combinations of the two (authoritarian and democratic) are a viable possibility.

In the light of this I am really trying to argue two things. First, the authoritarian features of the Imperial Constitution are not to be equated automatically with 'archaism', 'backwardness', or political inefficiency. Neither the exclusivist (the checks on popular participation), executive (the relative weakness of direct parliamentary control), nor aristocratic (privileges of the titular nobility) features of the political system were particularly unusual by the contemporary European standards of the later nineteenth century. In some ways the Second Reich seemed terribly 'modern' to commentators elsewhere—in the technocratic efficiency of its bureaucracy and military machine, in its more interventionist state, in the vaunted excellence of its municipal administration, in its system of social administration, and (from a different point of view) in the existence of universal suffrage and the extent of popular political mobilization.[24] Conversely, the other states of Europe were certainly not lacking in authoritarian features of their own, whether we look to the limited franchise and hereditary elements of the British Constitution, the extremely oligarchic character of the political system in Italy, or the more obviously absolutist systems further to the east in Austria-Hungary and Tsarist Russia. To say this is not to say that there were no differences between the *Kaiserreich* and Britain, or the *Kaiserreich* and

---

[24] See here the voluminous works of William Harbutt Dawson, an extended hymn of praise to the German model of efficient modern administration. See in particular: *Bismarck and State Socialism* (2nd edn., London, 1891); *The German Workman: A Study in National Efficiency* (London, 1906); *The Evolution of Modern Germany* (London, 1908); *Social Insurance in Germany, 1883–1911: Its History, Operation, Results, and a Comparison with the National Insurance Act, 1911* (London, 1912); *Municipal Life and Government in Germany* (London, 1914); and many others. Dawson is a badly neglected figure. Virtually the only significant discussion of him may be found in G. Hollenberg, *Englisches Interesse am Kaiserreich. Die Attraktivität Preussen-Deutschlands für konservative und liberale Kreise in Grossbritannien 1860–1914* (Wiesbaden, 1974), pp. 230ff.

Russia. But the respective stability of those states depended on the breadth, popularity, and cohesion of their social base, and the relative adequacy of their institutional apparatuses for organizing the necessary degree of consensus amongst both dominant and subordinate classes. And there is no reason why authoritarian features *per se* should render them totally disabled for this purpose.

Thus we can concede the Imperial state's authoritarianism without accepting the normal corollary, that it was inevitably condemned to some 'permanent structural crisis'. To put it another way, the authoritarian parameters of the Imperial Constitution allowed considerable latitude for manœuvre, negotiation, and compromise before the inner limits of the Bismarckian settlement (the prerogatives of the monarchy, the survival of the landowning aristocracy, and the social and economic power of the dominant classes) began to be breached. Within the same fundamental limits the Imperial state showed itself reasonably adaptable (certainly in the circumstances of its foundation, and for large parts of the subsequent four decades) to the tasks which a capitalist state is called upon to perform—securing the conditions of capitalist reproduction, doing the work of legitimation (in the Wehler–Habermas sense), organizing the unity of the dominant classes, mobilizing the consent of the people. In fact, I would suggest (this is the second argument I am trying to make) that the strictly reactionary elements were considerably more isolated in the political system, that the Constitution was considerably more flexible, and that 'modernizing' forces had achieved considerably more penetration—indeed that the 'traditional' elements were considerably less 'traditional'—than recent historians have tended to believe. In particular, the common equation between authoritarian social and political structures, right-wing politics and imperialist foreign policies on the one side, and 'backwardness', archaism, and 'pre-industrial traditions' on the other, is potentially extremely misleading. It may be, in fact, that precisely the most vigorous 'modernizing' tendencies in the *Kaiserreich* were the most pugnacious and consistent in their pursuit of imperialist and anti-democratic policies at home and abroad. If this is so (or at least worthy of discussion), then perhaps we should think again about what exactly the 'traditional' and the 'modern' mean, both in general and in the specific context of the *Kaiserreich*.

What I want to suggest is that in the past we have had our starting-point wrong. If we believe that the German bourgeoisie missed the boat, that it failed to establish its social, cultural, and political ascendancy in a manner commensurate with the dominance of capital in the economy, that 'pre-industrial traditions' survived when they should have been swept away, and that German industrialization unfolded within a framework of political institutions unsuited to the tasks of modernity—in short that the political system of the *Kaiserreich* was out of time—then that whole vocabulary of 'secondary integration', 'negative integration', 'social imperialism', 'manipulation', 'Caesarism', and 'plebiscitary dictatorship' becomes necessary to explain how the whole irrational system held together. If we believe that the Imperial state was so radically incapable of organizing consensus amongst the electorate, articulating the interests of the dominant classes into some workable basis of unity, co-ordinating the construction of social coalitions for the purposes of government, and generally integrating the divergent regional and economic sectors of the newly created German social formation, then the thesis of structural instability and the idea of a 'permanent structural crisis' makes eminent sense.

If on the other hand we believe that the feebleness and subordination of the bourgeoisie have been exaggerated, that the degree of 'positive' integration in Germany's social and political order was much greater, and that the 'mixed' authoritarianism of the Imperial Constitution was less a sign of pathology than of rational fittedness to historically specific circumstances, then an alternative perspective begins to emerge. I have spent some time in this essay suggesting how one particular issue—that of industrial paternalism and the prospects for a decisive liberalizing departure before 1914—might benefit from such a shift of perspective. I would argue further that we have reached the point in German historiography where future advances in our understanding of the Imperial period will require systematic exploration of this perspective from other points of view as well. This is the only way in which interesting new questions—as against the predictable rehearsal of old knowledge—will ever take shape.

IX
Some Provisional Conclusions

In bringing this essay to a conclusion—and to provide a basis for future discussion—it is worth formulating programmatically the main arguments I have been trying to make.

(a) First, we can make a reasonable case for arguing that Germany did, after all, experience a successful bourgeois revolution in the nineteenth century. This did not take the form of a pitched battle between bourgeoisie and aristocracy, in which the former seized state power from traditional monarchy and replaced it with parliamentary democracy. But then it didn't anywhere else in Europe either, certainly not in Britain in the seventeenth century, and certainly not in France in 1789. This view of the bourgeois revolution, where the insurgent bourgeoisie triumphantly realizes its class interests in a programme of heroic liberal democracy, is a myth. But if we associate bourgeois revolution with a larger complex of change—instead of a narrowly defined political process of democratic reform—which cumulatively established the conditions of possibility for the development of industrial capitalism, then there are good reasons for seeing the process of 'revolution from above' between the 1860s and 1870s as Germany's distinctive form of the bourgeois revolution, so that we focus more on the material or objective consequences of events than their motivational origins. We have to accept that the national forms of bourgeois revolution may vary considerably, and certainly can't be identified straightforwardly with either the British or French examples, not least because the latter are themselves in serious historiographical dispute. In other words, the German pattern of 'revolution from above' (spanning the two concentrated periods of 1807-12 and 1862-71) was just as capable of ensuring bourgeois predominance as the different developmental trajectories of Britain, the United States, or France. This leaves open the question of whether 'bourgeois revolution' is the best term for describing this process. In this

144

essay I have preferred to retain it. But the argument would stand perfectly well in its absence.

(b) Secondly, on this basis, rather than stressing the reactionary qualities of the Bismarckian settlement and the 'capitulation' of the liberals, we should accept the broadly 'progressive' character of German unification. I mean this in two specific senses, neither of which is, I trust, too teleological: on the one hand, to refer to the conditions of existence of the emergent capitalist mode of production, the institutional consolidation of the national market, and a German-wide process of industrialization; on the other, to invoke the characteristically bourgeois vision of a new social order as that was understood at the time, by enemies and exponents alike. The new Empire was certainly not the summit of constitutionalist perfection, let alone the enthronement of liberty (but where was?). But between 1867 and 1873 liberal demands for national institutions and constitutional regulation, national economic integration, and the rule of law became the centrepiece of the new constitutional settlement, which consummated the process begun by the *Zollverein* (Customs Union) several decades earlier.[1] Moreover, behind this political achievement were deeper processes of institutional growth and cultural coalescence—the outwardly visible side of the bourgeoisie's class formation—which brought bourgeois notabilities to regional, municipal, and local predominance, and allowed liberals to stake their claims to moral leadership in society ('hegemony', in Gramsci's

---

[1] To specify the nature of the emergent social order, we can do far worse than quote Marx, summarizing the cumulative effects of the English and French Revolutions: 'the proclamation of the political order for the new European society . . . the victory of bourgeois property over feudal property, of nationality over provincialism, of competition over guild, of the partition of estates over primogeniture, of the owner's mastery of the land over the land's mastery of its owner, of enlightenment over superstition, of the family over the family name, of industry over heroic laziness, of civil law over privileges of medieval origin.' In this litany of transformations there is no mention of a liberal-democratic constitution, and the whole burden of my argument has been that we should not necessarily expect to find one. At the same time, a good case can be made in the abstract that liberal forms are at least *not inconsistent* with these other objectives, and indeed during the mid-nineteenth-century liberalism was the creed generally thought best to express them. See Marx, 'The Bourgeoisie and the Counter-Revolution', pp. 192 f.

sense). The *Kulturkampf*—literally a struggle to unlock the potential for social progress, to free the dynamism of German society from the 'dead hand' of archaic institutions—perfectly expressed this combative unity of social, cultural, and political aspirations. This general buoyancy of the liberal presence in the political culture of the 1870s, and the liberals' straightforward domination of the state governments, the Reichstag, and the content of Bismarck's legislative programme, belies the usual view of liberal demoralization and ineffectuality. In other words (to adapt a phrase), the German bourgeoisie was very much present at its own making, and liberalism supplied the materials of its construction.[2]

(c) Thirdly, it is quite wrong to see the bourgeoisie under the German Empire as being somehow politically weak or 'immature', or as failing by some obscure criteria to realize its collective interests as a class. In any case, it is both theoretically misconceived and empirically impossible to view the bourgeoisie as a single inter-subjective unity in this way, because politically (though not economically or sociologically) there can only be different tendencies within the bourgeoisie, which in different situations may achieve a higher or lower degree of cohesion. But more specifically, this hides the fact that the interests of the bourgeoisie (or more exactly, the different fractions within it) may be pursued and secured by other than liberal democratic means. In other words, it is necessary finally to accept that the Imperial state between 1871 and 1918 was actually compatible with the adequate realization of legitimate interests and aspirations of the bourgeoisie. The *Kaiserreich* was not an irredeemably backward and archaic state indelibly dominated by 'pre-industrial', 'traditional', or 'aristocratic' values and interests, but was powerfully constituted between 1862 and 1879 by (amongst other things) the need to accommodate overriding bourgeois capitalist forces.

(d) Following on from this, we need to re-evaluate both

---

[2] I have discussed the process of German unification in G. Eley, 'State Formation, Nationalism and Political Culture in Nineteenth Century Germany', R. Samuel and G. S. Jones (eds.), *Culture, Ideology and Politics. Essays for Eric Hobsbawm* (London, 1983), pp. 277-301. The same questions are taken up by David Blackbourn in his companion essay in this volume.

the origins and significance of the Second Empire's evident 'authoritarianism' (i.e. the limited extent of its parliamentary-democratic development). This partly requires a revision of theoretical perspective. German 'authoritarianism' was not unavoidably bequeathed by an iron determinism of 'pre-industrial continuities', but was specifically overdetermined by the evolving disposition of forces within the German social formation as it entered its predominantly capitalist phase—above all by the simultaneous coexistence of significant aristocratic enclaves within the structure of the state and a powerful Socialist labour movement in German society, and by important contradictions between different fractions of the bourgeoisie. The complex interaction of these factors produced a high degree of fragmentation and instability in the post-Bismarckian power bloc—the coalition of dominant social forces on which effective government had to depend. This was exacerbated during and after the 1890s by the appearance of sharper contradictions amongst the dominant classes (setting industry against agriculture, protectionists against free traders, manufacturers against primary suppliers, small against big capital), and by the persistent volatility and independent mobilizations of the subordinate classes. This made it difficult to construct the necessary degrees of internal unity and popular support which the dominant classes needed to effect a genuinely organic relationship to government. This situation—which elsewhere I tried to characterize as a dual difficulty of the power bloc, a prolonged crisis of its internal cohesion and hegemonic capability—helps explain both the government's relative independence from a stable parliamentary bloc in the Reichstag for most of the period 1890-1914 and the heavily segmented appearance of the German party system.[3] While this did not necessarily prevent the political system from functioning, it did have the effect of seriously inhibiting the putting together of a sufficiently powerful liberal reformist coalition before 1914, in ways which I tried to discuss above.

Thus in tackling the problem of 'Germany's persistent failure to give a home to democracy in its liberal sense'

---

[3] Eley, *Reshaping*, esp. pp. 293-315, 203-5, 349ff.

(Dahrendorf), we have to be extremely clear about exactly what kind of question we are asking, because in previous discussions two distinct problems are frequently confused. On the one hand, there is the question of the conditions under which a bourgeois capitalist society could successfully reproduce itself, or to put it another way, the legal, political, and ideological conditions of existence for a successful German capitalism. Then on the other hand, there is the question of how a more liberal political system might have been achieved. *These are not the same question.* To take an example discussed extensively above, there can be no disputing that the practices of the most powerful fractions of German capital before 1914 were extremely reactionary by most of the standards we have become accustomed to after 1945. But whether they were really in conflict with the needs of capitalist reproduction is a very different matter. To put this more positively, it may be that such practices owed far more to the special circumstances of the industries concerned (in the ways dealt with earlier in this essay) than to the influence of any 'pre-industrial' mentalities.

(e) Next, it is worth drawing attention to a problem of rather surprising neglect amongst German historians, namely the area of social policy in the broadest sense. This is the point at which the two problems distinguished in the previous paragraph—the legal, political, and ideological preconditions for a viable capitalist society, and the chances for a more liberal political system—begin more clearly to separate. For the unstable dialectical unity of bourgeois interests and liberal politics held together quite successfully in the 1860s and 1870s; it was mainly in the 1880s and particularly the 1890s that things fell apart, so that liberal conceptions of the parliamentary state and the bourgeoisie's capacity for reproducing its social domination began to diverge. In the space that opened there crystallized a distinctive field of public activity, some of it centralized in agencies of government, some borne by different kinds of civic initiative, which aimed at regulating and organizing the new social environment of a rapidly industrializing and urbanizing economy. This encompassed everything from social investigation (e.g. the statistical movement, the public-health movement, the *Verein für Sozialpolitik*, and so on), to specific movements of social reform (housing reform, poor law, town planning, local financing, public health), educational activity of different kinds, processes of professionalization, and the more obvious areas of labour legislation (accident and sickness insurance, provision for old age, factory inspection, labour exchanges, unemployment provision, and so on). The point about this type of activity is that in practice it was concentrated in the city, and proceeded regardless of the liberal parties' parliamentary fortunes. In fact, the impressive accomplishments of German municipal administration were articulated only very ambiguously with the concerns of parliamentary liberalism. This was an authentic domain of bourgeois political achievement, in other words, that owed nothing to the existence of a liberal democratic state. It was perfectly compatible with the latter, but certainly did not require it.[4]

(f) In trying to define the Imperial state, Wehler's concept of Bonapartism is probably the best point of departure, provided that we give it Perry Anderson's specific inflection ('a capitalist apparatus, overdetermined by its feudal ancestry, but fundamentally homologous with a social formation which by the twentieth century was massively dominated

---

[4] Sheehan is quite suggestive on this subject. See J. J. Sheehan, 'Liberalism and the City in Nineteenth Century Germany', *Past and Present*, 51 (1971), 116-37. See also the following: D. Lindenlaub, *Richtungskämpfe im Verein für Sozialpolitik* (Beihefte zu den Vierteljahresheften für Sozial- und Wirtschaftsgeschichte, 52 and 53), Wiesbaden, 1967; K. Schwabe (ed.), *Oberbürgermeister 1870-1945* (Boppard, 1980); W. Hofmann, *Zwischen Rathaus und Reichskanzlei. Die Oberbürgermeister in der Kommunal- und Staatspolitik des Deutschen Reiches von 1890 bis 1933* (Stuttgart, 1974); D. Rebentisch, *Ludwig Landmann. Frankfurter Oberbürgermeister der Weimarer Republik* (Wiesbaden, 1975); R. Lembke, *Johannes Miquel und die Stadt Osnabrück* (Osnabrück, 1962; D. Berger-Thimme, *Wohnungsfrage und Sozialstaat* (Frankfurt, 1976); L. Niethammer (ed.), *Wohnen im Wandel* (Wuppertal, 1979); L. Niethammer, 'Some Elements of the Housing Reform Debate in Nineteenth Century Europe: Or, On the Making of a New Paradigm of Social Control', B. M. Stave (ed.), *Modern Industrial Cities. History, Policy, and Survival* (Beverly Hills and London, 1981), pp. 129-64; K. M. Pearle, 'Poverty, Charity, and Poor Relief in Imperial Germany, 1873-1914' (PhD, SUNY Stony Brook, 1980); C. Sachsse and F. Tennstedt, *Geschichte der Armenfürsorge in Deutschland. Vom Spätmittelalter bis zum Ersten Weltkrieg* (Stuttgart, 1980); F. Redlich, 'Academic Education for Business: Its Development and the Contribution of Ignaz Jastrow (1856-1937)', *Steeped in Two Cultures. A Selection of Essays* (New York, 1971), pp. 199-257. I have also benefited from unpublished work by Nick Bullock on the housing-reform movement, and by Michael John on the Code of Civil Law.

by the capitalist mode of production').[5] Valuable here is the stress on the large-scale confrontation of social forces articulated around the central axis of 'coalition of progress-coalition of order', which released the potential for autonomy of the Prussian state executive, realized through the breathtaking pragmatism of Bismarck's policies in the 1860s ('revolution from above'). It is this theoretical content of the idea of Bonapartism—the creative independence of the state executive, inside the limits imposed by the political dynamic of capitalist social development, in the context of a general social and political crisis—that defines its value, rather than the exactness of any descriptive comparisons between Bismarck and Napoleon III.[6] A wide range of problems—the deliberately disjointed characteristics of the Prusso-German Constitution, the individual role of Bismarck, the ideological manipulation of universal suffrage, the use of war scares, cultivation of extra-parliamentary structures based on economic interest groups, the oblique lines of representation between government and society—are at least partially illuminated in its light.[7] If we can get away from the

---

[5] Anderson, *Lineages*, pp. 277 f.

[6] After a promising start in the late 1960s in the work of Wehler and Stürmer, discussion of Bonapartism has become bogged down in needless empirical comparisons of Bismarck and Napoleon III and in arguments about contemporary meanings. Though valuable in themselves, such discussions have not vitiated the theoretical potential of the idea. In this sense I am not persuaded by the otherwise stimulating critiques by Mitchell and Gall. See Wehler, *Bismarck*, pp. 455 ff.; M. Stürmer, 'Konservatismus und Revolution in Bismarcks Politik', Stürmer (ed.), *Das kaiserliche Deutschland*, pp. 143 ff.; M. Stürmer, *Regierung und Reichstag im Bismarckstaat. Cäsarismus oder Parlamentarismus* (Düsseldorf, 1974); H. Boldt, 'Deutscher Konstitutionalismus und Bismarckreich', Stürmer (ed.), *Das kaiserliche Deutschland*, pp. 119 ff.; L. Gall, 'Bismarck und Bonapartismus', *Historische Zeitschrift*, 223 (1976), 618-37; A. Mitchell, 'Bonapartism as a Model for Bismarckian Politics', *Journal of Modern History*, 49 (1977), 181-209 (with comments by O. Pflanze, C. Fohlen, and M. Stürmer); E. Fehrenbach, 'Bonapartismus und Konservatismus in Bismarcks Politik', *Bonapartismus* (Beihefte zur Francia, 6), 1977, pp. 39-76. See also O. Pflanze, 'Bismarcks Herrschaftstechnik als Problem der gegenwärtigen Historiographie', *Historische Zeitschrift*, 234 (1982), 562-99. For an orthodox Marxist account, see E. Engelberg, 'Zur Entstehung und historischen Stellung des preussisch-deutschen Bonapartismus', F. Klein and J. Streisand (eds.), *Beiträge zum neuen Geschichtsbild* (Berlin, 1956), pp. 236-51.

[7] On the other hand, to call Bismarck's rule a 'plebiscitary dictatorship' is going too far. The degree of popular mobilization involved in Bismarck's politics (e.g. in the colonial agitation of the early 1880s and the elections of 1884) has

search for exact parallels between the two regimes of Bismarck and Napoleon III (centring on the issues of *coup d'état*, plebiscitary dictatorship, foreign adventures, popular support of the peasantry, etc.), and if we can avoid certain reductionist temptations (like Wehler's belief in Bonapartism's relationship to 'a certain phase of industrial growth'), then the core of the concept (the enhancement of the state's autonomy under circumstances of extreme conflict amongst the dominant classes) also has a definite typological potential. It facilitates comparisons not only between Germany and France, but between authoritarian manifestations in other periods (e.g. 1930-3) and other parts of the world (e.g. Latin America, Spain, inter-war Poland, the Balkans).[8]

At the same time we should be wary of the concept's limitations. In the classical usages (e.g. Marx, Engels, Gramsci) the key stress is on the temporary or exceptional character of the bonapartist state as a response to a short-term crisis— an 'equilibrium of forces heading towards catastrophe', as Gramsci put it. Attempts can certainly be made to institutionalize the resulting executive autonomy, but over the longer term these invariably prove unsatisfactory. Surely, the striking thing about Imperial Germany in this respect is the relative strength and workability of its parliamentary system before 1914. Unlike say Spain or Italy or Greece in the same period, the Bismarckian system was refreshingly free of clientelism and *caciquismo*, of direct military intervention in the political process (as in *pronunciamiento*), and of *trasformismo*, oligarchy, and extreme forms of political brokerage.[9] By contrast with these European examples and with,

been consistently overestimated by Wehler and others. The real period of systematic popular agitation (mobilization/self-mobilization) begins only in the 1890s.

[8] Here the ideas of August Thalheimer become very interesting. See the useful discussion in M. Kitchen, *Fascism* (London, 1976), pp. 71-82.

[9] See, e.g., the excellent discussion in G. Th. Mavrogordatos, *Still-born Republic: Social Coalitions and Party Strategies in Greece, 1922-1936* (Berkeley, 1983), pp. 1-23. In particular, see Mavrogordatos's definition of clientelism, which stands in sharp contrast to the salient characteristics of the Imperial German party-political and parliamentary system: 'What does clientelism mean? Its immediate implications are primarily structural and organizational: it inhibits the formation, or subverts the expected operation of ostensibly modern institutions and groups. Political parties in particular, regardless of labels, programs, and other paraphernalia of modernity, merely consist of unstable coalitions of patrons

say, many of the independent states of Latin America in the nineteenth and most of the twentieth centuries, the new German nation-state contained a relatively well integrated social formation, with national economic institutions which functioned very successfully between unification and the First World War. Moreover, while regional differences clearly remained, on the whole particularist interests were handled either constitutionally (through the *Bundesrat*) or politically (through the integrative efforts of the various parties) without ever crystallizing into the full-blooded separatist pursuit of independent regionalist blocs. In these and other respects the Imperial state demonstrated an impressive functional vitality, even without an advanced republican constitution or a stronger system of parliamentary responsibility. This puts the *Kaiserreich* in an interesting intermediate category, between the purer parliamentary states of Britain, France, the USA, Scandinavia, and so on, and the far less developed states to the south and east of the European continent.

(g) One series of questions which remains, particularly if Bonapartism is to be principally confined to the period of unification, concerns the problem of periodization between the dissolution of the Bismarckian system at the end of the 1880s and the new situation created by the outbreak of the First World War. What are the periods of crisis and of stability within this broad span, for instance, and how are the boundaries of specific conjunctures to be defined? The basic division between the Great Depression and the succeeding period of prosperity in 1895-6 is one of the most popular periodizations, and this is clearly important, though the

---

at the head of their respective clienteles—coalitions put together solely for the conquest of office, which is essential (and sufficient) if protection and services to clients are to be provided. Voters in turn behave as clients, each supporting his own patron and switching parties with him. Moreover, they respond to private inducements rather than policies, issues, or group identification and interests. The political system is thus constantly flooded with an amorphous mass of particularistic or rather specifically *personal* demands, which it can meet only erratically, while collective or categorical demands are not made or at least not met. Politics are fundamentally issueless and nonideological. The performance of the state bureaucracy is characterized by corruption, inefficiency, and waste. Economic development and long-term policies in general cannot be effectively undertaken, etc.' Anything further from the reality of Imperial Germany would be hard to imagine. See Mavrogordatos, *Stillborn Republic*, p. 12.

dangers of reducing political movements to economic ones should also be clear enough. My own preference is for a four-fold periodization, based on the phases of unification (1860s to later 1880s), flux (1890s), relative parliamentary stabilization (summer 1897 to roughly 1911), and domestic crisis (1911–12 to 1914). But the explanation of these designations must await another occasion. Here it is important simply to raise the issue of periods and to emphasize just how ignorant we still remain about the detailed political history of the *Kaiserreich*. This is particularly true of the 1880s, for instance.[10] Beyond this, we desperately need some serious analytical discussion of the domestic political crisis on the eve of the First World War, its dimensions, and possible range of outcomes. Only then will the difficult question of the Imperial state's viability (whether expressed as 'parliamentarization' or in some other way) be properly adjudicated.[11]

(h) In conclusion, the general conceptual issue motivating this essay should be rejoined. Basically, I have tried to argue that the option of the German bourgeoisie's leading fractions for a politics of accommodation with the landowning class after 1871 was fully compatible with the pursuit of bourgeois interests in the sense I have tried to define. The bourgeoisie entered the agrarian alliance not from a lack of

---

[10] The general paucity of first-rate scholarship on the 1880s cannot be emphasized too strongly. The recent argument of Margaret Anderson and Kenneth Barkin is very compelling here, for they show conclusively that prevailing perceptions of the political climate in the 1880s depend too an extraordinary degree on a few speculative, undeveloped, and wholly unverified remarks by Eckart Kehr in a book review of 1929. See M. L. Anderson and K. Barkin, 'The Myth of the Puttkamer Purge and the Reality of the *Kulturkampf*: Some Reflections on the Historiography of Imperial Germany', *Journal of Modern History*, 54 (1982), 647–86. Aside from a few competent biographies and Stürmer's *Regierung und Reichstag in Bismarckstaat*, to which may now be added Lothar Gall's new biography of Bismarck, *Der weisse Revolutionär* (Frankfurt, 1980), it is hard to find a substantial recent literature on the domestic politics of these years. Margaret Anderson's own *Windthorst: A Political Biography* (Oxford, 1981) must count as the most important new contribution for many years. I have not yet seen O. Pflanze (ed.), *Innenpolitische Probleme des Bismarck-Reiches*.

[11] The best discussion of this question is in Schmidt, 'Parlamentarisierung oder "Präventive Konterrevolution"?'. The works of the Fischer school have been especially disappointing in this particular respect. See details in p. 119 n. 2 above.

'political self-confidence', but as the best means of securing certain political goals. The indifference to further 'parliamentarization' came less from any 'pre-industrial tradition' of authoritarianism, than from a rational calculation of political interest in a situation where greater parliamentary reform necessarily worked to the advantage of the left. Likewise, it made perfect sense for German capitalists to refuse the 'just' demands of the working class, once a given level of private economic power and monopoly organization bequeathed the ability to do so. In this sense it was not the absence of bourgeois revolution that forced a supine bourgeoisie into junior partnership with a 'pre-industrial power élite', but the particular form of Germany's bourgeois revolution (revolution from above under the aegis of the Prussian state through military unification) that combined with the accelerated character of Germany's capitalist transformation to impose a specific logic of class alliance. The latter entailed no renunciation of bourgeois political ambition *per se*. But it did mean that ambitions were articulated in ways considerably different from those in Britain, France, and elsewhere. To that extent we should speak not of German peculiarity, but of British, French, and German *particularities*.

(i) Finally, this also has implications for our understanding of fascism, which cannot be discussed in detail here. For once we become sceptical about the argument from 'pre-industrial traditions' when applied to the political culture of the *Kaiserreich*, the deep historical view of the origins of fascism is also cast into doubt. At the very least this means shifting our attention from the *longue durée* of Prussian history (the bureaucratic, militarist, and authoritarian traditions which embodied the special position of the Junkers as a feudal or 'pre-industrial' ruling class) towards the internal dynamics of the Imperial period itself (i.e. the specific contradictions of a society experiencing accelerated capitalist transformation). Personally, I would take this further and stress the more immediate circumstances under which the Nazis rose to power—namely, the succeeding conjunctures of the First World War, the post-war crisis of 1917-23, and the world economic crisis after 1929.[12] At all events, it is surely

[12] See the discussion in Eley, 'What Produces Fascism'.

time to stop blaming the Junkers for all the ills of German history—not (obviously) to exculpate them morally or to demonize the capitalist bourgeoisie in their stead, but to get a better grasp on the full complexities of the German social formation.

In general, this is an argument against notions of German exceptionalism. It suggests that we should think again about the assumed absence of bourgeois revolution in nineteenth-century Germany and accept that the bourgeoisie may come to social predominance by other than liberal routes. Finally, it is meant to query the simple continuity thesis which locates Germany's vulnerability to fascism in a 'pre-industrial' blockage of 'modernization'. On the contrary, it might now be far more useful to examine the particular forms of German capitalist development and the new structures of politics they helped broadly to determine. In other words, Germany's failure to develop a native liberalism of comparable vitality to that of Britain may have lain more with the conditions of capitalist reproduction themselves than with the continuing domination of a 'pre-industrial power élite'. At least this is worth discussing.

The Discreet Charm of the Bourgeoisie:
Reappraising German History in the Nineteenth Century

David Blackbourn

I
German Peculiarities

1. *The Arguments*

'Wie es eigentlich gewesen'—as it really happened—was Ranke's
celebrated dictum on the way history should be written.
'Wie es eigentlich *nicht* gewesen' would better describe the
way many have been tempted to write the history of Germany
in the nineteenth and twentieth centuries. For it is striking
how often what did not happen has been regarded as more
important than what did. Historians who otherwise differ
considerably in approach seem agreed that modern Germany
failed to take the course it should have taken. Two widely
read post-war works, one English the other German, may be
taken as illustrations. A. J. P. Taylor, surveying 'The Course
of German History', suggests at one point that in 1848
German history reached its turning-point and 'failed to turn'.
Nor is this the only turning that he believes was missed.
Helmuth Plessner, in a very different but equally influential
book on *Die verspätete Nation* (The Belated Nation), also
has much to say about the peculiar incompleteness of modern
German history.[1] This preoccupation with German history's
sins of omission has continued to exercise commentators of
various persuasions. It is strikingly captured in a phrase of
Leo Kofler's: 'Just as England is the eternally "finished"
country in Europe, so Germany is the one that is eternally
stuck half-way.'[2]

Common to these and similar accounts is their attribution
of sins of omission to the German bourgeoisie in particular.
Taylor takes it to task for its political immaturity and civic
quietism. Plessner subtitled his book 'On the susceptibility
to political seduction of the bourgeois mind'. For Kofler,

[1] A. J. P. Taylor, *The Course of German History* (London, 1945); H. Plessner,
Die verspätete Nation (Stuttgart, 1959).
[2] L. Kofler, *Zur Geschichte der bürgerlichen Gesellschaft* (Neuwied and
Berlin, 1966), p. 537.

'the historical chain of failures on the part of the bourgeoisie in Germany is the cause of "Prussianism" pure and simple.'[3] This pin-pointing of bourgeois failure can be widely found in monographs as well as general accounts. Two recent examples of this approach are books published in the 1970s on the German peace movement and the German feminist movement.[4] Both succeed as studies by showing that the movement in question failed. One author, indeed, uses as a motto the well-known comment by Sherlock Holmes about the significance of the dog that failed to bark. The failure in each case, moreover, is attributed to the absence in nineteenth-century Germany—by contrast with England, for example— of the sort of bourgeois political culture in which reformist movements like pacifism and feminism could take root. Their failure was connected, that is, with the absence in Germany of a proper bourgeois revolution. Many other examples of this approach could be cited, especially in the German literature, and I shall be considering some of them in more detail below. The general point is that the German bourgeoisie has had a bad press. True bourgeoisies are supposed to rise, casting social relations and political institutions in their own image. We expect them to be the breakers of historical moulds. The German bourgeoisie, however, seems to have been an exception: its weaknesses, not its strengths, its failures rather than its successes, occupy the centre of the historical stage. These observations provide the point of departure of the present essay. The intention in what follows is not to engage in retrospective apologetics on behalf of the German bourgeoisie. It is to suggest that there are more fruitful ways of approaching modern German history, and the role of the bourgeoisie in particular, than to address it with questions to which the answer is always 'No'.

Historians have naturally explored these sins of omission in a variety of different ways, but two kinds of approach are worth singling out. The failures we have been considering

---

[3] Ibid., p. 539.

[4] R. Chickering, *Imperial Germany and a World without War* (Princeton, 1975); R. J. Evans, *The Feminist Movement in Germany 1894–1933* (London, 1976).

have been located, first, at the level of values, in a distinctively German pattern of thought. This is the approach that tries to anatomize the 'German Mind'.[5] At least since the Romantic period, so it has been argued, figures like Fichte, Wagner, Nietzsche, and Spengler, along with countless epigoni, have both addressed and reflected a certain cast of mind, especially among the educated German bourgeoisie (*Bildungsbürgertum*). This pattern of thinking embodied a belief that dominant German values were superior to those of the west, less sullied by arid rationalism. A peculiarly intense relationship to nature, and a tendency to prefer the 'organic' to the 'mechanical' society, supposedly went together with this. Hostility towards 'modernity' and a strong leaning towards 'cultural despair' have usually been fitted into the same framework. As a corollary, it has often been argued that this 'vulgarised idealism',[6] as one historian calls it, formed a substitute for a healthy and proper engagement in social and political affairs. A retreat into the private world of sensibility and inwardness therefore helps to explain the fateful figure of the 'unpolitical German', symbolized by Thomas Mann's defence of these peculiarly German virtues during the First World War.[7] Thus, in turn, a star-struck and supine response to authority has been diagnosed. This amounts to an indictment of the German bourgeoisie, especially its university-educated part, for its divergence from western standards of rationality and pragmatism. Irrationalism, inwardness, and cultural pessimism appear as burdens which prevented the German bourgeoisie from fighting for its own proper objectives.

Arguments of this kind have sometimes been incorporated into a second approach, which concerns itself with the fraught relationship between economic, social, and political developments in Germany. Here the centre of attention is the interplay between class, status, and power—the 'great triad' as one

---

[5] Plessner, *Die verspätete Nation*; H. Kohn, *The Mind of Germany* (London, 1961), translated in 1962 into German with the revealing title 'Wege und Irrwege: Vom Geist des deutschen Bürgertums'; F. Stern, *The Politics of Cultural Despair* (Berkeley, 1961); G. L. Mosse, *The Crisis of German Ideology* (London, 1966).

[6] The phrase comes from Fritz Stern.

[7] Mann's *Betrachtungen eines Unpolitischen* (1918) has recently been translated as *Reflections of a Nonpolitical Man* (New York, 1983).

prominent historian has called them.[8] The relationship
between these three in the German case has been viewed as
out of joint. Elsewhere economic, social, and political developments moved in tandem; in Germany they did not.
Hence Germany's 'modernization' at the social and political
levels was impeded and only partial. Thus it has been maintained that Germany did not pass through the stages which
countries further west passed through: it simply did not have
a bourgeois revolution of the normal kind. Bourgeois economic objectives, for example, were not achieved by the
bourgeoisie's own efforts, but provided by the state, 'from
above'. Industrial and commercial capital therefore never
won a struggle against the landed aristocracy, represented
by the Junkers. Instead they compromised. The period of
the Great Depression (1873-96) is usually cited as crucial
in this respect. The 'marriage of iron and rye', in which both
heavy industry and landed estates were aided by the re-
introduction of tariff protection, is seen as an economic
distortion with serious political consequences. Industry
obtained what it wanted in material terms, so it is argued,
but only at the cost of a continuing defensive partnership
with the unreconstructed landed élite.[9]

The real price of achieving economic success in this way
was paid at the social and political levels. For 'faulted'
economic development (or misdevelopment) was accompanied by bourgeois social compromise. The bourgeoisie, so
the argument runs, had already been weakened by the failure
of 1848 and the achievement of unification by Bismarckian
blood and iron. Now, by putting material interest above
principle, it signalled its acquiescence in the role which the
Junkers were to play in the new Reich. In subsequent years
the bourgeoisie failed to assert itself as a class: instead it

[8] H. Rosenberg, *Machteliten und Wirtschaftskonjunkturen* (Göttingen,
1978), p. 14.
[9] Standard German accounts of this include the various works of Hans
Rosenberg: *Grosse Depression und Bismarckzeit* (Berlin, 1967), *Probleme der
deutschen Sozialgeschichte* (Frankfurt/M., 1969), *Machteliten*; H. Böhme, *Deutschlands Weg zur Grossmacht* (Cologne, 1966); D. Stegmann, *Die Erben Bismarcks*
(Cologne, 1970). In English, see M. Kitchen, *The Political Economy of Germany
1815-1914* (London, 1978) and H. Böhme, *An Introduction to the Social and
Economic History of Germany* (London, 1978).

aped the values of the old élite whose survival it had helped to ensure. It bought up landed estates, angled after titles, and emulated the reactionary values of the Prussian officer corps. It underwent, in short, a process of self-humbling which has been dubbed the feudalization of the bourgeoisie. This, so it is maintained, also proved disastrous in a political sense. For the traditional élite continued to dominate and set the tone of court, army, and bureaucracy, and through them political decision-making. Thus 'pre-industrial' forces were enabled to survive in Germany beyond their natural span. Through a combination of repression and the threat of it, co-optation and indoctrination, they kept their hands on the crucial levers of power through to 1918 and beyond. The problems of the Weimar Republic followed from a democratic and parliamentary superstructure being erected on this unreformed institutional base. Only the Third Reich and total defeat finally dislodged this stubborn élite from its anachronistic perch. Hence 1945 should be regarded as a genuine 'year zero' (*Stunde Null*). Only after 1945 did the German bourgeoisie (at least in the west) finally come into its own, and Germany itself make the vital breakthrough to modernity.[10]

Historians who have argued along these lines, like those principally concerned with intellectual peculiarities, have therefore seen 1945 as a turning-point when German history really did turn. And in the Federal Republic at least, the crucial point is that it turned towards the west: after 1949 the Federal Republic rejoined a western tradition of liberalism, pluralism, and modernity which had previously been rejected. Conversely, German history's sins of omission supposedly stretched back into the last century, the product of a critical divergence from western, and especially British, norms of development. It is the absence of a successfully class-conscious and liberal bourgeoisie, by contrast above all with Britain, that provides the linchpin of this argument. Implicit or explicit contrasts of this kind between Germany and Britain can be found in the work of many historians and

---

[10] See, generally, the works cited in the previous footnote. E. J. Feuchtwanger, *Prussia: Myth and Reality* (London, 1970), also makes some of these arguments available in English.

political scientists writing in the last decades. They are present, within a much more ambitious framework, in Barrington Moore's pioneering book on *The Social Origins of Dictatorship and Democracy*. And they can be found in the work of a man who combines elements of both the approaches outlined above: Ralf Dahrendorf. His important book on *Society and Democracy in Germany*[11] acquired its cutting edge by addressing the previous hundred years with the question 'Why wasn't Germany England?'

In the essay below I want to look at the idea of a German special road (*Sonderweg*) in the light of this central proposition that the German bourgeoisie somehow failed to conduct itself in a properly bourgeois manner. The following chapter offers some general bearings, discussing the yardstick against which Germany has been measured and found wanting. The intention here is to question what might be called 'normal' bourgeois behaviour, and to address the vexed question of bourgeois revolution. I try to suggest how we might redefine this so that the heroic idea of political struggle which attaches to the term is relegated in importance, yet without the crucial connections between the economic, the social, and the political being lost sight of. Chapter II argues for the substantial achievements of a silent bourgeois revolution in nineteenth-century Germany, in the fields of property relations, economic organization, the law, and free public association. These amounted to a programme, half conscious and half unconscious, which created not only a new *homo oeconomicus*, but also a new kind of public man. Chapter III then explores the shadow side of this achievement, its contradictions and the ways in which the reality of the new society fell short of its public rhetoric. It is in this context that I locate and try to reconsider some common arguments noted above concerning cultural despair, civic quietism, and the feudalization of the bourgeoisie. After attempting to characterize these double-edged and ambiguous features of bourgeois society as it developed in Germany, I move in Chapter IV to the problem of the form assumed by the state. Some general observations about the

---

[11] R. Dahrendorf, *Society and Democracy in Germany* (London, 1968).

lack of fit between the economic, social, and political begin the section. The argument continues with a consideration of the German state as Janus-faced: an unreconstructed shell in many crucial respects, yet capable in others of fulfilling the ambitions vested in it by a bourgeoisie for whom a powerful state 'above' society had many attractions. The discussion here leads on to an examination in Chapter V of politics in the broadest sense. For if the state was seen by some as a welcome arbiter of social antagonisms, so it was also perceived by others as a means of redressing grievances which found no redress elsewhere. Conflicts generated in Germany's exceptionally dynamic society could be fought out in the political arena, via universal male suffrage, with more hope of success than in the market-place or the law-court. I hope to show, in particular, how the advent of a vigorous mass politics eclipsed the modest notable politics established around the 1860s; and I consider the various effects this had. It is here, in the context of bourgeois divisions and the rise of a new popular politics, that I discuss the particular problems of German liberalism. This also provides the background finally for an examination of the options for political and constitutional reform in the years before 1914.

An essay of this length can clearly make no claim to be comprehensive. I have been selective, although I hope not unfairly so. The aim throughout has been to try, where it seemed appropriate, to de-mystify the idea of a German *Sonderweg*: to question assumptions about German peculiarity, while at the same time indicating what was actually distinctive about the German nineteenth-century experience. Even though it is not possible to calibrate degrees of peculiarity, I hope that the arguments which follow will at least have the effect of chipping away at certain over-ready assumptions. Above all, perhaps, I hope that we may come to hear a little less about the German problem as the outcome of a thwarted breakthrough to modernity. For arguments of that kind can obscure important truths about western modernity as much as they do about German peculiarity.

2. *The Role of the Bourgeoisie: A General Perspective*

If the German bourgeoisie appears in so many accounts as resolutely unheroic, it is worth asking the question first how unusual this really is. Are we not, perhaps, pitching our expectations rather high? If that is indeed the case in general, then possibly we should revise our views on the historical role played by the German bourgeoisie in particular. An obvious starting-point here is to consider the part so often attributed to an assertive bourgeoisie in the emergence of capitalism. And it is proper to begin with two German commentators—Marx and Weber—whose influence on historical writing about Germany has been very great, and whose names will recur fairly often in this essay. In an important sense the bourgeoisie plays a heroic role in Marx's writings. In *The Communist Manifesto*, this class was

the first to show what man's activity can bring about. It has accomplished wonders far surpassing Egyptian pyramids, Roman viaducts, and Gothic cathedrals; it has constructed expeditions that put in the shade all former Exoduses of nations and crusades. . . It has created enormous cities, has greatly increased the urban population as compared with the rural, and has thus rescued a considerable part of the population from the idiocy of rural life.[12]

This paean to bourgeois energy finds a certain counterpart in Weber. In his celebrated work on *The Protestant Ethic and the Spirit of Capitalism*, but not only there, Weber identified the bourgeoisie as the historical agent of a new and revolutionary principle of economic organization. For him, the entrepreneurial spirit continued to offer a hope of dynamism in both economy and society, to counteract the adverse effects of an increasingly rationalised and bureaucratized world. Not without justice has Weber been labelled a 'bourgeois Marx'.[13]

For neither Marx nor Weber was this, of course, anything

---

[12] K. Marx and F. Engels, *Selected Works* (London, 1968), pp. 38-9.

[13] The phrase comes from Albert Salomon, cited W. J. Mommsen, *Max Weber und die deutsche Politik 1890-1920* (Tübingen, 1959), p. 112. For English accounts, see Mommsen, *The Age of Bureaucracy* (Oxford, 1974), A. Giddens, *Politics and Sociology in the Thought of Max Weber* (London, 1972), and most recently, G. Marshall, *In Search of the Spirit of Capitalism* (London, 1982).

like the whole story. I shall be dealing later with the various ways in which each addressed the shadow side of capitalism and the place of the bourgeoisie in sustaining it. What is important here is that our view of the bourgeoisie's dynamic role has often remained stuck at this rather simple level. Many historians have taken Marx as a warrant to play the game of Hunt the Bourgeoisie, and its variant, Hunt the Nascent Bourgeoisie. This game has been played on a board which covers many centuries. It has rightly attracted critics. But there is also a line of vulgarization running down from Weber, which might be called Spot the Entrepreneurial Initiative. This approach has found creative expression in the hands of a Schumpeter; it has also spawned the writings of those who, like Walt Rostow, are over-impressed by the bourgeois contribution to industrial take-off and 'modernity'. Historians may affect to despise either or both of these approaches to the past; the fact remains that such ideas have a stubborn hold on our minds, even when we believe that we have consciously rejected them. The relevance of this for our purposes should be clear. The standard against which the conduct of the German bourgeoisie has been judged and found wanting is a very exacting one. It is, arguably, rather too exacting. And it is also a standard based on the implicit assumption that what occurred in England was the norm.

We are often told that the German bourgeoisie compromised its birthright in the course of economic modernization from above: that its victories were not the result of its own exertions, but delivered on a plate. There is considerable truth in this, as we shall see; but how do we evaluate it? It might well be argued that, in European terms, this seemingly modest measure of initiative constitutes the norm rather than the exception. Seldom do we encounter commercial and industrial classes that rolled up their sleeves and carved out a capitalist world for themselves in quite the manner attributed to their English exemplars. *Laissez-faire* may have been made in England and Adam Smith in Scotland; but cameralism and *dirigisme* were by no means made in Germany, or felt in Germany alone. The British road to a developed industrial capitalism, precisely because it was the first, has not been followed. There has normally been some kind of short cut, whether in the form of the role played by the state, or the banks, or foreign capital, or all of these, which telescoped the classic British process of capitalist transformation. That is by no means an original point,[14] but it ought to serve as a reminder that the independent and assertive bourgeoisie lurking behind so many assumptions, which consciously made itself in the course of building capitalism, has been a historically elusive class. Indeed, many would question how far it existed even in Britain. As research continues to accumulate on the importance in Britain of landed wealth and the agrarian origins of capitalism, so the notion of an 'embourgeoisement avant la bourgeoisie' becomes more plausible.[15] And so, too, some of the more extravagant ideas about the self-raising properties of the bourgeoisie seem even less convincing. This is very much in line with the approach of those who have argued more generally against the idea of an assertive bourgeoisie as the *deus ex machina* of the painful 'transition from feudalism to capitalism'.[16] It is also consistent with the most recent arguments of German historians about proto-industrialization and about the commercialization of agriculture, with their emphasis on the growth of petty-commodity production in the one case and on Prussian agrarian capitalism in the other.[17] Both approaches tend, once again, to scale down our expectations about the role assumed by a dynamic bourgeoisie in the making of capitalism. The bourgeoisie, it would seem, has not generally played the heroic part so often ascribed to it—and the absence of which in the German case is held against it. It was as much the product of capitalism

---

[14] The pioneering comparative work here is A. Gerschenkron, *Economic Backwardness in Historical Perspective* (Cambridge, Mass., 1962). A similarly stimulating comparative perspective informs D. Landes, *The Unbound Prometheus* (Cambridge, 1969).

[15] R. S. Neale, ' "The Bourgeoisie, Historically, has played a Most Revolutionary Part. . ." ', in E. Kamenka and R. S. Neale (eds.), *Feudalism, Capitalism and Beyond* (London, 1975), p. 94. See also the work of British historians such as G. E. Mingay and J. H. Plumb.

[16] Neale, loc. cit., also Paul Sweezy *et al.*, *The Transition from Feudalism to Capitalism* (London, 1976).

[17] See, respectively, P. Kriedte, H. Medick, and J. Schlumbohm, *Industrialisierung vor der Industrialisierung* (Göttingen, 1977); and H. Schissler, *Preussische Agrargesellschaft im Wandel* (Göttingen, 1978).

as its instigator. One might almost say, varying a familiar metaphor, that the bourgeoisie was unable (reasonably enough) to act as midwife at its own birth.

A further point follows from this. If we question the bourgeois role as an active agent in the making of capitalism, should we not question the heroic idea of the bourgeoisie in the making of bourgeois society more broadly? Was the seeming absence of a class-conscious bourgeoisie in Germany really all that peculiar? Once again, German writers seem to be operating with an implicit standard of judgement based on England and in this case France as well. It is the English and French bourgeoisies that stand for social success historically. This is another of those cases where the grass appears to be greener on the other side of the Rhine and the Channel. For specialists in British and French history have fairly effectively disposed of the notion of anything resembling bourgeois social transformation in either country, at least of the kind that still seems to govern the categories in which German if-only history is constructed. This emphasis is common to the revisionist writing on England in the seventeenth century and France during the revolutionary period. In neither case is there much left of the idea that we can identify, either sociologically or ideologically, a bourgeois class pursuing clear class interests of its own.[18] A similar scepticism about the power, unity, and self-consciousness of the bourgeoisie has been voiced in much of the influential recent writing on the nineteenth century. Writing on nineteenth-century France, Theodore Zeldin betrays a marked resistance to the notion that this can be labelled 'the age of the bourgeoisie'. Rather, the bourgeoisie was above all 'deeply fragmented';[19] indeed in his account it seems to dissolve entirely into a kaleidoscope of occupations, ambitions,

---

[18] On England, J. H. Hexter, 'The Myth of the Middle Class in Tudor England', *Reappraisals in History* (London, 1961); L. Stone, *The Causes of the English Revolution* (London, 1972); J. Morrill, *The Revolt of the Provinces* (London, 1980). On France: A. Cobban, *The Social Interpretation of the French Revolution* (Cambridge, 1964); F. Furet and D. Richet, *La Révolution française*, 2 vols. (Paris, 1965-6); F. Furet, *Interpreting the French Revolution* (Cambridge, 1981).

[19] T. Zeldin, *France 1848-1945*, vol. 1: *Ambition, Love and Politics* (Oxford, 1973), pp. 11, 13.

and manners. The bourgeois as social hero has been replaced by the bourgeois as expectorating doctor or cautious local notary. Much the same case has been put by British historians. We are repeatedly reminded about the wealth, power, influence, and sheer capacity for survival through adaptation of the landowing aristocracy. The bourgeoisie, for its part, has been viewed as fragmented, socially modest, and largely immersed in local affairs. Once again therefore, as in the work of John Vincent, we find the heroic bourgeois cut down to size, coupled with an austere rejection of the idea that Victorian England witnessed 'an insurrection of "bourgeois" ideas against the old ways of thought'.[20] One recent writer does no more than summarize an emerging consensus when he suggests that, at least before 1850, the English bourgeoisie constituted neither a class in itself nor a class for itself.[21]

In discussing German aberrations, therefore, historians seem to be working with a model of the 'normal' pattern of social development in England and France which is not accepted by historians of those countries. Perhaps this explains the fact that argument over Germany's special road has been paralleled by debate among historians of England and France over their own historical peculiarities. It is habitually argued that Germany has paid the social price of her economic advantages as a late-comer, while Britain has paid an economic penalty for her social advantages as a pioneer. That is the thrust of Ralf Dahrendorf and many others. Yet there has been a curious mirror-image of that position in the debate that has taken place between Perry Anderson, Tom Nairn, and E. P. Thompson on the 'peculiarities of the English'.[22] That argument has centred on the social and political, not simply economic, price Britain has paid and continues to pay as a result of her early and

[20] J. Vincent, *The Formation of the Liberal Party 1857–1868* (London, 1968), p. xxvii.

[21] Neale, ' "The Bourgeoisie, Historically" ', p. 90.

[22] See P. Anderson, 'Origins of the Present Critis', *New Left Review*, 23; T. Nairn, 'The British Political Elite', ibid.; E. P. Thompson, 'The Peculiarities of the English', in R. Miliband and J. Saville (eds.), *The Socialist Register* (1965), now reprinted in Thompson's *The Poverty of Theory* (London, 1978), pp. 35–91.

exceptional transition to capitalism. And within that framework, England's historically 'supine bourgeoisie'[23] has been
singled out for attention. There is, of course, an obvious trap
awaiting the British historian who makes such a point: that
of special pleading in reverse. Hans-Magnus Enzensberger has
given us a cautionary account of that 'macabre competition'
in which 'the shades of the former powers try to settle the
question of who has sunk furthest and who has the greatest
afflictions'.[24] This kind of self-abasement is really a form of
pride. It is therefore as well to note that there has also been
spirited argument among historians of France about the
extent to which the French bourgeois supposedly lacked the
proper appetites and instincts.[25] More generally, Arno J.
Mayer has recently disparaged European bourgeoisies as a
whole for their lack of social muscle, arguing that the 'Old
Regime' persisted everywhere until 1914.[26] I shall return
later to consider the problems posed by arguments of this
kind. What should be stressed for the moment is the need
for reticence in considering German peculiarity. We should
not operate with unrealistic assumptions about the role
played by a buoyant bourgeoisie in the forging of bourgeois
society.

There are important implications here for the sphere of
state power and politics. It is there, above all, that the
'failure of Western-style liberal democracy to take root in
Germany'[27] has been causally connected with a supine

[23] Anderson, 'Origins', p. 43. Nairn also compares England unfavourably
with 'other countries with an old and unified bourgeois culture': 'British Political
Elite', p. 22.
[24] H. M. Enzensberger, *Deutschland, Deutschland unter anderm: Äusserungen
zur Politik* (Frankfurt/M., 1968), p. 10.
[25] See Landes, 'French Entrepreneurship and Industrial Growth in the Nineteenth Century', *Journal of Economic History* (1949), pp. 45-61; F. Sawyer, 'The
Entrepreneur and the Social Order: France and the United States', in W. Miller
(ed.), *Men in Business* (Cambridge, Mass., 1952), pp. 7-22. C. Kindleberger,
Economic Growth in France and Britain 1851-1950 (London, 1964) is a useful
guide to the arguments. More generally, see Zeldin, *Ambition, Love and Politics*.
[26] Arno J. Mayer, *The Persistence of the Old Regime* (London, 1981), esp.
ch. 2: 'The Ruling Class: The Bourgeoisie Defers'.
[27] J. M. Diefendorf, *Businessmen and Politics in the Rhineland* (Princeton,
1980), p. 6. This excellent study provides a good example of Ralf Dahrendorf's
deep influence. Cf. Dahrendorf's desire 'to find out what it is in German society
that may account for Germany's persistent failure to give a home to democracy
in the liberal sense.'

bourgeoisie. Once again we find Marx and Weber frequently cited as witnesses. In the latter case, historians have drawn particularly on the celebrated Freiburg inaugural address, when Weber vigorously attacked the 'political immaturity' of his fellow-bourgeois.[28] Weber's arguments continue to have widespread currency ninety years later. But the earlier criticism of Marx and Engels has also been drawn on to similar effect, by marxists and non-marxists alike. Hans-Ulrich Wehler, for example, has offered his own variant on Marx's forthright critique of the neo-absolutist Bismarckian Reich with its minimal formal bourgeois influence.[29] Michael Stürmer, in an essay on 1848, reminds us of Engels's strictures on the German bourgeoisie; Stürmer goes on to underline what he calls the absent 'revolutionary thrust' of the bourgeoisie as a class in Germany.[30] Leo Kofler, out of Marx by Georg Lukács, has posed the question in sharper language still. Contrasting Germany unfavourably with England and France, he suggests that 'only an uncompromising bourgeois revolution could have forced Germany once and for all on to the road of social and political development.'[31] But this, argues Kofler, was what did not occur.

In view of this impressive testimony from Marx and Engels for the idea of German peculiarity it is worth looking briefly at the broader context of their views. It is certainly true that both were trenchant critics of the politically 'cowardly' German bourgeoisie. Writing in the aftermath of 1848, Engels made this a major theme both of *Revolution and Counter-Revolution in Germany* and of *The Peasant War in Germany*, which dealt with the peasant revolt of 1525. He was to repeat the argument in later years, especially in various descriptions of Imperial Germany as a 'mish-mash of half-feudalism and Bonapartism'.[32] The Bonapartist theme, which

[28] W. G. Runciman (ed.), *Max Weber: Selections in Translation* (London, 1978), pp. 263–8.

[29] H.-U. Wehler, *Das deutsche Kaiserreich 1871–1918* (Göttingen, 1973), pp. 64–7.

[30] M. Stürmer, '1848 in der deutschen Geschichte', in H.-U. Wehler (ed.), *Sozialgeschichte Heute. Festschrift für Hans Rosenberg* (Göttingen, 1974), p. 236.

[31] Kofler, *Zur Geschichte*, pp. 555–6.

[32] K. Marx and F. Engels, *Werke*, 41 vols. (Berlin, 1957–68), 36, p. 54, Engels to Bernstein, 27 Aug. 1883. This is quoted in H. A. Winkler, 'Zum Verhältnis von

runs back to an equally scathing Marx (and was echoed by Weber), has proved particularly attractive to German historians. Bourgeois failure has thus been read off from the establishment in 1871 of an authoritarian, sham-constitutional regime, bolstered by military and bureaucratic support and covered with a plebiscitary fig-leaf.[33] We should nevertheless exercise caution in using these embittered contemporary writings to support arguments about German exceptionalism. Bonapartism may well have useful application to the German case, as also to twentieth-century fascism;[34] but Marx did not have Germany in mind when he originally outlined his thoughts on the subject. Engels, in fact, suggested that Bonapartism had become the natural state-form of the French bourgeoisie as well after 1848; indeed he argued that it was the form of state most agreeable to bourgeoisies in general, where there was no governing oligarchy—'as here in England'.[35] Again, Marx in characteristically caustic vein, attacked the English bourgeoisie in the mid-1850s for its craven political nature. It was, he suggested, tyrannical to those below, but servile to those above.[36] Richard Cobden, as we shall see, took a similar view. All this sounds very familiar to the German historian. What is clear is that Marx and Engels held generally malevolent views on the political capacity of European bourgeoisies in general, something which emerges again and again in their writing.

bürgerlicher und proletarischer Revolution bei Marx und Engels', in Wehler (ed.), *Sozialgeschichte Heute,* pp. 326-53.

[33] See W. Sauer, 'Das Problem des deutschen Nationalstaats', in H.-U. Wehler (ed.), *Moderne deutsche Sozialgeschichte* (Cologne and Berlin, 1966), pp. 407-36; M. Stürmer, *Regierung und Reichstag im Bismarckstaat 1871-1880. Cäsarismus oder Parlamentarismus* (Düsseldorf, 1974). Hans-Ulrich Wehler's account of Bismarck's politics has also drawn heavily on the Bonapartist concept. Critical voices include L. Gall, 'Bismarck und Bonapartismus', *Historische Zeitschrift,* 223 (1976), pp. 618-37, and A. Mitchell, 'Bonapartism as a Model of Bismarckian Politics', *Journal of Modern History,* 49 (1977), 181-209. This issue of the *JMH* also includes comments by O. Pflanze, C. Fohlen, and M. Stürmer. See, most recently, O. Pflanze, 'Bismarcks Herrschaftstechnik als Problem der gegenwärtigen Historiographie', *Historische Zeitschrift,* 234 (1982), 562-99.

[34] For an introduction, see J. Dülffer, 'Bonapartism, Fascism and National Socialism', *Journal of Contemporary History,* 11 (1976), 109-28.

[35] Marx-Engels, *Werke,* 31, p. 208: Engels to Marx, 13 Apr. 1866.

[36] From an article in the *New-York Daily Tribune,* 1 Aug. 1854, on 'The English Middle Class': Marx-Engels, *Articles on Britain* (Moscow, 1971), p. 218.

In this they were surely right. If one looks at nineteenth-century Europe it is difficult to identify an unambiguous instance where the bourgeoisie ruled as a class, without the help of an old élite or oligarchy, without a strong man or allies from some other class or classes. It is even more difficult to find bourgeois revolutions of the supposedly classic type, in any period. Historians who have worked in the last decade or so on seventeenth-century England and late eighteenth-century France are largely agreed in dismissing the idea of bourgeois revolution as a category that signifies the transfer of political power to the bourgeoisie as a class. One author with more general ambitions, reviewing the experiences of England, France, and Germany, contends that 'no paradigm case of the bourgeois revolution can be found'. He adds, significantly, that 'one very striking point common to every case should be noted: namely the bourgeoisie's lack of political capacity . . . successfully to lead its own revolution in open action.'[37] A recent discussion of nineteenth-century Italy arrived at similar conclusions.[38]

It is possible that we should actually be better off without the label bourgeois revolution at all. Certainly East German historians, more concerned to preserve the baggage than the label, have been fecund in producing alternatives: 'cycle of bourgeois revolutions', 'bourgeois transformation', 'bourgeois upheaval', 'bourgeois revolution in the broad sense'.[39] Their own recent arguments on this question have been thoughtful. And their unease with the term bourgeois revolution underlines the problem of a label that seems to imply an overt transfer of political power. Of course, their colleagues in the Federal Republic do not really believe in bourgeois revolution in this sense either—certainly not explicitly. But they do often appear to believe in the idea of a failed bourgeois revolution; and their criteria of success and failure are implicitly those that have been discredited elsewhere. Certainly

[37] N. Poulantzas, *Political Power and Social Classes* (London, 1975), p. 183.
[38] P. Ginsborg, 'Gramsci and the Era of Passive Revolution in Italy', in J. A. Davis (ed.), *Gramsci and Italy's Passive Revolution* (London, 1979), pp. 31-66.
[39] See esp. W. Schmidt, 'Zu einigen Problemen der bürgerlichen Umwälzung in der deutschen Geschichte', in H. Bleiber (ed.), *Bourgeoisie und bürgerliche Umwälzung in Deutschland 1789-1871* (Berlin, 1977), pp. 1-33.

if we do retain this term, it makes more sense (and not just in the German case) to apply it rather differently. We should direct our attention to long-term processes rather than short-term events, to quiet changes in economy and society rather than dramatic public episodes, to the effects of actions rather than the intentions of actors. Before the present century at least, the bourgeoisie characteristically became the dominant class in European countries, although seldom the ruling class and never the sole ruling class, through means other than the heroic, purposive conquest of power. Its real strength and power were anchored in the capitalist mode of production and articulated through dominance in civil society. This, rather than one specific state-form, is what deserves the label bourgeois revolution, or whatever equivalent label comes to replace it.

This should not be construed as an attempt to remove either bourgeois self-consciousness in general or political objectives in particular from the record. Clearly both existed and were important; and both have a significant place in the discussion below. But there are grounds for arguing that the more openly bourgeois interests were articulated, the more problematic their realization became. The great strength of bourgeois revolution, in many respects, was its very lack of 'open action'. It is therefore appropriate to turn next to what I have called the silent bourgeois revolution in nineteenth-century Germany.

II
Economy and Society:
A Silent Bourgeois Revolution

1. *Capitalism and the Brave New World*

In considering the form of bourgeois revolution that took place in nineteenth-century Germany we shall have to look at changes at many levels: in the law, in the advance of mechanical civilization, in patterns of sociability and the formation of a 'public'. But the bedrock of these changes was the emergence and consolidation of the capitalist economic system, based on the sanctity and disposability of private property and on production to meet individual needs through a system of exchange dominated by the market.

In Germany, as elsewhere, the establishment of capitalism owed much to the active role played by the state. There is a long tradition of German historical writing which rightly stresses the importance of *dirigisme*, and more recent studies have continued to underline the centrality of the state's role, both directly and as a catalyst.[1] As Wolfram Fischer, Reinhart Koselleck, and others have shown, such was the commitment of some German states to economic and institutional reform in the pre-1848 period that it eclipsed the role played by the bourgeoisie.[2] An economically progressive bureaucracy served almost as a kind of surrogate bourgeoisie, levelling the ground on which the capitalist order would stand, as well as undertaking some of the preliminary construction work on its own account. Secularization removed

---

[1] Two classic works in this tradition are G. Stolper, *German Economy, 1870–1940* (London, 1940) and F. Facius, *Wirtschaft und Staat. Die Entwicklung der staatlichen Wirtschaftsverwaltung in Deutschland vom 17. Jahrhundert bis 1945* (Boppard, 1959).

[2] R. Koselleck, *Preussen zwischen Reform und Revolution* (Stuttgart, 1967); W. Fischer, *Der Staat und die Anfänge der Industrialisierung in Baden 1800–1850* (Berlin, 1962), and his later writings, many of them now collected in *Wirtschaft und Gesellschaft im Zeitalter der Industrialisierung* (Göttingen, 1972).

property from the 'dead hand' of the Church; the peasantry was emancipated and a free market in land confirmed; guild restrictions were pruned away; and internal tariff barriers to freedom of trade were removed, most notably by the *Zollverein*. More positively, the individual states undertook wide-ranging programmes of technical education in the first half of the nineteenth century, establishing model workshops, rewarding new industrial products with prizes, and encouraging new standards of taste and achievement through schools and evening classes for craftsmen. As early as 1826 it was reported from Passau in Bavaria that small businessmen were prepared to travel for as long as four to five hours in order to attend classes. By the middle of the century even the small Grand Duchy of Hesse had thirty such schools for craftsmen. The virtues of the new economic order were also spread by exhibitions of industrial production, like those mounted in Lüneburg (1837), and Osnabrück and Villingen (1858). The most important of these exhibitions attracted enormous attendances. The Karlsruhe exhibition of 1861 had 100,000 visitors, equivalent to 10 per cent of the population of Baden over the age of fourteen.[3] In all this we see confirmation of Richard Saage's proposition that 'possessive individualism' in Germany could progress only when it was 'positively fostered by the Mighty Leviathan'.[4]

By the 1850s and 1860s individual industrialists and merchants were undoubtedly stronger, wealthier, and more self-conscious than they had been even a generation earlier. But as Dieter Langewiesche has shown in detail for one southern state, there were fields in which the bureaucracy continued to make the running during these decades, while the economic bourgeoisie was content to welcome innovations like new commercial codes and the greatly expanded railways.[5] Even those classic mouthpieces of capitalist interests, the chambers of commerce, were fostered by the state

[3] B. Deneke, 'Fragen der Rezeption bürgerlicher Sachkultur bei der ländlichen Bevölkerung', in G. Wiegelmann (ed.), *Kultureller Wandel im 19. Jahrhundert* (Göttingen, 1973), pp. 55-7.
[4] R. Saage, *Eigentum, Staat und Gesellschaft bei Immanuel Kant* (Stuttgart, 1973), p. 142.
[5] D. Langewiesche, *Liberalismus und Demokratie in Württemberg zwischen Revolution and Reichsgründung* (Düsseldorf, 1974).

as hybrid, semi-public, and semi-private bodies. This pattern was reproduced at national level in the period 1866–79, when German industry and commerce received many cherished objectives from above, following successful unification. These included a national market, the Reichsbank, the beginnings of a national communication system, favourable conditions for the establishment of limited companies and uniform currency, weights and measures, and patent laws. The role of the state was therefore crucial. Its authority was necessary to clear many of the obstacles in the way of economic development, for defenders of corporate privilege or 'backward' enclaves of the natural economy often fought tenacious rearguard actions. At the same time, the state stepped in more positively when a first generation of entrepreneurs hesitated through lack of confidence: railways provide the obvious example. Above all, through institutional reform, changes in communication and educational provision the state helped to establish the possibility and desirability of a new kind of *homo oeconomicus*. It lent an imprimatur of naturalness to developments which, at the time, were by no means automatically perceived as natural.[6]

Yet it is also true that German capitalism had acquired a powerful momentum by the 1850s and 1860s. The symbol of this is the emergence of the public limited company as a new means of financing large-scale investment. Made possible by favourable legal codes and a broad climate of business confidence, stimulated by the hunger for capital of railways, steamship lines, and growing mining concerns, limited companies became an increasingly important economic force after mid-century. They provided a means of mobilizing savings and wealth which would have been impossible a generation earlier. Shares became more easily acquired and disposed of as the system of exchanges burgeoned, and investors in the public company began to feel that they were outflanking the more conservative who kept their capital in immovable property and state paper. Against this background the German economy—especially, in the first instance, mining,

---

[6] There is an outstanding account of this in G. Zang (ed.), *Provinzialisierung einer Region. Zur Entstehung der bürgerlichen Gesellschaft in der Provinz* (Frankfurt/M., 1978).

iron and steel, and engineering—registered impressive rates of growth. The detail here is familiar, and so is the further career of the now-Unbound Prometheus: the 'second wave' of industries, including chemicals, optics, and electrics, which developed during the last quarter of the century; the further extension of the communications network via railway branch lines and urban transportation; the rapid growth of the tertiary sector, which accounted for one in seven of those gainfully employed by 1907; and the overtaking of agriculture by industry and commerce as the centre of gravity of German economic activity, and the major sources of national wealth.[7]

Surveying evidence of this kind, Ralf Dahrendorf has argued that Germany 'developed into an industrial, but not into a capitalist society'.[8] But this is surely misleading. For all the impressive scale of its purely industrial manufacturing performance, the emergence of German capitalism had predated the flowering of industry. More important, it was more extensive in the nineteenth century than industry as such. Petty-commodity production provides a good example of why we need to consider capitalism as something different from, and more all-embracing than industrialism. In the eighteenth and early nineteenth centuries, home-workers as well as urban craftsmen in many branches were dependent on merchant capitalists: middlemen who provided credit, raw materials, sometimes even tools. In branches such as textiles (and later ready-made clothing) outwork did at least as much as the formal demise of the guilds to undermine the independence of master artisans.[9] Ostensibly, factory industry soaked up labour of this kind in the second half of the century; and we are accustomed to view the many small

---

[7] General accounts in Kitchen, *Political Economy*, and Böhme, *Introduction*. J. H. Clapham's *The Economic Development of France and Germany 1815–1914* (Cambridge, 1921) retains high value among the works in English. On relations between agriculture and industry, see esp. K. D. Barkin, *The Controversy over German Industrialization, 1890–1902* (Chicago, 1970).

[8] Dahrendorf, *Society and Democracy*, p. 43.

[9] Kriedte *et al.* (eds.), *Industrialisierung vor der Industrialisierung*; on master craftsmen, see P. Ayçoberry, 'Probleme der Sozialschichtung in Köln im Zeitalter der Frühindustrialisierung', in W. Fischer (ed.), *Wirtschafts- und Sozialgeschichtliche Probleme der frühen Industrialisierung* (Berlin, 1968), esp. pp. 519–24; K. Assmann and G. Stavenhagen, *Handwerkereinkommen am Vorabend der industriellen Revolution* (Göttingen, 1969).

businesses that survived as independent, 'pre-industrial' remnants. Indeed, the presence of a sizeable 'Mittelstand' of small producers is often seen as evidence for the peculiar incompleteness of German economic and social modernization, as a symbol of archaism which coexisted uneasily with the hot-house growth of the industrial sector.[10] In reality, however, the dominant capitalist economy extended its hold on small-scale production, although its control often assumed a form different from that of earlier periods. Through the control of capital, raw materials, and market outlets, middlemen (whether factories, wholesalers or retailers) used notionally independent shoemakers, tailors, turners, and cabinet-makers as contracted outworkers. The use of 'independent' craftsmen by contractors in the building sector followed a similar pattern. Small producers provided, in fact, a very useful safety-valve at times of cyclical or seasonal down-turn in demand. Like the perpetuation of outwork, especially through female labour in the clothing industry, this pattern of production did not always find its way cleanly into the statistics. It is easy enough to overlook, when set against the more obvious presence of the factory chimney. But it is testimony to the flexibility of a German capitalism which did not only assume an industrial guise.[11]

Indeed, it is this ubiquitous and protean quality that is most important in the present context. It is possible to be sceptical of impressionistic remarks about shares becoming 'fashionable' in the 1850s and 1860s,[12] although there is little doubt that many 'small men' (and women) invested heavily prior to the crash of 1873.[13] What cannot be disregarded is the broad impact of capitalist market forces in

[10] H. A. Winkler, *Mittelstand, Demokratie und Nationalsozialismus* (Cologne, 1972); Winkler, 'From Social Protectionism to National Socialism: the German Small Business Movement in Comparative Perspective', *Journal of Modern History*, 48 (1976), 1-18; S. Volkov, *The Rise of Popular Antimodernism in Germany: The Urban Master Artisans 1873-1896* (Princeton, 1978).

[11] I have discussed these points in 'The *Mittelstand* in German society and politics, 1871-1914', *Social History*, 4 (1977), 409-33, and at greater length in 'Between Resignation and Volatility: The Petite Bourgeoisie in Nineteenth-Century Germany', in G. Crossick and H.-G. Haupt (eds.), *Shopkeepers and Master Artisans in Nineteenth-Century Europe* (London, 1984).

[12] Böhme, *Introduction*, p. 39.

[13] On the popular speculative boom which preceded the crash of 1873, see H. Rosenberg, *Grosse Depression*, pp. 63ff.; Kitchen, *Political Economy*, pp.

flooding previous enclaves of a natural subsistence economy. The demise of this can be appropriately read off from the rising volume of paper money in circulation: the value of bank notes in circulation in Prussia increased from 18 million to 290 million Taler between 1850 and 1875.[14] There is plenty of evidence of what this meant in practice, then and later. A lively market developed in land, for example, especially around the growing towns and cities. There is also a mounting and impressive body of evidence of the market-rationality of the German peasant, *pace* many received opinions about 'backwardness'. The steep fall in subsistence production of food, drink, and household goods—a result both of the relative decline of peasant households within the population and of new patterns of rural consumption—fits into the same picture.[15] This particular trend, among the urban lower classes as well as the peasantry, was most clearly revealed by the sharp rise in retail turnover.[16]

Small-commodity and agricultural production were not 'industrial'; but they did not remain pre-capitalist. Capitalist agriculture was, of course, practised on the largest scale (although not always with the greatest success) on big estates. Even before the agricultural export boom of mid-century, many Junkers ran their estates on thoroughly capitalist lines,[17] a fact ironically obscured by the insistence of self-consciously bourgeois novelists such as Gutzkow, Freytag,

---

133–8; G. Craig, *Germany 1866–1945* (Oxford, 1978), pp. 78–85. There is evidence of speculative investment by better-off members of the petty bourgeoisie in the 1840s, as for example on the part of the butchers who made up Cologne's 'sausage brigade'. See Ayçoberry, 'Probleme', pp. 517–18; and more generally, J. Bergmann, 'Ökonomische Voraussetzungen der Revolution von 1848', in H.-U. Wehler (ed.), *200 Jahre amerikanische Revolution und moderne Revolutionsforschung: Geschichte und Gesellschaft, Sonderheft* 2 (Göttingen, 1976), 277–8.

[14] R. Engelsing, *Sozial- und Wirtschaftsgeschichte Deutschlands* (Göttingen, 1976), p. 131.

[15] See Blackbourn, '*Mittelstand*', pp. 426–7; J. C. Hunt, 'Peasants, Grain Tariffs and Meat Quotas', *Central European History*, 7 (1974), 311–31; R. G. Moeller, 'Peasants and Tariffs in the Kaiserreich: How Backward were the Bauern?', *Agricultural History*, 55 (1981), 370–84.

[16] R. Gellately, *The Politics of Economic Despair: Shopkeepers and German Politics 1890–1914* (London and Beverly Hills, 1974), pp. 12–27.

[17] Rosenberg, *Probleme*; Schissler, *Preussische Agrargesellschaft*.

and Spielhagen on depicting all Junkers as effete and indolent.[18] Max Weber came much closer to the truth in his famous enquiry of the early 1890s into East Elbian agriculture, when he stressed how the estate owners' methods had eroded former patriarchal relations.[19] Of course many Prussian estate owners were simply indigent *Krautjunker*. It is also true that the old families so often described by Fontane —'the Jagows and Lochows/the Stechows and Bredows/the Quitzows and Rochows'[20]—did not, like their wealthier landed counterparts in England, play an active role in the urban land market.[21] But they were often assiduous at winnowing an extra profit from auxiliary concerns such as brick-works and distilleries. The largest landowners, moreover, like the Counts Ballestrem and Henckel von Donnersmarck, were multi-millionaires from the exploitation of mineral deposits on their estates. It is also worth reminding ourselves that the Junker landowners of the nineteenth century were notably infused with bourgeois blood. By 1859, 57 per pent of Prussian *Rittergüter* were already in non-noble hands. By the 1880s bourgeois estate owners possessed two-thirds of the total number of estates even in the eastern provinces of Prussia.[22] This is a subject on which I shall have more to say later.

It is clear that the 'natural laws' of capitalism were not confined solely to an advanced industrial sector. Their writ ran more extensively. There is little doubt, for example, that inherited status or *Stand* increasingly gave way to property, wealth, and achievement as criteria of social worth, just as the cash nexus eclipsed concepts such as the primacy of social harmony and the just price. The growing self-consciousness of professional groups such as surveyors,

---

[18] E. K. Bramsted, *Aristocracy and the Middle-Classes in Germany* (Chicago, 1964), pp. 47 ff.

[19] First published in the *Preussische Jahrbücher*, 77 (1894). English transl. as 'Developmental tendencies in the situation of East Elbian rural labourers', *Economy and Society*, 8 (1979), pp. 172–205.

[20] Bramsted, *Aristocracy and Middle-Classes*, p. 267.

[21] On England, see F. M. L. Thompson, *English Landed Society in the Nineteenth Century* (London, 1963); D. Cannadine, *Lords and Landlords* (Leicester, 1980). A useful comparative work is D. Spring (ed.), *European Landed Elites in the Nineteenth Century* (Baltimore, 1977), esp. the articles by Spring and Stern.

[22] Rosenberg, *Probleme*; Engelsing, *Sozial- und Wirtschaftsgeschichte*, p. 113.

accountants, architects, and schoolteachers was a by-product of, and in turn reinforced, these changes. A society which placed a growing emphasis on access to and disposability of property, on material calculation and the discipline of the timetable, came to value their professional expertise accordingly.[23] Generalizations of this kind are necessarily hazardous, but the broad contours of change seem clear enough. Certainly intelligent conservatives, like Wilhelm Riehl in *Die bürgerliche Gesellschaft*,[24] unhappily offered this diagnosis of what was happening. Indeed, those who variously disliked the threat, the ruthlessness, the efficiency, or the 'materialism' of the new order sought at many points to turn the clock back. They resisted the emancipation of the peasantry and the dismantling of the guilds; they resisted new commercial codes and the erosion among craft masters of the principle of subsistence (*Nahrungsprinzip*); they resisted the railways and more rigorous, compulsory education. They warned of a Hobbesian 'war of all against all', and variously couched their objections in religious, aesthetic, moral, parochial, or political terms. Their importance was considerable, as we shall see. But they were nevertheless unable to reverse the ratchet effect of the newly established bourgeois order.

In fact, a recognition of bourgeois standards of profit and slide-rule calculation can be found in some rather unlikely quarters. The 'backwardness' of Catholic Germany was much remarked on by contemporaries; it provides the background to Weber's celebrated thesis. But the closing decades of the century saw a growing tendency among bourgeois Catholics —businessmen, officials, lawyers, publicists—to complain about the relatively small number of their co-religionists who entered the worlds of business, commerce, or the professions.[25] One of them noted with asperity that Jewish merchants

---

[23] See *Geschichte und Gesellschaft*, 6 (1980), No. 3, for a special issue on professionalization.
[24] First edition 1851.
[25] Evidence for this changing sentiment is legion. A useful source on bourgeois Catholic embarrassment about 'backwardness' is the compilatory work of J. Rost, *Die wirtschaftliche und kulturelle Lage der deutschen Katholiken* (Cologne, 1911). See also C. Bauer, *Deutscher Katholizismus. Entwicklungslinien und Profile* (Frankfurt/M., 1964).

appeared to have cornered the market in rosaries and ginger-bread Virgins, at a time when a revived and strongly com-mercialized popular piety offered new opportunities.[26] All the critics agreed that too many talented young Catholics were drawn off into the priesthood, to the detriment of Catholics' standing in a society now ordered on rather different principles. The efforts of those who sought to establish Catholicism as 'a principle of progress'[27] had some effect in changing this state of affairs. The German Catholic Church itself also bowed to the logic of prevailing values. At the close of the nineteenth century it moved a growing number of saints' days from work days to weekends, so that Catholic wage and salary earners need not remain idle when they could be contributing to gross domestic product.[28] This worldliness—and the arguments adduced to support the policy were fairly blunt—makes us less surprised to learn of the brisk trade in black-market tickets for the confessional queue during the great popular missions of the 1860s.[29]

A similar market—and black market—developed in the granting of official titles. In tiny Coburg they were available, as one contemporary sourly noted, 'for cash down'.[30] Saxony and Württemberg made large sums from stamp duties and fees; Prussia was recognized by *aficionados* to be cheaper, but the parsimonious Hohenzollern economized by asking for the physical return of orders on the death of the holder, leaving relations with only the parchment. More important, though, it was widely known that unofficial fixed rates existed for the various honours: in Prussia, 60,000 marks of

[26] Rost, *Lage*, pp. 202–3.
[27] H. Schell, *Der Katholizismus als Prinzip des Fortschritts* (Würzburg, 1897). This sentiment was not, however, confined to 'Reform Catholics' and 'Modernists'. For further detail and references, see Blackbourn, 'Die Zentrumspartei und die deutschen Katholiken während des Kulturkampfs und danach', in O. Pflanze (ed.), *Innenpolitische Probleme des Bismarck-Reichs* (Munich and Vienna, 1983), pp. 73–94, and 'The Centre Party and its Constituency: Catholic Politics in Imperial Germany', in D. Blackbourn, *Populists and Patricians: Essays in Modern German History* (London, 1987), pp. 188–214.
[28] Rost, *Lage*, p. 211.
[29] E. Gatz, *Rheinische Volksmissionen im 19. Jahrhundert* (Düsseldorf, 1963), p. 124.
[30] G. A. Ritter and J. Kocka (eds.), *Deutsche Sozialgeschichte: Dokumente und Skizzen*. vol. II: *1870-1914* (Munich, 1974), p. 80.

disbursements in a cause approved by the state sufficed for the rank of commercial councillor; commercial privy councillor cost rather more, with other titles pro rata. In the 1880s, when the Lord High Steward Baron von Mirbach collected 30 million marks for a church-building fund on behalf of the Kaiserin, it transpired that countless contributors had correctly believed they were in fact purchasing orders, titles, patents as royal deliverers and even ennoblement. There were indeed forty or fifty men in Wilhelmine Berlin who offered their services as title brokers; the more reputable offered money-back guarantees.[31]

These were not everyday occurrences. But a glance at the exceptional helps to throw into sharper relief—as it did for contemporaries, when the story of the church-building fund emerged—the everyday and often unnoticed workings of the cash nexus and system of exchange. For the most part the market worked in more prosaic ways; and in this lay one of its principal strengths. It is nevertheless true that there were ways in which the form assumed by Germany's dynamic capitalism brought about more dramatic shifts in perception. Nowhere is this more evident than in attitudes towards nature, the machine, and mechanical civilization. This may seem curious at first sight. We have become accustomed to associate paeans to Progress, in the shape of the railway for example, with England and France, not Germany. It is the French who celebrated their bridge- and canal-building heroes, England to which we owe Martin Tupper's doggerel in honour of the Great Exhibition of 1851 and on the links between the railway and human happiness.[32] Germany, by contrast, was the 'land of poets and thinkers', with an educated class especially which rejected the mechanical in favour of the 'organic'. I shall consider below in more detail the place occupied by this tradition in German thought. What needs to be stressed here is the presence in Germany of a palpably affirmative attitude to material progress: a self-satisfied and pervasive strain of optimism which trumpeted the advances of mechanical civilization. In Germany, no less

[31]   R. Lewinsohn, *Das Geld in der Politik* (Berlin, 1930), pp. 26-32.
[32]   For an example of Tupper's work, see A. Briggs, *Victorian People* (London, 1967), p. 23.

than in England or France, the 'triad of railway, steamship, telegraph'[33] served as the symbols of a progress which was held to go beyond the merely economic. They underpinned a buoyant, if often superficial, belief in the liberating power of material advance, a victory over man's cramped and superstitious nature. Karl Beck's 'The Railway' or Anastasius Grün's 'Poetry of Steam' capture the spirit of this 'railway poetry' with Tupperesque crassness.[34] Writing in a similar vein, Max Maria von Weber, the eldest son of the composer, was credited by his publisher with having invented the 'technological novella'. A director of engineering and then of railways in Saxony, later a financial official, Weber had the similar claim made for him by a friendly critic that he had 'discovered the poetry of rails'. Certainly the publisher's introduction to Weber's posthumous collection of essays left little doubt about their stance: 'Mightier beyond compare than steed or chariot, than oar or sail, it is the new and powerful motor of our day: steam, which, with aquiline speed, guides ocean castles and rolling towns.' For Weber himself, the steam engine allowed men 'to triumph in the struggle against the forces of Nature.'[35] We encounter this cast of mind again and again in nineteenth-century Germany. It can be heard in the characterization by the physicist and scientific popularizer, Helmholtz, of the 'animal body as a steam engine'; it can be seen in such a picture as Adolph Menzel's *Iron Rolling Mill* of 1875.

The importance of the new machine world and the metaphorical significance which became attached to it lay in its very universality. In this it resembled the new economic order as a whole. The first German to ride on a railway may have been Prince Pückler-Muskau (in London in 1828).[36] But the opening of new bridges, such as the Rhine Bridge at

[33] W. Schivelbusch, *The Railway Journey* (Oxford, 1980), p. 187.
[34] M. Riedel, 'Vom Biedermeier zum Maschinenzeitalter. Zur Kulturgeschichte der ersten Eisenbahnen in Deutschland', *Archiv für Kulturgeschichte*, 43 (1961), 106-7.
[35] D. Sternberger, *Panorama of the Nineteenth Century* (Oxford, 1977), pp. 20-3. Cf. the similar sentiment in Switzerland: O. Walzel, *Wirklichkeitsfreude der neueren Schweizer Dichtung* (Stuttgart and Berlin, 1908), pp. 52 ff., which cites Swiss works of the period 1830-95 that made the railway their theme.
[36] Riedel, 'Vom Biedermeier zum Maschinenzeitalter', p. 110.

Strassburg-Kehl or the Ravenna viaduct in the Black Forest, captured the popular imagination and drew large crowds, as did the major exhibitions.[37] There is a parallel here with the public festivities that accompanied the opening of Brunel bridges in England, and with the crowds that attended the Crystal Palace. Artisan autobiographies of the last century show the fascination the new mode of transport exercised on the former 'tramping' artisans.[38] By the end of the century the railway was used on a large scale for pilgrimages, as well as for the more modest annual outing of the Brown Cow Insurance Society.[39] Even variations of local time between different parts of Germany had been standardized on the basis of 'schedule time'.[40] The universality of the railway in social terms was, then, a crucial feature of its impact. But it is nevertheless true that the fêting of the railway, like other aspects of the brave new mechanical world, was particularly associated with the bourgeoisie. The novels of Spielhagen and Gutzkow are full of gloating references to outmoded aristocrats, wearing out their horses in fruitless, Quixotic attempts to race the iron steed, and with stories of countesses unable to come to terms with the public nature of the railway carriage. In the middle decades of the century especially, the new means of communication, together with discoveries in the natural sciences and their popularization, engendered an unmistakable and often strident bourgeois identification with Progress. This tendency saw its full flowering during the *Kulturkampf,* the grandiloquently titled 'struggle of civilization' which drew so much of the German bourgeoisie into battle against the Catholic Church. During this period of the 1860s and 1870s it was not just the power of the Church that was thought to be at stake; for the protagonists it really was

[37] Sternberger, *Panorama,* pp. 27-9.
[38] See W. Fischer, *Quellen zur Geschichte des deutschen Handwerks* (Göttingen, 1957), which includes artisan autobiographies dealing with the 'tramping' experience.
[39] Blackbourn, *Class, Religion and Local Politics in Wilhelmine Germany* (London and New Haven, 1980), p. 17; H. Schiffers, *Kulturgeschichte der Aachener Heiligtumsfahrt* (Cologne, 1930). For a telling comparison between the Trier pilgrimages of 1844 and 1891, see L. Pastor, *August Reichensperger,* 2 vols. (Freiburg, i.B., 1899), I. 184.
[40] Schivelbusch, *Railway Journey,* p. 51.

seen as a struggle for civilization. On the one side stood the Church, symbol of the 'dead hand', backwardness, charitable hand-outs, and superstition, backed by residual corporate privilege; on the other stood the shining new civilization of material advance, productive labour, the model orphanage, and Progress, guaranteed by equality before the law.[41] As one opponent of compromise with the Church noted, 'going to Canossa will bring us no railways'.[42]

In the middle third of the century above all there was therefore a strong identification between the new order which was establishing itself and the bourgeoisie. Hostile commentators noted this identity, as in Wilhelm Riehl's remark that 'our whole era bears a bourgeois character, other estates are really only the ruins of the past.'[43] In other words, the bourgeois epoch was associated clearly with the bourgeois class—or 'estate' as Riehl preferred to put it. This certainly corresponded to a powerful element of bourgeois self-understanding. It is hardly an exaggeration to say that in the middle years of the century the idea of material and moral progress, the two being closely intertwined, held together the various subgroupings of the bourgeoisie: businessmen, officials, professionals.[44] If we accept this, however, does it not contradict the previous emphasis on the non-heroic role of the bourgeoisie, on the silent nature of its achievements? We seem to be faced, not with silent victories, but with a noisily self-aggrandizing bourgeoisie, bent on fulfilling its role of taming nature and conquering the idiocy of rural life. To a considerable extent this is a matter of chronology. The full flowering of bourgeois optimism was the effect, not the cause, of capitalist dynamism. But that leads in turn to a further point. The very speed and

---

[41] See Blackbourn, 'Die Zentrumspartei und die deutschen Katholiken', and 'The Centre Party and its Constituency'; Zang, *Provinzialisierung*; A. M. Birke, 'Zur Entwicklung und politischen Funktion des bürgerlichen Kulturkampfverständnisses in Preussen-Deutschland', in D. Kurze (ed.), *Aus Theorie und Praxis. Festschrift für Hans Herzfeld* (Berlin, 1972), pp. 257-79.

[42] J. B. Kissling, *Geschichte des Kulturkampfes im Deutschen Reiche*, 3 vols. (Freiburg i.B., 1911-16), III. 295.

[43] Cited in L. Beutin, 'Das Bürgertum als Gesellschaftsstand im 19. Jahrhundert', *Gesammelte Schriften zur Wirtschafts- und Sozialgeschichte*, ed. H. Kellenbenz (Cologne and Graz, 1963), p. 292.

[44] Ibid., pp. 292 ff.

force with which Germany was transformed in material terms during the 1850s and 1860s encouraged a particularly intense identification on the part of its bourgeois advocates.[45] This was all the stronger, given the sharp contrast with what had come before: the subaltern position of the bourgeoisie itself, together with the stifling economic and mental barriers between the small states. Hence that quasi-religious 'worldly piety' (*Weltfrömmigkeit*) so characteristic of the bourgeois encomia on Progress. Helmuth Plessner, one of the most acute and differentiated of all the writers on German peculiarity, has some valuable things to say about this. The text of *Die verspätete Nation* is peppered with words such as 'volcanic' and 'titanic', and these give an appropriate indication both of the scale and suddenness of material advance in Germany, and of the cast of mind it bred. Ironically, in the light of so much later writing, Plessner argues that this feature of nineteenth-century Germany represented the very acme of the 'bourgeois age' in Europe.[46]

This is less surprising than it appears at first sight. German backwardness, in bourgeois eyes (as in the eyes of German rulers), created a desire for over-compensation; it led to an enthusiastic embracing of what was 'titanic' in the new age which was actually more extravagant than comparable sentiment in England or France. In this respect the notion of the parvenu may be a helpful one. We may, that is, see the German bourgeoisie as a parvenu class within a parvenu nation. It is often noted that Engels once said Britain had a bourgeois bourgeoisie, a bourgeois aristocracy, and a bourgeois working class. It is less often pointed out that Max Weber, at different points in his writing, suggested that Germany had a parvenu bourgeoisie, a parvenu aristocracy, and a parvenu working class.[47] The distinction is well taken and it is a telling one. The dramatic advent of the new order

---

[45] Cf. Friedrich Harkort: 'The locomotive is the hearse on which absolutism and feudalism will be carried to the graveyard.'

[46] Plessner, *verspätete Nation*, p. 82. See, generally, chs. 4-6.

[47] See esp. 'National Character and the Junkers', in H. H. Gerth and C. Wright Mills (eds.), *From Max Weber* (London, 1974), pp. 386-95, and 'Economic Policy and the National Interest in Imperial Germany', in Runciman (ed.), *Selections in Translation*, pp. 263-8.

in Germany actually fuelled the stridency of the bourgeoisie: it heightened parvenu claims to a particular position within society as a whole. At the end of the eighteenth century and the beginning of the nineteenth, the bourgeois had still been widely regarded as an 'incomplete' and even risible figure: he had no answer to the question 'what are you?', only to the question 'what have you?' Thus Adam Müller, writing in 1809, identified, not the grubby *Spiessbürger*, but the nobility as the embodiment of society's general will. It was this class that represented 'the power and freedom of the invisible and absent members of society'. It was the nobility, again, which stood for 'the *intérêt générale* and *volonté générale*'.[48] By the middle of the nineteenth century, however, things had changed. Now it was the bourgeoisie that laid claim to represent the general interest of society. Nowhere was this more gloomily acknowledged than by Müller's spiritual successor, Wilhelm Riehl.

2. *Law, Voluntary Association, and the Rise of the Public*

How did the bourgeoisie exercise this claim to represent a 'general interest'? Part of the answer must be that it did so through the workings of the capitalist economy, as the norms of this system gradually acquired a patina of 'naturalness'. One historian has written of these changes in the material sphere of life as a 'silent victory' for the German bourgeoisie.[49] It should be noted immediately that the silence was as important as the victory. The new order was most successful where its achievements came to seem second nature. This quality of naturalness was also characteristic of another crucial sphere: the securing and consolidation of the rule of law. This was also a necessary foundation of a fully bourgeois society. Two powerful and complementary moves in this direction can be traced from the late eighteenth century onwards. The first saw the emerging concept of the citizen (*Staatsbürger*) within the legally based state (*Rechtsstaat*); the second, closely connected, firmly established the idea of

---

[48] Bramsted, *Aristocracy and Middle-Classes*, pp. 28-31, 39-40.
[49] Beutin, 'Das Bürgertum', p. 295.

the private individual (*Bürger*) within a society based on the inalienability and disposability of private property. Each of these legal frameworks embodied major bourgeois desiderata; and the clearly upheld distinction between public and private law was in itself a mark of the transition from the old corporate state and society (*Ständestaat*) to the new bourgeois *Rechtsstaat*. It is to the dual evolution of these ideas that I now want to turn.[50]

The concept of the equality of citizens before the law signalled a major break with the corporate state. It found expression in the legal codifications of both Prussia (the *Allgemeines Landrecht* of 1794) and Austria (the *Allgemeines Bürgerliches Gesetzbuch* of 1811). The dates demonstrate the importance of the reform period around the turn of the century, and indicate the parallels with legal changes in France during the revolutionary and Napoleonic periods. In Germany these years witnessed either the outright abolition or the serious pruning of many corporate, seigneurial, and ecclesiastical forms of jurisdiction which were obstacles to the realization of formal equality before the law. The emancipation of the peasantry, the stripping of corporate powers from the guilds, and the secularization of many charitable foundations were three major instances.[51] This pattern of change can be seen throughout Germany, in the small and medium-sized states as well as in the largest, and it was to reach a high point in the 1860s. This process of transformation was undoubtedly uneven, however. The vicissitudes in the movement towards full citizenship rights for Jews,

[50] An extremely useful guide to these areas is provided by two articles of Manfred Riedel's: 'Bürger, Staatsbürger, Bürgertum', in O. Brunner, W. Conze, R. Koselleck (eds.), *Geschichtliche Grundbegriffe. Historisches Lexikon zur politisch-sozialen Sprache in Deutschland*, vol. 1 (Stuttgart, 1972) esp. pp. 683–725; and 'Gesellschaft, bürgerlich', in J. Ritter (ed.), *Historisches Wörterbuch der Philosophie*, vol. 3 (Dortmund, 1974), cols. 466–73. Specialists will also recognize my general debt to J. Habermas, *Strukturwandel der Öffentlichkeit* (Neuwied and Berlin, 1962), whose ideas are outlined in English in 'The Public Sphere', *New German Critique*, 3 (1974).

[51] For French influence, see E. Fehrenbach, *Traditionelle Gesellschaft und revolutionäres Recht* (Göttingen, 1974). See also Koselleck, *Preussen zwischen Reform und Revolution*, and B. Vogel, ' "Revolution von oben"—Der "deutsche Weg" in die bürgerliche Gesellschaft?', *Sozialwissenschaftliche Informationen für Unterricht und Studium*, 8 (1979), 67–74.

or the strongly resisted reform of communal citizenship restrictions in the south-west are illustrations of this.[52] The politically restorationist leanings of monarchs such as Ernst August in Hanover and Friedrich Wilhelm IV in Prussia, during the 1830s and 1840s, also ran counter to the general direction of change. They found some intellectual backing in the reactionary doctrines of men such as von Haller and Adam Müller. Yet these monarchs and writers were clearly swimming against the current. Even in the 1830s it had an anachronistic ring to it when Ernst August of Hanover addressed himself to 'all Our Royal ecclesiastical and worldly servants, vasalls, freeholders, and subjects';[53] and this was equally true of the terms used by those who defended the distinctions made in south-west German communal codes between full citizens, half-citizens, and protected subjects. The process of emancipation from corporate ties of various kinds was in fact consolidated by the 1860s, following two further waves of institutional and legal reform. The concept of the equality of all citizens before the law was anchored in the constitution of both the North German Confederation of 1867 and the German Reich of 1871.

Inseparable from this transition were two further components of the move towards the legally based *Rechtsstaat*. The first of these was the principle of the legal accountability of the bureaucracy, finally achieved in Prussia in the 1870s after many years of effort. The second was the development of a public sphere (*Öffentlichkeit*), separate from and independent of the state: a sphere of activity and discourse through the press, and through legally guaranteed rights of association and assembly. These 'bourgeois freedoms', together with the rights of free speech and petition, constituted the formal attributes of equality before the law within a *Rechtsstaat*.[54] Taken as a whole, they worked against both corporate presumption and the danger of state arbitrariness. They embodied the principle of legal 'certainty'

---

[52] On these, see respectively R. Rürup, *Emanzipation und Antisemitismus* (Göttingen, 1975), and M. Walker, *German Home Towns* (Ithaca, NY, 1971).

[53] Riedel, 'Bürger, Staatsbürger, Bürgertum', pp. 704–5.

[54] D. Blasius, 'Bürgerliches Recht und bürgerliche Identität', in H. Berding *et al.* (eds.), *Vom Staat des Ancien Régime zum modernen Parteienstaat* (Munich, 1978), pp. 213–24. See, generally, Habermas, *Strukturwandel.*

which played such a large part in the thinking of German jurists and of bourgeois opinion more generally.[55] These changes provided the formal basis for a 'public opinion' to be formed.

This was only one side of the coin, however, in respect of equality before and within the law. The other side was the legal framework which emerged out of a similarly protracted process of change, and guaranteed the property rights of the private individual—that is, the rights of the 'Bürger' rather than the 'Staatsbürger'—through principles such as the freedom to acquire and dispose of property without restriction. The nineteenth century also saw the establishment of this central bourgeois credo. The Penal Code of the German Reich, for example, modelled on the Prussian Penal Code of 1851, was based squarely on bourgeois property rights. As one commentator has noted, it explicitly confirmed 'the value of property through the punishment laid down for theft'.[56] The parallels with changing penal codes in contemporary England and France are striking—although the relative neglect of the German case by historians is perhaps more striking still.[57] Civil law was similarly consonant with the needs of a society which rested on unrestricted individual property rights, as for instance in the principles that underlay the laws on bankruptcy and distraint. The way in which the rule of law underpinned and spoke the language of bourgeois society was perhaps most clearly manifested in the Civil Code (BGB) which came into effect in 1900 after decades of preparation. The Civil Code embodied individualist values which had their origin in Humboldtian humanism. It also flowed out of the Roman law tradition within the German historical school of jurisprudence, running from Savigny to Windscheid, with its emphasis on the primacy of the legal individual and contractual freedom.[58] In its confirmation

---

[55] M. Gugel, *Industrieller Aufstieg und bürgerliche Herrschaft* (Cologne, 1975), pp. 81–91; G. Dilcher, 'Das Gesellschaftsbild der Rechtswissenschaft und die soziale Frage', in Vondung (ed.), *Das wilhelminische Bildungsbürgertum*, pp. 53–79.

[56] Blasius, 'Bürgerliches Recht', p. 220. See also Blasius, *Bürgerliche Gesellschaft und Kriminalität* (Göttingen, 1976).

[57] Blasius notes this relative neglect in the introduction to *Bürgerliche Gesellschaft und Kriminalität*, pp. 9–13.

[58] Dilcher, 'Das Gesellschaftsbild der Rechtswissenschaft', p. 61.

of individual property rights, the equal treatment of landed and movable property, the law of mortgage, freedom of contract, and the freedom to bequeath, in its firm establishment of civil marriage, and even in its discrimination against women in the sphere of marriage law, it was a code which had 'codified the ideals of nineteenth-century bourgeois society'.[59] As one of its principal contemporary critics, Otto von Gierke, noted of an earlier version of the BGB, 'if the draft code had a hidden social tendency, it would be the individualistic and one-sidedly capitalistic notions of the pure Manchester theory.'[60]

It is therefore highly appropriate that one historian should have employed a legal term in describing the state as the 'executor' of bourgeois interests in Germany.[61] This corresponds to the central importance the bourgeoisie itself attached to this sphere. The rule of law, in the various telling forms it assumed in nineteenth-century Germany, provided an essential framework for the unfolding of a bourgeois society. This process of unfolding is not easy to pin down with any precision. This is partly because historians have, once again, directed less attention to it than they have in the case of England or France. But there is a more important reason for this difficulty which the German case has in common with the English and French. The developments in question were not especially dramatic events: like the rule of law which sustained them, they amounted to further silent victories; they came to seem natural. The very fact that bourgeois dominance was expressed through civil society makes it (and made it) less easy to identify than the overt prescriptions and proscriptions of the *Ständestaat*, although correspondingly more powerful. It is, however, possible to isolate some of the major channels of this dominance. One crucial conduit was certainly the professions.[62] As the professions emerged out of the corporate society in which their functions had usually been tied to court, church, or guild, their personnel

---

[59] F. Wieacker, cited in Blasius, 'Bürgerliches Recht', p. 222.
[60] O. Gierke, *Der Entwurf eines bürgerlichen Gesetzbuches und das deutsche Recht* (Leipzig, 1889), p. 3. I owe this reference to Michael John, from whom I have learned much about the history of the law in Germany.
[61] Schmidt, 'Zu einigen Problemen der bürgerlichen Umwälzung', p. 17.
[62] See n. 23 above.

was heavily bourgeois from the outset. Men from this background were numerically preponderant in the new and more
specialized spheres of civil society: the law, education,
science, art, music, medicine, the press. And they were able,
in the course of establishing the ground-rules of their own
increasingly self-conscious professions to define the ground-
rules of the broader society within which the professions
operated, and which they in turn helped to shape. In this
way, to take one example, science and medicine became
imbued with the tones of optimism and belief in progress
we have already noted; and these sentiments were in turn
asserted as general or universal values.

But the professions were probably not the major agency
through which the bourgeoisie set the tone in the material
and cultural spheres of civil society. A more important
conduit was, characteristically enough, less formal. This was
the increasingly dense network of voluntary associations
(*Vereine*). The voluntary association was made possible by
changes in the framework of law which confirmed the
existence of the public sphere as a new kind of social arena
between the family on the one hand and the state on the
other, where men could associate freely. There had been
associations of this kind from the last decades of the
eighteenth century, mainly reading clubs, musical societies,
or associations devoted to pure conviviality. By the beginning of the nineteenth century we can see the formation
of gymnastic and sporting clubs, and after around 1815 the
mushrooming of artistic, choral, and learned associations of
many kinds. The 1830s and 1840s also saw the burgeoning
of associations which concerned themselves with the social
question. Many attended in a general way to supporting the
'deserving poor'; others had more specific objectives, whether
discouraging the drinking of spirits, encouraging the cultivation of potatoes by the indigent, or 'encouraging school
attendance by poor children'. At the all-important local level,
associations were often formed with a particular project in
mind, like the construction of a hospital or ophanage.[63]

[63] T. Nipperdey, 'Verein als soziale Struktur in Deutschland im späten 18.
und frühen 19. Jahrhundert', *Gesellschaft, Kultur, Theorie* (Göttingen, 1976),
pp. 174–205.

Historians have spoken of a 'passion for association' by the
middle of the century, of a 'hypertrophic growth' of voluntary
associations in all areas of life.[64] They existed for business
and professional purposes, while others were largely sociable;
there were sporting, cultural, philanthropic, religious, and
educational associations; some, of course, were specifically
political. Voluntary association assumed the status of a
'universal elixir',[65] its concerns ranging from the Schiller
Association to the carnival association, from the workers'
education association to the Society for the Protection of
Animals.

Three important points should be noted about these associations. First, the association as such was non-corporatist,
and even anti-corporatist, in organization and intention: it
was 'public' and voluntary, an alternative way of forming
and expressing 'opinion' to the fixed and prescriptive channels
of the corporate state. Whether concerned with social discipline, welfare, or edification, the voluntary association
stepped into the gap left by the eroded functions either of
the state itself, or of ecclesiastical, guild, or other corporate
institutions.[66] Secondly, the association reflected the strength
of family, personal, and social ties among the propertied and
educated bourgeoisie (*Besitz- und Bildungsbürgertum*). All
empirical work on voluntary associations—local studies of
Augsburg, Hamburg, and Weinheim, as much as general
accounts—is agreed in stressing this characteristic. Indeed, it
has been argued that associational life was one of the principal
means by which the various constituent groups of the bourgeoisie actually came together as a class. The associations
constituted, in other words, an open and public arena which
was actually dominated by a relatively small class of those
who had money to disburse, access to meeting places, and the
education to draft formal rules and provide officers to follow

[64] Ibid., p. 175; R. Braun, 'Probleme des sozio-kulturellen Wandels im 19.
Jahrhundert', in Wiegelmann (ed.), *Kultureller Wandel*, p. 17.
[65] Braun, 'Probleme', p. 17.
[66] Nipperdey, 'Verein als soziale Struktur', pp. 177-83; Beutin, 'Das Bürgertum', pp. 299-300.

them.[67] Thomas Nipperdey has argued convincingly that the growth of associations was symptomatic of the emergence of a bourgeois society in Germany, while in turn it underwrote and accelerated this process.[68] The third point follows from this: the associations were a major vehicle for bourgeois aspirations to social leadership. The humanist strain in associational life testified to a belief in individual self-realization; the pedagogic strain broadcast this belief as a universal message to society as a whole. Hence the frequency of association names which alluded to the common good and the public welfare.[69] Underlying economic, social, and moral principles of bourgeois life were acted out publicly in the association; they were offered as a model.[70] Workers were exhorted to respectability through educational associations and the early co-operative movement; parts of the petty bourgeoisie—typically those who had links with the local bourgeoisie such as butchers, bakers, bookbinders, and better-off shopkeepers —played an important subsidiary role in associations; and from about the 1830s, the association spread into the countryside, often borne by local urban notables who invented a rustically gregarious 'way of life' after their own image.[71] Other classes were thus the recipients of philanthropic support, cultural edification, and social patronage provided by a bourgeoisie which translated its local ascendancy into a claim to social leadership.

It is possible to see voluntary association as the social counterpart to the market economy: one was based on the mutual exchange of goods between formally equal participants in the market place, the other on the mutual exchange of opinions between formally equal citizens. Both principles were underwritten by nineteenth-century legal changes. Also common to both was the idea of the public.

---

[67] H. Bausinger, 'Verbürgerliching—Folgen eines Interpretaments', in Wiegelmann (ed.), *Kultureller Wandel*, pp. 27–8.

[68] Nipperdey, 'Verein als soziale Struktur', pp. 182–3.

[69] Ibid., pp. 177–8.

[70] There are some thoughtful observations on this in W. Kaschuba and C. Lipp, 'Zur Organisation des bürgerlichen Optimismus', in *Sozialwissenschaftliche Informationen für Unterricht und Studium*, 8 (1979), 74–82.

[71] E. M. Wallner, 'Die Rezeption stadtbürgerlicher Vereinswesens durch die Bevölkerung auf dem Lande', in Wiegelmann (ed.), *Kultureller Wandel*, pp. 160–73.

This was central to the emergence and self-understanding of bourgeois society in Germany, as elsewhere. The public company, public association, public meeting, and public opinion were all made possible by the transition from a corporate society to one in which material and social life in the widest sense were differently organized. If we consider the development of German public life in this broad sense we can see many further instances of this pattern taking shape.

In many different spheres a form of actual bourgeois dominance operated anonymously through institutions which addressed a general public made up of formal equals. Writers, for example, became less dependent on princely or noble patronage, more dependent on a reading public. This change was naturally uneven: a number of writers continued to sustain themselves as state officials, or even received direct court patronage. Max II of Bavaria, Duke Ernst II of Saxe-Coburg, and Grand Duke Karl Alexander of Weimar were prominent in their efforts to attract literary talent to court. We should certainly not disregard this continuing form of patronage, which was often a product of the very multiplicity of surviving courts and of the rivalry between them. Wittelsbach cultural ambitions *vis-à-vis* the Hohenzollern were particularly pronounced.[72] More important overall, though, was the growing number of writers who were able to live from their writing, or from a combination of writing and journalism. The genesis of the professional writer—a parallel to professionalization elsewhere—was made possible by the rising number of publishers, bookshops, and reading customers; it was also facilitated by the growth of the press, especially by the literary *feuilleton* section of newspapers, copied from the French.[73] Writers achieved a new visibility as their audiences became more anonymous. A heightened

---

[72] Generally, see Bramsted, *Aristocracy and Middle-Classes*, esp. pp. 279–89. On the Wittelsbachs, see R. Lenman, 'Politics and Culture: the State and the Avant-Garde in Munich 1886-1914', in R. J. Evans (ed.), *Society and Politics in Wilhelmine Germany* (London, 1978), pp. 90–111. Mayer, *Persistence of the Old Regime*, pp. 189–273, has much to say about patronage in Germany and elsewhere.

[73] See E. Sagarra, *Tradition and Revolution. German Literature and Society 1830-1890* (New York, 1971); R. Pascal, *From Naturalism to Expressionism. German Literature and Society 1880-1918* (London, 1973).

form of this phenomenon can be seen in authors such as Herwegh and Freiligrath, who consciously set up their stalls against courtly patronage. On his triumphal journey through Germany in 1842, Herwegh 'was cheered by the bourgeoisie like a modern film-star'; Freiligrath achieved a similar public fame as 'the pride of the bourgeoisie' when he returned to Germany from English exile in 1868.[74] Less spectacular, but more weighty, was the gradual formation, not of a cheering, but of a reading, public. This we can broadly characterize, like English and French commentators on the same subject, as a bourgeois reading public.

This development had its counterparts in cognate spheres of life. The public park and gallery came to rival, although they by no means eclipsed, the princely or aristocratic park and gallery. The same is true of other places of public entertainment and edification such as the nineteenth-century concert hall or museum, financed by subscription or by municipal notables (often members of the appropriate association), not by the court or nobility. The advent of the public zoo is no less telling as a symptom of social change. Royal menageries and kindred institutions had long existed as a sign of royal prestige and a diversion for courtiers; but they had already found critics such as the French Encyclopedists. The menagerie at Versailles was actually destroyed in the French Revolution.[75] The nineteenth-century zoological garden was explicitly different; it addressed itself to the 'public' and was commonly the product of subscriptions and appeals mounted through voluntary associations. It is certainly not without significance that the Berlin zoo, completed in 1844 between its counterparts in Amsterdam (1838) and Antwerp (1848), was constructed on the site of the former Royal Prussian Pheasantry.[76] The development of the spa resorts and great hotels of the nineteenth century as rivals to, or replacements of, the aristocratic hunting party or weekend gathering falls into a similar category. So does the

---

[74] Bramsted, *Aristocracy and Middle-Classes*, p. 335.

[75] H. F. Ellenberger, 'The Mental Hospital and the Zoological Garden', in J. and B. Klaits (eds.), *Animals and Man in Historical Perspective* (New York, 1974), pp. 62–5.

[76] R. Michaelis-Jena, *The Brothers Grimm* (London, 1970), p. 129.

rise of famous public restaurants such as Wilkens Keller in Hamburg or Helms in Berlin.

It may seem curious to discuss the public hotel and restaurant together with apparently weightier and more 'serious' institutions like the law or philanthropic association. But it is important to recognize that not only did they rest on the same principle of accessibility to all on a formally equal basis; they were also perceived by contemporaries as sharing this quality. Thus we find a prominent anti-vivisectionist talking of 'putting up large pictures of the horrors of vivisection at street corners, on kiosks, in railway stations, hotels and restaurants'.[77] Here we see the campaigner treating each of these places as part of the public sphere, no less important than the public meeting called by the anti-vivisection association to influence 'opinion' in its favour. In bourgeois society it was possible to mobilize outrage through public opinion, just as it was possible to mobilize capital through the public company. The very principle embodied in free public association was held by many, in fact, to offer the possibility of a civilizing or moralizing effect. We can see this same assumption operating with regard to some of the other institutions noted above, such as the museum and the zoo. Both were, after all, a tribute to bourgeois self-confidence: symbols of the power of science and witnesses to how Progress could edify man while taming the natural order. Let us take the zoo as an example. When the new zoological garden was built in post-revolutionary Paris it was constructed on the principles laid down by Philippe Pinel of the Natural History Society of Paris: 'A menagerie like those that princes and kings are accustomed to maintain is nothing but a costly and unnecessary imitation of Asiatic pomp; but we think that a menagerie without frills could be extremely useful to natural history, to physiology and to the economy.'[78] It would also, so it was believed, contribute to public instruction. Similar ideas lay behind the building of zoos in German cities. And the same values were clearly at play in the modern open zoological garden pioneered by Carl Hagenbeck near Hamburg: Hagenbeck's Stellingen was to

[77] Sternberger, *Panorama*, p. 65.
[78] Ellenberger, 'The Mental Hospital and the Zoological Garden', p. 65.

make money, serve the cause of animal psychology, and elevate the public at the same time. One of his scientific assistants, Alex Sokolovsky, remarked that 'the animal park has the effect of a temple dedicated to nature, which educates, enlightens and edifies its visitors.' This 'instructive, enlightening, and educational influence on the popular masses', he added, should be 'valued as a cultural factor.'[79]

Sokolovsky noted that the mood of visitors to Stellingen was 'almost pious'.[80] This kind of reverential approach was one which the new custodians of public culture clearly welcomed and sought to encourage. It was a feature of many of the artistic and musical associations.[81] At the theatre, audience restraint became a mark of public respectability: by the 1870s both the theatre- and concert-going public had ceased to interrupt proceedings with calls for the repetition of a particular aria, scene, or movement, and concentrated their applause instead at the end of the performance. Talking during the performance came to be equally frowned upon, and the dimming of house lights reinforced this taboo. This significant pattern of public behaviour began around the middle of the century and soon became general. Wagner insisted on it at Bayreuth.[82]

This discussion of respectability and 'correct' forms of public conduct brings us to a final subject to which German sociologists and ethnologists as well as historians have devoted valuable attention: taste, fashion, and dress. Just as the public restaurant, zoo, and philanthropic association were, in their different ways, manifestations of a new form of public life in which the bourgeoisie *de facto* set the tone, so something of the same was true in the emergence of correct forms of public dress. In the corporate state, *Kleiderordnungen* had

[79] A. Sokolovsky, *Carl Hagenbeck und sein Werk* (Leipzig, 1928), pp. 42, 56. See in general the chapter on 'Carl Hagenbeck als Erzieher', pp. 23–66.

[80] Ibid., p. 41.

[81] Nipperdey, 'Verein als soziale Struktur', pp. 192ff.

[82] R. Sennett, *The Fall of Public Man* (Cambridge, 1972), p. 206. It is noteworthy that Sennett draws the majority of the illustrative material for his stimulating book from Britain and France. As in so many areas of this kind—'bourgeois' taste, the 'bourgeois' reading public, the rise of the 'bourgeois' novel (and especially the detective novel)—the German bourgeoisie is tacitly passed over and thereby rendered exceptional to an extent that scarcely seems to accord with the evidence available.

laid down the appropriate form of dress for the various estates.[83] State, ecclesiastical, seigneurial, and guild authorities had sanctions with which to police these regulations. But these sartorial prescriptions had never been absolutely enforced, and they were palpably breaking down after the middle of the eighteenth century. The debate over 'luxury' was a symptom of this, and the process was later discussed with characteristic relish by novelists such as Freytag.[84] What came to replace the *Kleiderordnungen* was the market. Fashion, in both its narrow and broad meanings, was therefore a product of the new material and social order. Within good society, fashion (especially for women) became canonized by the fashion magazines which began in the eighteenth century. Parallel to this, the top hat and frock coat, trousers, and boots, became the badges of male respectability. They stood sartorially in contradistinction to both the breeches and stovings worn by the aristocracy, and to the peasant smock or workers' fustian.[85] The establishment of gentlemen's outfitters such as the Goldene Hundertzehn in Berlin set the standard.

It was important, however, that this form of dress was strictly neither required nor prohibited by law. In this sphere, as in others, respectability was formally permitted to all, just as all were formally permitted to bequeath property, join the philanthropic society, or dine at Wilkens Keller. It does, in fact, seem to be the case that 'correct' dress became standardized in the nineteenth century along the lines described above. Fashion, in this broader sense, grew out of the development of a larger market for clothing. This resulted from the decline of household subsistence, the availability of new fabrics like cotton which allowed clothing to be changed more often, and by the appearance of ready-made clothing. This became available for men from the 1830s, for women from the following decade. Like the great

---

[83] O. Lauffer, 'Ausstattung nach Stand und Rang', in *Wirtschaft und Kultur. Festschrift zum 70. Geburtstag von Alphons Dopsch* (Leipzig, 1938), pp. 512–34.

[84] Deneke, 'Fragen der Rezeption bürgerlicher Sachkultur', pp. 50–1; Lauffer, 'Ausstattung', p. 523.

[85] Deneke, 'Fragen der Rezeption bürgerlicher Sachkultur', p. 59; Sagarra, *Tradition and Revolution*, p. 23.

nineteenth-century exhibitions, these changes in dress prompted renewed complaints about 'false taste and vanity'.[86] So did the newspaper advertisements and travelling sales-men later used to popularize cheap, standard clothing. Un-fortunately for the advocates of 'tradition', however, they discovered the virtues of the peasant costume about the same time that the peasant discovered the mail-order catalogue. (In much the same way, the arts-and-crafts movement began at the time when a truly independent craft mode of pro-duction was disappearing.) It is worth noting, anyway, that the praise heaped on the peasant *Tracht* by zealous advo-cates was itself a highly stylized affair of fashion. Urban enthusaists did much to invent rural 'tradition' in the nine-teenth century. The commercialization of stylized peasant costume was the sartorial counterpart of the way in which urban notables formalized and helped to commercialize rural processions and small-town carnivals. The *Trachtverein*, or costume association, perfectly summed up this example of new wine in old bottles. Here, too, 'anti-materialism' worked with the grain of the new market, not against it.[87]

There are two distinct, but closely connected, respects in which we can view the changes discussed above as evi-dence for the arrival of a new kind of bourgeois society. It is the tension between these two meanings that will occupy us in the next chapter of the essay. The first respect in which such a view makes sense does not require us to see the in-dividual bourgeois as a social hero, as a Promethean figure at the root of everything. Quite the reverse, in fact. Like the market system, legal codes, voluntary associations, the sub-scription concert hall, and the public zoo were not exclusively founded, operated, supported, and patronized by socio-logically copper-bottomed bourgeois. That was precisely the point. It had been the hallmark of the corporate state and society that the different estates had different, prescribed

[86] Deneke, 'Fragen der Rezeption bürgerlicher Sachkultur', pp. 60-5; R. Koenig, *The Restless Image* (London, 1973), pp. 112-15, 148-53.
[87] Blackbourn, *'Mittelstand'*, pp. 426-7; Deneke, 'Fragen der Rezeption bürgerlicher Sachkultur', pp. 62-5; T. Gantner, 'Brauchtumsvorführungen in Festumzügen des 19. Jahrhunderts', in Wiegelmann (ed.), *Kultureller Wandel*, pp. 83-7; *Masken zwischen Spiel und Ernst. Beiträge des Tübinger Arbeitskreises für Fasnachtforschung* (Tübingen, 1967), pp. 58-60, 80ff., 211-15.

forms of material expenditure, sociability, and edification. The law, in turn, underwrote this state of affairs. The point of bourgeois society was that such prescriptions and pro-scriptions fell, to be replaced by the formally non-prescriptive disciplines of the market. These were also supported by a corresponding legal system. It is manifestly the case that non-bourgeois exchanged goods and services, were treated under a common legal system, and constituted formal mem-bers of the 'public'. Here the sociological identity of the individual actor was less important than the status of the action. It made a difference that artisan or peasant living standards became a matter of income and fashion, not of corporate regulation. It made a difference when an aristocrat supported an association on voluntary terms, rather than demand that others support him on the basis of caste loyalty or corporate subordination. It made a difference whether the prince supported a writer by procuring his works through a bookseller, or through direct patronage. Artisans and aristo-crats, peasants and princes were notionally bound by the same ground rules of a single, anonymous bourgeois society. The very universality of the claims made by that society was one of its chief recommendations.

The problem was that this universality was more impressive as rhetoric than as reality. In practice it was the bourgeoisie that occupied a dominant position in the newly ordered society: that was the second sense in which we may speak of a bourgeois society. This dominance in practice was a liability which set limits to the bourgeois achievement. As I have already tried to indicate, bourgeois dominance in Germany was most effective where it was most silent and anonymous, where its forms and institutions came to seem most natural. It was correspondingly most vulnerable where *de facto* bourgeois strength was most evident, where achieve-ments were noisily celebrated, and where the anonymous forces of the market and the rule of law were believed to veil a more particular class interest. At these points the claim to embody a universal or general interest within society came to seem threadbare, and the very visibility of dominance threatened to defeat its own purpose. The central paradox of the bourgeois revolution in Germany was therefore that the more openly it appeared to be successful, the more its claims could be challenged and the more visible the target at which opponents could aim.

III
Economy and Society: The Shadow Side

1. *Organized Capitalism and Cultural Despair*

It should be clear from what has already been said that this essay is not concerned to foster the myth of a heroic bourgeois success story. The emphasis of the previous section on positive achievements has nevertheless been necessary for two main reasons. First, it redresses the balance by providing a counterpoint to those familiar arguments about the relentless failures of the German bourgeoisie. Secondly, it provides the necessary context for considering some arguments about the limitations of German bourgeois society which are rather different in emphasis from those often advanced. Usually, as we saw earlier, the stress has been placed on sins of omission. The German bourgeoisie, we have been told, failed to find a public role commensurate with its economic strength, preferring to take the money and run; it failed to embrace the 'modern', turning instead to pessimism and cultural despair; it failed to develop a responsible sense of social engagement, retreating rather into civic quietism; it failed to impose its own values on society, allowing itself to become feudalized; and it failed, finally, to muster sufficient self-confidence as a class to do more than genuflect before the mighty state. It will be suggested below that these arguments, as usually posed, amount to a series of half-truths. The principal problem with bourgeois society in Germany was not its absence but its ambiguity: the bourgeoisie was as much a victim of its contradictory successes as its outright failures. It is in the light of this proposition that I want to consider now some problems and contradictions of the society which emerged in nineteenth-century Germany. These might be labelled its shadow side. Like the matters discussed in the previous section, these problems bear a family resemblance to those in other European countries. That is something I shall try to indicate as I look at the particular form these problems assumed in the German case.

I want to start by exploring the shadow side of the most basic bourgeois achievement: the capitalist system itself. Its positive achievements were clear enough. It could plausibly claim advantages of both efficacy and equity over what it had replaced. The unlocking of productive capacity and the creation of a national market within an international economy banished the necessity of dearth which had been visited on German populations up to 1848.[1] Employment was generated and increased levels of consumption brought about. Opportunities became available for entrepreneurial talent as old restrictions, both material and institutional, were pushed aside. The heady optimism of the 1850s and 1860s reflected confidence in this 'natural' progress.

Both efficacy and equity had their limits, however, and progress became less automatic than many hoped. Instability of a new kind, that of the business cycle, replaced the earlier cycles of dearth and pauperization. One thinks especially of the Great Depression between 1873 and 1896, the most obvious caesura in the development of German capitalism between mid-century and 1914. This period included three major economic down-turns within a quarter of a century.[2] But the Great Depression was also flanked by other cyclical troughs: 1857, 1901-2, 1907-9. All had adverse effects in varying degrees on employment, output, investment, profits, and dividends.[3] No less important, they had their impact on business confidence, with important consequences flowing from this. One effect was to accelerate an already apparent tendency towards business concentration, and the idyll of a society of middling property-owners lost any vestige of reality. Germany became noted for the size and number of its largest concerns and for the cartels that they formed. Initially the latter were defensive and tactical, 'horizontal' cartels of manufacturers in the same branch looking for market stability at a time of recession. But 'vertical' cartels

[1] See esp. the works of Wilhelm Abel, e.g. *Der Pauperismus in Deutschland am Vorabend der industriellen Revolution* (Dortmund, 1966).
[2] The outstanding account remains Rosenberg, *Grosse Depression.*
[3] The statistical indices are usefully brought together in G. Hohorst, J. Kocka, G. A. Ritter (eds.), *Sozialgeschichtliches Arbeitsbuch II. Materialien zur Statistik des Kaiserreichs 1870-1914* (Munich, 1978), esp. pp. 78-81.

208 The Discreet Charm of the Bourgeoisie

also appeared, uniting different stages of production under one controlling interest and seeking the strategic objective of institutionalized market domination. Thus, to the extent that we can talk of a natural self-righting of the capitalist economy, this was achieved at the cost of significant levels of concentration.[4] Naturally, the rhetoric of opportunity continued, in business and other circles. In 1880, for example, we find a clergyman assuring workers that 'the poorest journeyman can work himself up to be the greatest factory owner. Legislation can hardly guarantee a greater freedom than this.'[5] But it is clear that the direct avenues of upward mobility were closing for 'journeymen', and indeed for small businessmen and master craftsmen.[6] In the new industrial branches it is true that there were examples of men from humble backgrounds who had risen to entrepreneurial prominence. Bosch and Daimler spring to mind. But these remained more exceptional than their counterparts of fifty years earlier; and in the new sectors, concentration followed the buccaneering phase of growth more quickly than it had in the older industrial branches.

We have seen that business concentration was stimulated by uncertainty about the market. But lack of confidence and anxiety on this score were not confined to the major owners and controllers of capital. An event such as the panic of 1857 or the crash of 1873 had a broader ripple-effect which created a wider public sense of instability: on labour, on small investors and on the small producer who was especially hard hit by recession, as he had been in earlier and rather different crises. Crises of the new kind reinforced criticism of the 'natural laws' of capitalism as unnatural. Often this criticism was couched in language taken from older pre-capitalist traditions, like the just price or the principle of a right to subsistence; sometimes the critics strained for an idiom appropriate to the novelty of the

---

[4] Kitchen, *Political Economy*; Böhme, *Introduction*; Rosenberg, *Grosse Depression*.
[5] Engelsing, *Sozial- und Wirtschaftsgeschichte*, p. 148.
[6] For a concise and differentiated summary of a large body of evidence, see J. Kocka, *Unternehmer in der deutschen Industrialisierung* (Göttingen, 1975), esp. pp. 47–50. See also Blackbourn, 'Between Resignation and Volatility'.

offence. It should not be imagined that we are dealing here only with working-class insecurity and anger. The young German labour movement did indeed argue against the 'iron law of wages' or the prospect of 'immiseration'. But the last quarter of the century also witnessed sharp hostility from small investors and (especially) from small producers towards the alleged 'swindles' of 'parasitic mobile capital'. It is significant in all these cases that not only did a breakdown in the natural working of the capitalist economy occur; it was also seen to occur. For that was another novelty, albeit involuntary, of the new order. It was in the logic of share prices and dividends that they could hardly remain a secret; and their very public quality provides a metaphor of capitalism's potential vulnerability.[7]

Two important developments were given impetus by this complex of new instabilities and anxieties. Both have a considerable bearing on the general argument of this essay. First, we can identify a growing preference on the part of the economic bourgeoisie in the narrow sense for retreating behind the scenes, away from critical public scrutiny. The boundlessly optimistic prospectuses of railway, steamship, and mining promoters in the 1850s and 1860s gave way to the discreet conclaves of cartel managers, the off-stage machinations of interest-group functionaries.[8] The advent of the time-and-motion man in the same period suggested a further retreat in a different sense: technological considerations and 'efficiency' often came to be regarded as ends in themselves, divorced from the heady language which had accompanied earlier business salesmanship. This was partly a matter of bureaucratization in big business. But the parallel retreat of businessmen from public life and politics at its various levels, and the preference for forceful but discreet

[7] Basic details in Kitchen, *Political Economy,* and Böhme, *Introduction.* Rosenberg, *Grosse Depression* and *Die Weltwirtschaftskrise von 1857–59* (Stuttgart, 1934) provide excellent pointers. I have tried to discuss the ideas of 'scandal' and 'swindle' in 'Between Resignation and Volatility'. For some thoughtful observations on 'natural' and 'unnatural' laws, see Gugel, *Industrieller Aufstieg,* pp. 167–79.

[8] See esp. H. Jaeger, *Unternehmer in der deutschen Politik* (Bonn, 1967); H. Kaelble, *Industrielle Interessenpolitik in der wilhelminischen Gesellschaft* (Berlin, 1970); D. Stegmann, *Die Erben Bismarcks: Parteien und Verbände in der Spätphase des Wilhelminischen Deutschlands* (Cologne, 1970).

lobbying cannot be explained in organizational terms alone.[9] This public reticence born out of prudent anxiety was not a uniquely German phenomenon, any more than the uneven growth of mature capitalism.[10] But the nature and timing of economic change in Germany seem to have made the problem especially pronounced.

The second major outcome of instability and anxiety was a qualitatively new interlocking of business and state towards the end of the century. This, no less than growing levels of concentration, became a characteristic of what historians in the Federal Republic have dubbed 'organized capitalism' and their colleagues in the Democratic Republic 'state monopoly capitalism'.[11] It will be necessary to return in Chapter IV below to consider the implications of these two approaches for our view of the German state. It is enough here to note that both interpretations are agreed that the increased interlocking of state and economy had two main purposes. First, it sought to steady uneven economic development by means of tariffs, arms contracts, and the opportunities afforded by *Weltpolitik* (world policy); secondly it aimed to contain social conflict through the granting of concessions to specific classes and interests. It was a response, in short, to features of the economic order which belied the possibility that it could spontaneously generate material and social harmony. When the virtues of 'natural' economic laws became less self-evident, the state was required to lend its own authority to try and restore equilibrium. Business cooperation with state authority on closer terms, and its retreat from open public life, were two sides of the same coin. Each was the product of social anxiety. As businessmen disappeared from parliaments, they reappeared in government

[9] The decline of businessmen in parliaments, both local and national, is detailed by Jaeger, *Unternehmer,* pp. 25-106. For a differentiated analysis of a particular group and region, see T. Pierenkemper, *Die westfälischen Schwerindustriellen 1852-1913* (Göttingen, 1979), pp. 61-70.

[10] On the pre-1914 background in France, Italy, and Germany to a 'corporatism' which short-circuited parliament, see C. Maier, *Recasting Bourgeois Europe* (Princeton, 1975), pp. 3-39.

[11] See H. A. Winkler (ed.), *Organisierter Kapitalismus* (Göttingen, 1974). For a discussion of the terms, see G. Eley, 'Capitalism and the Wilhelmine State: Industrial Growth and Political Backwardness in German Historiography, 1890-1918', *Historical Journal,* 21 (1978), 737-50.

commissions. The character of the chambers of commerce, part interest group and part government agency, perfectly expressed these twin responses of the business élite to economic uncertainty. [12]

The same combination of anxiety and narrowing horizons helps to set the phenomenon of cultural pessimism into context. This has so often been noted as a symptom of German peculiarity that the terms of the indictment are familiar: the rejection of western rationalism, the tormented relationship to nature, with its blood-and-soil undertones, the yearning for the organic rather than mechanical society. Central to most accounts has been the argument that Germans of the educated class celebrated the peculiar virtues of their own culture by way of contrast to the mere civilizations of the superficial and degenerate French and the money-grubbing English. And the reaction against western modernity in its various forms has been viewed as culminating in the rejection of advanced industrial society from the last decades of the nineteenth century.

This approach has enjoyed much popularity, and it would certainly be a wilful historian who failed to acknowledge that it has something of importance to tell us. In the work of Fritz Stern, George Mosse, and others the writings of selected intellectuals have been used to isolate and examine such a cast of mind; others have added valuable detail on the mandarin other-worldliness in the universities, and on the prevalence of hostility towards the 'asphalt city'. [13] The yearning for a 'whole' and 'organic' society is as well attested among the 'agrarian' intellectuals as it is in the Youth Movement. It is clear that cultural pessimism was a powerful current in the *Bildungsbürgertum* generally and in the academic milieu in

---

[12] W. Fischer, *Unternehmerschaft, Selbstverwaltung und Staat. Die Handel-skammern in der deutschen Wirtschafts- und Staatsverfassung des 19. Jahrhunderts* (Berlin, 1964). Diefendorf, *Businessmen and Politics*, has valuable material on this 'incorporation' of businessmen during an earlier period. Gugel, *Industrieller Aufstieg*, also has much to say on the issue.

[13] Stern, *The Politics of Cultural Despair*; Mosse, *The Crisis of German Ideology*; F. Ringer, *The Decline of the German Mandarins* (Cambridge, Mass., 1969); K. Bergmann, *Agrarromantik und Grossstadtfeindschaft* (Meisenheim am Glan, 1970).

particular.[14] Paul Honigsheim, a young member of Max Weber's Heidelberg circle before the First World War, has written of the 'trend away from the bourgeois way of life, city culture, instrumental rationality, quantification, scientific specialisation, and everything else then considered abhorrent phenomena'.[15] Nor can we miss the evidence that suggests the anti-western thrust of such attitudes. German music, for example, was widely praised for its greater 'spiritual' value as against the prosaic—in every sense—novel of the French and English. Diederich Hessling, Heinrich Mann's fictional creation, can be seen as an embodiment of these and similar values.[16] Indeed the hostility to the supposed superficiality of French and English *mores* extended across a broad spectrum. Nineteenth-century fashion historians such as Friedrich Vischer and Max von Boehn were savage in their criticism of French artificiality and refinement. They contrasted this frivolity and affectation with German naturalness.[17] In a similar way, German hunting was compared favourably with the courtly affectation of the French *Parforcejagd* and the shallow brutality of the English *Reitjagd*.[18]

As a means of getting to grips with the German bourgeois mind, this approach nevertheless has its limitations, at least in the familiar form. In the first place, the presumption of German peculiarity fares poorly on the comparative test. There are clear analogues elsewhere in Europe to the irrationalism, rediscovery of nature, and rejection of arid modernity which have been so relentlessly catalogued in the German case. One thinks of *fin de siècle* France, Karl Kraus's Vienna, the generation of 1898 in Spain. Here, too, cultural pessimism had a powerful purchase on the minds of the educated bourgeoisie, and such currents of thought commonly contained a powerful rhetoric about the need to preserve national

[14] Vondung (ed.), *Das Wilhelminische Bildungsbürgertum*, is a valuable collection of essays whose editor and authors take reception studies of these phenomena seriously.

[15] Cited in M. Löwy, *Georg Lukács—From Romanticism to Bolshevism* (London, 1979), p. 38.

[16] Heinrich Mann, *Der Untertan* (1918), available in English as *Man of Straw*.

[17] Koenig, *Restless Image*, pp. 32, 136.

[18] M. Marx-Kruse and E. von Campe, *Chronik der deutschen Jagd* (Ebenhausen, 1937), pp. 295-7. The Prussian cavalry, however, adopted a modified version of English hunting.

cultural virtue from foreign contamination. In the late-Victorian and Edwardian period, claims about a peaceful and uniquely harmonious 'English way of life'[19] occupied an equivalent place: they were a typically understated cele-bration of national cultural superiority.

If we compare like with like, moreover, there is a further parallel which can be drawn between England and Germany. Let us consider educated bourgeois reactions to English industrialism in the first half of the nineteenth century with the equivalent reactions in Germany at the end of the cen-tury. For each was a reaction to the most advanced and predatory European capitalism of its time: just as Marx saw the alienated future inscribed in Manchester of the 1840s, so Max Weber saw a new 'iron cage' being created by Germany's American-style, time-and-motion capitalism. When we make this comparison it is clear that many of the charges later levelled in Germany against dehumanizing modernity were already prefigured in England by the indictment of Coleridge, Southey, Carlyle, and other members of the clerisy. Even the terms of the argument were very similar: culture vaunted as more organic and superior to merely mechanical civi-lization. It is, in fact, a pleasing irony that the vocabulary of German Romanticism should have provided English critics with ammunition against the new order. Raymond Williams is only the most prominent of those who have addressed this problem.[20] It is not, in fact, the incidence of such ideas that ought to surprise us in itself, but rather the treatment of the German case as an aberration. As James Sheehan has re-cently reminded us, in talking about late nineteenth-century cultural pessimism, 'there was, of course, nothing especially new or uniquely German about this; self-criticism seems to be a persistent and pervasive part of bourgeois culture.'[21]

This is not to say, of course, that Germany was just like everywhere else; but the weight that should be attached to cultural pessimism, and the particular context in which it

[19] See M. Wiener, *English Culture and the Decline of the Industrial Spirit 1850-1980* (Cambridge, 1981), esp. pp. 41-80.

[20] R. Williams, *Culture and Society 1780-1950* (London, 1958).

[21] J. J. Sheehan, *German Liberalism in the Nineteenth Century* (Chicago, 1978), p. 254.

should be placed, needs close examination in the German case, as it does in others. The point is certainly well taken that we should, at least, place the German experience on a continuum, not isolate it as something *sui generis*. But Sheehan also makes another important point: that cultural pessimism was actually characteristic of bourgeois societies. We return here to one of the central arguments of this essay. At least in the middle decades of the nineteenth century, as we have seen, German businessmen and educated bourgeoisie alike were often fulsome in their optimism about the new mechanical civilization. Subsequent pessimism should be viewed in that light. For cultural despair, in its more or less differentiated forms, was only one possible response to a more general anxiety. That anxiety has already been touched on in the strict context of the economy. There it arose from bourgeois doubts about the implications of its own achievement. In the case of cultural despair more generally it was the fruits of success, not of failure, which proved to be sour.

Take the railway as an example. We have seen how it became a paramount symbol of the brave new world of Progress. From the beginning, however, there had been a shadow side: paeans of praise were mingled with expressions of fear. The very speed of the new means of communication excited alarm among many; there was widespread anxiety that the passengers became mere 'projectiles', sustaining harmful physiological and psychological effects from being shaken and jolted. A sizeable medical and pseudo-medical literature, similar to that of other European countries, gave voice to these anxieties.[22] As the railway came to seem more natural, such anxieties became submerged: a sentimental *Heimat* author like Auerbach was even able to write about an 'idyll on the railway'.[23] A major accident or boiler explosion could nevertheless serve to trigger a sense of alarm and induce a flutter in public opinion. Hope and fear were always two sides of the same coin.

This double-edged quality to the reception of the railway takes on added significance when it is placed in a social

[22] Schivelbusch, *Railway Journey*, pp. 58–60, 118–25; Sternberger, *Panorama*, p. 21; Sagarra, *Tradition and Revolution*, p. 19.

[23] Riedel, 'Vom Biedermeier zum Maschinenzeitalter', p. 123.

context. In the 1840s it had been reluctant kings who complained that their cobblers and tailors were now able to travel as fast as they could.[24] But the general point was not lost on a bourgeoisie which became more socially defensive in the course of the nineteenth century. Compartments of different class were one way of preserving the necessary distinctions. But this could also prove an ambiguous solace, as demonstrated by the 'panics' of the 1860s over a series of murders, assaults, and robberies in isolated first-class railway compartments. As one commentator noted in the 1870s, 'the passenger is so pleased when he finds a vacant compartment; but he is not so fortunate when he acquires a fellow passenger who robs him in his sleep, or perhaps even murders him, and then ejects his body from the compartment piecemeal, without attracting the train personnel's attention.'[25] Such panics, as we know from recent studies of similar English and French outbreaks of the same period, had relatively little to do with the objective degree of danger.[26] But they do offer a telling commentary on the way in which half-submerged social anxieties could turn into outright social panic. It is likely that the genre of 'railway murder' detective stories (which flourished in Germany, as in England) reinforced fearful bourgeois imaginations.

The railway had another effect which could heighten social anxiety: the impact of railway construction on the urban landscape. It was reported from one German city that after the building of a new railway terminal, the bourgeois character of the adjacent street was disagreeably transformed: 'The solid, massive buildings reverberate from the continuous shocks, and inhabitants who formerly . . . looked for quietness and greenery lose their "serenity".' This writer concluded gloomily that 'in the future, the great Leipziger Strasse will

[24] W. Pöls, (ed.), *Deutsche Sozialgeschichte. Dokumente und Skizzen*, Band I: *1815-1870* (Munich, 1973), p. xiv.
[25] Heusinger von Waldegg, cited in Schivelbusch, *Railway Journey*, p. 88.
[26] J. Davis, 'The London Garotting Panic of 1862: A Moral Panic and the Creation of a Criminal Class in Mid-Victorian England', and R. Tombs, 'Crime and the security of the State: the "dangerous classes" and insurrection in 19th Century Paris', both in V. A. C. Gatrell, B. Lenman, G. Parker (eds.), *Crime and the Law. The Social History of Crime in Western Europe since 1500* (London, 1980).

most probably be a thoroughfare of factories.'[27] The town, like the railway, was of course a double-edged achievement itself. It was the seat of bourgeois material wealth, social power, and cultural pre-eminence; and it testified to a power which could tame disordered nature. But the town and city were also conceived as the incubators of social disorder, spawning crime and social movements which seemed to threaten private property. Werner Sombart's remarks about the 'barbarism' of 'unrooted and uprooted proletarians' were not exceptional.[28] They illuminate a widespread anxiety about the unintended effects of material and social development, in a period when uneven economic growth and the rise of a strong labour movement had weakened the belief in harmonious social progress.

It is difficult to suppress a degree of cynicism when fears of this kind were voiced in the extravagant language of 'barbarism' and cultural decline. One is tempted to lay down a plank labelled hypocrisy to bridge the distance between inflated rhetoric and everyday reality. This temptation is probably best resisted. Cultural pessimism was not simply a mandarin affair, however, floating above class perceptions. The mingled hostility and anxiety towards organized labour and criminality (which were often conflated), as towards servants and prostitutes (also often conflated),[29] was the product of a bourgeois disenchantment with the ambiguous results of its own success. The degree and speed of this success only increased the degree of disenchantment, for it sharpened the sense of what stood to be lost. That fears of this kind were frequently based on alarmed misperceptions does not entitle us to call them hypocritical; it no more allows us to treat them as a form of cultural despair in the abstract.

Responses of this nature were probably sharper in Germany than they were elsewhere: the speed of demographic and economic change helped to intensify them. To that extent,

---

[27] Schivelbusch, *Railway Journey*, pp. 172–3.
[28] Bausinger, 'Verbürgerlichung', pp. 38–9.
[29] R. Schulte, *Sperrbezirke. Tugendhaftigkeit und Prostitution in der bürgerlichen Welt* (Frankfurt/M., 1979); R. J. Evans, 'Prostitution, State and Society in Imperial Germany, *Past and Present*, 70 (1976), 106–29.

those who have laid stress on bourgeois cultural despair in Germany appear to be right after all, even if their angle of vision has sometimes seemed rather narrow. But pessimism, in whatever context, was still only half the story. Undue emphasis on it, moreover, threatens to obscure what was actually distinctive in the German case. For it was not cultural despair as such that was peculiarly German; it was the fact that it was so strikingly conjoined with a continuing affirmation of so many features of urban, mechanical life, with all its attendant artefacts and cultural forms. This continuing strain of shallow optimism produced widespread pride in the powerful electrical and chemical industries; it produced the enormous respect accorded to the natural and applied sciences; it produced complacent allusions to the ever more complete provision of sewerage pipes; it produced enthusiasm for the Zeppelin; and it produced a strong sense of identification, in bourgeois circles above all, with the growth of the navy, supreme symbol of Germany's burgeoning industrial and commercial power. These artefacts and institutions were very decidedly 'made in Germany', alongside yearnings for the harmonious and organic society.

It is not the case that between the middle and the late nineteenth century cultural optimism simply gave way to cultural pessimism, that belief in progress yielded to despair. The reality was a complex juxtaposition of the two. On the one hand, anxiety did indeed give rise to a sense of cultural disenchantment. But this was seldom a blanket rejection of the modern world, and anxiety could also manifest itself in an optimism which was more brittle and often therefore more facile and narrowly conceived than that associated with earlier decades. Earlier material advances had often been welcomed effusively; but they were still usually connected with a fairly vigorous sense of social and moral progress. By the last decades before 1914 it is difficult to escape the impression that statistics on industrial production and sewerage pipes had assumed a more complacently materialistic importance. A self-satisfied statistical compilation such as Karl Helfferich's *Deutschlands Volkswohlstand*[30] may stand as an

---

[30] *Deutschlands Volkswohlstand 1888–1913* (Berlin, 1913).

example of this unthinkingly technocratic cast of mind. For many German bourgeois, material advances were best contemplated in isolation, shorn of awkward social or moral questions. They were treated as providing their own justification, rather as the 'interesting facts' in newspapers and children's encyclopedias were left simply to speak for themselves. This suggests parallels with the attitude of large capitalists which we have already noted. Narrowly conceived materialism of the kind described above was the counterpart of their retreat into economic interest groups, time-and-motion studies and organized capitalism. As we shall see in the following chapter, there are further parallels in the spheres of law, culture, and associational life.

Vulgar materialism and 'vulgar idealism' thus existed side by side: both assumed a heightened form in Germany and each reinforced the other. Although there were clearly exceptions, the line between the two ran roughly between business and allied, more technocratic professions on the one hand, and the classic *Bildungsbürgertum* on the other. The former tended towards a brittle optimism, the latter towards a stylized pessimism. What had united the propertied and educated during the buoyant middle decades of the century now came to divide them in a period of greater self-doubt. But it would be no less true to add that the German bourgeoisie as a whole was ambivalent: individuals from varied backgrounds harboured divided feelings of optimism and pessimism, of 'shallow western' materialism and 'deep German' disenchantment. Perhaps the most intellectually impressive individual who maintained these two positions in a state of constant creative tension was Max Weber. Weber, who saw himself very self-consciously as a member of the bourgeois class, may be seen in this respect (as in others) as the exceptional individual who represents the heightened form of a more general condition. Weber, on the one hand, was acutely aware and proud of Germany's civilizing mission: he identified himself strongly with the liberating features of modern capitalism and technical organization, a position which was confirmed when he visited the United States and witnessed the dynamism of American society at first hand. He was scathing about those who sought a lazy-minded return to an imagined Arcadia. Yet he was fully alive to what, following a long line of German writers, he saw as the 'disenchantment of the world' (*die Entzauberung der Welt*) through the advance of cold rationality. Weber wrote with passion on the implications for society of rational calculation and 'this passion for bureaucracy'. 'The key question', he argued, 'is not how to further and stimulate this tendency, but how to oppose this machine-mentality and keep a part of humanity free from such fragmentation of the soul, from ultimate domination by the bureaucratic form of life.'[31] We have already noted the comments of Paul Honigsheim, a member of Weber's Heidelberg circle before 1914, on the prevalence of contemporary cultural despair. The adherents of this neo-Romanticism, he suggested, 'knew on whose door they should knock: Max Weber's door.'[32] But that, of course, is only half true. For Weber was able to combine his hopes and fears in a tortuously hard-won personal position of 'heroic pessimism'. This ambivalence remains one of the most compelling features of his thought.

At a lesser level we find many other examples of a comparable ambivalence. Heinrich von Treitschke was a coarse-grained advocate of material progress; but he frequently argued along lines which correspond closely to the received idea of 'German' cultural criticism—his remark that the English confuse soap and civilization, for example.[33] Similarly, it has often been noted that Walter Rathenau was a successful businessman of the most dynamic kind who liked to see himself as a prophet of cultural despair. Here, once again, the modern and anti-modern existed in an unstable compound.[34] Another prominent Wilhelmine entrepreneur,

[31] M. Weber, *Gesammelte Aufsätze zur Soziologie und Sozialpolitik* (Tübingen, 1924), p. 412. Cf. 'Science as a Vocation', in Gerth and Mills (eds.), *From Max Weber,* p. 155: 'The fate of our time is characterized by rationalization and intellectualization and, above all, by the "disenchantment of the world".' The best guide remains Mommsen, *Age of Bureaucracy.*
[32] Cited in Löwy, *Georg Lukács,* p. 38.
[33] On Treitschke, see G. Iggers, 'Heinrich von Treitschke', in H.-U. Wehler (ed.), *Deutsche Historiker,* II (Göttingen, 1971), 66–80. On the broader tradition of Anglophobia in academic historical circles, see B. Faulenbach, *Ideologie des deutschen Weges* (Munich, 1980), esp. pp. 122–67.
[34] J. Joll, *Intellectuals in Politics* (London, 1960), pp. 59–129; and 'The Contradictory Capitalist', *Times Literary Supplement,* 25 Aug. 1978.

Albert Ballin, is described by his biographer as 'forever oscillating between an optimistic exuberance and a neurotic, despairing and cynical fatalism'.[35] In each of these cases it is the ambiguity that strikes us. The same is true when we turn to look finally at attitudes towards nature and 'organic' rural society. Ulrich Brache has written with insight on 'the contradictory bourgeois self-consciousness' concerning changes in the countryside.[36] On the one side was a strongly idealized sense of the 'loss' sustained in the quality of life as the town came to dominate the country; on the other side was a feeling of pride and superiority that the new civilization should have effected such changes. A measure of this ambivalence was expressed, perhaps only half-consciously, in the way the German bourgeoisie reassured itself with a stylized vision of traditional rusticality, even while it took for granted the necessity for transforming rural society. The costume association was one manifestation of this sentiment. In a comparable way, the bourgeois reading public of the towns was able to enjoy a sentimental *Heimatsroman*, or the stories of yodelling peasants and cherry-picking maidens printed in the pages of the *Gartenlaube* and *Fliegende Blätter*.[37] There is a significant parallel here with England, where, as Raymond Williams has argued, 'a triumphant urban and industrial economy remade the countryside . . . in its own compensating image.'[38] The compensating image in Germany was perhaps more often elemental than pastoral by comparison with England. But it certainly embraced a range of responses to mountains, forests, and animals which make sense only if we remember the cosy and usually urban domesticity which nurtured them. It is illuminating to find that even the railway engine was clothed in the reassuring

[35] L. Cecil, *Albert Ballin* (Princeton, 1967), p. 29.

[36] U. Brache, 'Rezeption städtisch-bürgerlicher Formen und regionale Formen im bäuerlichen Wohninventar der Elbmarschen', in Wiegelmann (ed.), *Kultureller Wandel*, p. 72.

[37] Bausinger, 'Verbürgerlichung', pp. 34-9. Bramsted, *Aristocracy and Middle-Classes*, is illuminating on the *Gartenlaube* family journal. So is Hermann Glaser, *The Cultural Roots of National Socialism* (London, 1978), which explores the significance of its name ('The Arbour'), pp. 82-5. Glaser's sensitive study stands out from most works of its kind.

[38] Cited in Wiener, *English Culture*, p. 51. This is also one of the central arguments in Williams's stimulating *The Country and the City* (London, 1973).

language of nature, referred to constantly as an 'iron steed' or a 'winged wheel'. This 'blend of the technological and the organic' was characteristic.[39] The ambiguity it suggests offers a more convincing approach to patterns of German bourgeois thought than the habitual emphasis on the anti-modern alone. In its coy evasiveness, as well as in its ambiguity, it also sums up two of the major themes of this chapter.

2. *Legal Positivism, Civic Quietism, and 'Feudalization'*

The previous chapter considered the shadow side of German bourgeois society from a number of different angles. The central point was the advent of new anxieties, generated by the new social order itself, which expressed themselves through a narrowing of bourgeois horizons and a retreat from earlier optimism. I want to extend this argument now by examining, from a different perspective, three other developments which were identified earlier as major bourgeois achievements: the rule of law, the emergence of a vigorous associational life, and the rise of new public institutions and manners. I shall suggest that each of these advances shared the same double-edged quality as the capitalist market economy and mechanical progress. And in each case this aroused anxieties, more or less consciously voiced, which in turn prompted a retreat from the heroic postures of earlier decades. We encounter the same change of emphasis in the practice of law, the character of associational life, and the value placed on aspects of the new public domain like culture. Common to all was the increasingly ritual and formalized inflection given to what had earlier been proclaimed as the universal panaceas of bourgeois society. It is in this context, so I shall argue finally, that the 'feudalization' of the German bourgeoisie can most usefully be located.

In the middle decades of the nineteenth century many saw the achievement of formal legal equality and the secure anchoring of property rights in law as a litmus test of a true bourgeois society. Both principles were portrayed as an

---

[39] Sternberger, *Panorama*, pp. 23–5.

advance over the arbitrariness and the restrictions of absolutist state and corporate society. Equality before the law
and the sanctity of property rights nevertheless stood in a
potentially awkward relationship to each other. Formal
equality at one level matched substantive inequality at
another. In a society of citizens who were middling property-
owners this discrepancy would have been less obvious; but
nineteenth-century German society was moving in the
opposite direction. Law and its interpretation became, in
fact, an arena of potential conflict between different social
interests. The debate over the Civil Code made this clear,
when critics like Gierke argued that substantive inequality
undermined the principle of formal equality.[40] But this particular debate had many lesser counterparts. Lawyers sympathetic to labour, and those who were close to agrarian
interests, argued in their very different ways against what
they claimed to be the in-built bias of the legal system.
Like the peasant advocates of the earlier nineteenth century,[41] they sought to turn that system against itself, trying
to exploit its very flexibility to specific social ends. So, for
example, labour law, contract law, mortgage law, master and
servant law, and the legal principle of 'good faith' became
potentially matters of substantive social dispute dressed up
as formal legal disputation.

This tendency remained, however, marginal to the practice
of law in general. The possibility of social conflicts finding
legal expression in this way was perceived as a danger. This
produced its own reaction: a retreat into an increasingly
formal, even formalized definition of the law and its role.
'Legal certainty', a progressive idea in the middle decades
of the century, now took on the conservative overtones of
'legal positivism'. Imperial Germany has been dubbed an era
of legal positivism. What is meant by the term is that questions of law were addressed in the most restricted and narrow
spirit, stripped of their broader social, economic, and moral
significance. Public and private law came to be treated in

---

[40] Dilcher, 'Das Gesellschaftsbild der Rechtswissenschaft', pp. 55–66.
[41] For a description of one such 'peasant advocate' in south-west Germany,
Andreas Wiest, see C. Bauer, *Politischer Katholizismus in Württemberg bis zum
Jahre 1848* (Freiburg i.B., 1929), p. 128.

even more rigid isolation from each other, while the humanist background which had informed the work of legal theorists from Savigny to Windscheid was lost from sight. In an epigoni generation of academic jurists at the end of the century, Gierke was an exception in insisting that the law should not be divorced from broader considerations. Gierke, however, devoted attention increasingly to his Germanic and historical work, just as other prominent legally trained academics moved away from mainstream law into specialized fields such as ancient legal history (Theodor Mommsen), church law (Rudolf Sohm), or political science, economics, and sociology (Max Weber). The opponents of legal positivism within the universities were isolated and remained marginal.[42] The universities trained the legal officials and private lawyers; and legal positivism was not confined to academic jurists. Its spirit permeated the legal system, and it reflected a more general shift in bourgeois sentiment. Retreat into a narrow conception of law was a response to the possibility that law might become an arena invaded by social conflict. What has been called an 'evolutionary fatalism' enjoyed wide currency: a highly formalized notion of the law which held that the stage of legal development which had been reached must be defended as such; what was, had to be. At the same time it is possible to detect a parallel shift in bourgeois attitudes away from the idea of law as an offensive weapon against absolutist restrictions and corporate privilege, towards a more conservative view that what had to be inculcated was a 'sense of the law'. Law, in short, had started to become synonymous with order.[43]

There are marked similarities between this and the changing pattern of civic involvement and associational life in nineteenth-century Germany. The issue of civic quietism is, as we know, an important one. Beneath this common criticism of the bourgeoisie lies the idea that it failed to take a sufficiently active role in public life—that it lacked a developed civic spirit. As it stands, this charge is at best a half-truth. It hardly stands up to scrutiny even if we measure Germany against Anglo-Saxon societies, with their strong traditions of

---

[42] Dilcher, 'Das Gesellschaftsbild der Rechtswissenschaft', pp. 58–66.
[43] Gugel, *Industrieller Aufstieg*, pp. 89–91, 190–95.

voluntarism; it is actively misleading if we make the comparison with France. The problem in Germany was not civic quietism as such; it was the changing form assumed by civic activism in the course of the century. It is here, as we shall see, that the parallels with the law are so illuminating.

At its high point the 'passion for association' was the repository of extravagant claims. The association supposedly had a universal appeal, and in this respect enjoyed two advantages over corporate institutions. The association was universal in the sense of being accessible to the whole public as potential members; and it was universal in its objectives, addressing the 'common good' or 'public welfare'. Neither claim stood up very well in practice. Although notionally open to all, associations tended to be dominated in fact by a narrow élite. The possession of a certain level of education served as a filter which restricted access. In major associations, the level of membership fees and the method of recruiting new members (by personal recommendation and ballot) tended to reinforce this restrictiveness. Many associations became socially closed bodies which developed patterns of ritual, hierarchy, and narrow control which echoed those of the churches, courts, and aristocracies against which they had once tilted.[44] In this they closely resembled the professions which provided so many of their notables. By the end of the century the professions themselves had assumed many of the features of the old, closed corporations they had often replaced, with education rather than birth as the new arbiter.[45] This exclusive structure can be seen especially in the large and influential urban associations such as Museum Societies, Monday Clubs, and *Casinos*. Even in organizations like the gymnastic *Turner*, where an explicitly egalitarian rhetoric included the use of the familiar *Du* form, actual dominance fell to students and academics. There were, of course, still numerous links between the social classes in associational life. But what evidence we have suggests that

[44] Nipperdey, 'Verein als soziale Struktur', pp. 186-7.
[45] For a local study which places the advent of a 'self-recruiting' educated bourgeois élite in the first half of the century, see R. Elkar, *Junges Deutschland in polemischem Zeitalter. Das schleswig-holsteinisches Bildungsbürgertum in der ersten Hälfte des 19. Jahrhunderts* (Düsseldorf, 1979), esp. pp. 81-151.

the interlocking networks of voluntary associations typical
of so many towns were often, in fact, constellations around
one major club. Major social influence was located here, in
the Museum Society or *Honoratiorenclub*; and recruitment
to this was certainly tightly controlled.[46]
Bourgeois claims to exercise social leadership were therefore realized, in a sense, through associational life. But where
this leadership was too visibly apparent, a price might be
paid in terms of suspicion from other social classes. Certainly there was a tendency which grew in the course of the
century for other classes or excluded groups to adopt the
principle of association and form societies of their own. This
was the case, on the one hand, of the aristocracy and the
Catholic Church.[47] It was true, in the opposite direction, of
workers, who began to free themselves in the 1860s from
bourgeois tutelage (especially in the form of workers' educational associations) and establish their own workers'
associations.[48] In the case of both the Catholic Church and
the working class, the second half of the nineteenth century
witnessed the creation of a dense and impressive associational
network which presented an explicit challenge to the hallowed
idea of the association as a universal elixir which cut across
class and religious lines.[49] Some peasant associations at the
end of the century similarly constituted themselves as peasant-
only bodies. And there is considerable evidence that, as the
petty bourgeoisie became increasingly divided socially from

[46] Nipperdey, 'Verein als soziale Struktur', pp. 186-7. Zang (ed.), *Provinzialisierung*, has some excellent detail on the Konstanz Monday Club; and a
description of the Stuttgart Museum Society can be read in Pöls (ed.), *Deutsche
Sozialgeschichte*, pp. 94-5.

[47] An excellent study of the Westphalian aristocracy and its associations is
H. Reif, *Westfälischer Adel 1770-1860* (Göttingen, 1979), pp. 398-431. Reif
also has some very good general observations on the significance of associational
life.

[48] Most books on the emerging labour movement make some mention of this.
A good local study focused on the 1860s and workers' educational associations
is W. Schmierer, *Von der Arbeiterbildung zur Arbeiterpolitik* (Hanover, 1970).

[49] On the working-class associational 'subculture', see most recently W.
Guttsman, *The German Social Democratic Party 1875-1933* (London, 1981),
chs. 4-5. Similarly, as the Boniface, Pius, Kolping, and countless other associations testified, Germany (unlike, say, France or Italy) was 'the classic land
of the Catholic associational movement': H. Jedin (ed.), *Handbuch der Kirchen-
geschichte*, vol. VI. 2: *Die Kirche zwischen Anpassung und Widerstand (1878
bis 1914)* (Freiburg i.B., 1973), p. 220.

the bourgeoisie proper, so it too deserted the established societies and set up associations of its own.[50]

In terms of social access, therefore, the rhetoric of universality became rather threadbare. This had its effect, in turn, on the scope of societies' activities. The mosaic of associational life came to reproduce, rather than transcend, the class and sectional divisions of society; and the claim that association conduced to the common good or human happiness in general was seriously strained. Thus, in a second sense, the association began to reproduce the particularist features of the corporate society. Associations did not, in their areas of interest, cut across the divisions between household, family, and profession; they tended rather to confirm these divisions. Associations became more specialized and narrow in function in the latter part of the century. Cultural organizations, for instance, took an attitude to their particular fields of concern which was increasingly hardened and ritualized, bereft of any humanist or pedagogic imperative to reach beyond the narrow circle to a broader public. The growing specialization of academic and learned societies followed a similar pattern, and so did the increasingly important and strictly professional associations. Equally telling evidence of these changes is provided by the transformation of the association into the pressure group, above all the pressure group based on material interests. Business *Verbände* had a necessarily restricted membership, they worked for limited objectives, and they often operated (certainly in the case of the influential industrial organizations) as much behind closed doors as they did in public. Nothing could have been more removed in spirit or practice from the early association, with its broad social-cultural mission and its high public profile. The trend towards more specialized organizations therefore marked a diminution of public

[50] Paul Adam, a relatively prosperous and self-consciously respectable bookbinder, furnishes an example. On leaving Giessen in 1885 he gave up his post as secretary of the veterans association and his committee membership of the fire brigade and art association. Such honorary posts, he had already concluded, 'simply cost money and bring nothing in'. P. Adam, *Lebenserinnerungen eines alten Kunstbuchbinders* (Stuttgart, 1951), p. 95. Further detail in Blackbourn, '*Mittelstand*', pp. 409–33.

ambition; it also reinforced socially exclusive tendencies, since the preconditions for membership became self-evidently restricted to a narrower circle. This was one way in which civic concern became chanelled into increasingly specialized and narrow outlets; and associations, as a result, became depoliticized in the broadest sense.[51] Of a piece with this development was the degeneration of many societies into solely recreational gatherings. These clubs, in a sense, specialized in gregariousness, just as others came to specialize in medieval local history or in furthering the interests of the bottled beer trade.[52] Hence the plethora of cards and skittles clubs which have helped to form the image of German *Vereinsmeierei* since the last half of the nineteenth century.

Here, then, is civic quietism of a kind. But it is really much more a form of gelded civic activism, shaped by changes within German bourgeois society itself. It was a product of what I have described as a universal claim which was flawed in a twofold sense: in terms of access to public life, and in terms of function within public life. The narrowing horizons we can see, in both these senses, in the associations had obvious counterparts elsewhere: the retreat of businessmen into cartels and interest groups, of lawyers into a narrow positivism, of the professions generally into a tightly corseted professional ethos. The transformation of 'culture' into a frozen and exclusive property of the initiated was of a piece. Half a century of social experience divides the good intentions of the workers' education associations from the harsh strictures of a Werner Sombart on the 'barbarism' of proletarians who 'never listened to Schubert *Lieder* or Chopin *Nocturnes*'.[53] Practices such as dimming the house lights and new forms of audience restraint similarly underlined the cultic and socially exclusive nature of the actual cultural 'public'. This pattern of social exclusiveness extended even to the sartorial sphere. Here, too, what had once stood for social openness acquired a more formalized and conservative

[51] Nipperdey, 'Verein als soziale Struktur', pp. 190–205.
[52] There is a good local account of this process in K. Köstlin, 'Schleswig-Holsteinische Gilden im 19. Jahrhundert', in Wiegelmann (ed.), *Kultureller Wandel,* pp. 135–45.
[53] Bausinger, 'Verbürgerlichung', pp. 38–9.

meaning. The black suit had once been (like the moustache) a challenge to corporate restrictions; but it became the acme of 'bourgeois fashion',[54] a means of reinforcing new forms of exclusiveness rather than of challenging old ones. It represented, as Rene König has argued, a barrier as well as a standard. Dress was a means by which the bourgeoisie could be sure they were 'among their own kind', that they were not in a 'mixed crowd'.[55] Wealth, not corporate privilege, may have determined who was able to dine at the Ratskeller. The approved form of dress and etiquette nevertheless strengthened the barriers created by material natural selection. It is hardly surprising that the term *standesgemäss*, denoting correct conduct and appearance, was preserved from the vocabulary of the corporate society and pressed into service by the notables of bourgeois society. For they, in their professions, Museum Societies, and Ratskeller, came to exhibit a sense of caste which echoed that of the old nobility.

It is in this context that arguments about the feudalization of the bourgeoisie can usefully be placed. The susceptibility of the bourgeoisie to aristocratic influence and values has become a staple of historical writing on Germany. Few books dealing with this period neglect to mention the buying up of rural estates by the bourgeoisie, their hunt for honours and adoption of an aristocratic life-style. And indeed the evidence on the subject seems impressive. From the last third of the century especially, Rhenish and Westphalian manufacturers, Berlin bankers, and even Hanseatic patricians did buy up rural seats.[56] Max Weber was one contemporary who noted this. Another, Adolf von Wilke, remarked in his memoirs that if Fontane had lived to write a sequel to his *Wanderungen durch die Mark Brandenburg*, he would have found fewer old Junkers. These were dying out: but Fontane would have found that 'the new lords of the manor before the gates of Berlin are not just stupidly proud parvenus; they have partly themselves become ennobled.'[57] The research of

---

[54] Koenig, *Restless Image*, p. 158.
[55] Ibid., pp. 112–15, 148–53.
[56] See, e.g., F. Zunkel, *Der rheinisch-westfälische Unternehmer 1834–1879* (Cologne-Opladen, 1962).
[57] Cited in Ritter and Kocka (eds.), *Deutsche Sozialgeschichte*, p. 76.

Hans Rosenberg and others has amply vindicated these contemporary impressions. Buying a rural estate was only the first step for some bourgeois commoners; acquiring a title, even ennoblement, was the next. Certainly the bourgeois demand for titles and orders was intense, and the increased supply of them in Prussia under Wilhelm II was not enough to satisfy it.[58] At the same time, intermarriage between the wealthy bourgeoisie and the more impecunious nobility was a further feature of the late nineteenth century. The von Hoesch, von Haniel, and von Stumm dynasties exemplify this process of absorption.[59] In addition to this, historians have often pointed to the reserve officer corps and student duelling corporation as institutions that acted as a conduit through which aristocratic values were transmitted to the bourgeoisie. Heinrich Mann's Diederich Hessling is, once again, a favourite example. But more striking perhaps is the case of Theodor Heuss, later to become the first president of the Federal Republic. Born into a notably liberal family in a notably liberal state of the Reich, he felt obliged to study in Munich because of an accident which would have made it impossible for him to follow his brothers into a duelling corporation at Tübingen.[60]

All this is incontrovertible. But let us stop for a moment, surrounded by seemingly unmistakable evidence of 'feudalization', to consider the implications of what was happening. Max Weber himself had written that 'the entailed estate of the parvenu is one of the characteristic products of capitalism in an old country with aristocratic traditions and a military monarchy.' That seems clear enough. Weber continues, however: 'In the German East the same thing now takes place which has been going on in England for centuries.'[61] On this point Weber's judgement was sounder than on many things English. We could find no better witness to confirm his view than the English liberal Richard Cobden. In the 1860s he

---

[58] Jaeger, *Unternehmer,* pp. 160–3; Lewinsohn, *Das Geld in der Politik*, pp. 25–7.

[59] Lewinsohn, op. cit., pp. 21–2.

[60] T. Heuss, *Preludes to Life* (London, 1955), p. 119.

[61] M. Weber, 'Capitalism and Rural Society in Germany', in Gerth and Mills (eds.), *From Max Weber*, p. 383.

argued with some asperity that 'feudalism is every day more and more in the ascendant in political and social life. . . . Manufacturers and merchants as a rule seem only to desire riches that they may be enabled to prostrate themselves at the feet of feudalism.'[62] The point will hardly surprise a present-day English reader. Martin Wiener is only the latest in a long line of commentators who have noted this pattern. Wiener discusses how the English bourgeoisie turned away from the industrial and productive origins of its wealth and embraced instead the values of the old landed aristocracy. It did so through the purchase of landed property, building country houses, emulating an imagined gentry style of life, and educating its children in a manner which removed the stigma of trade. A similar debate has also exercised French historians, centred on the propensity of the dynastically minded French entrepreneur to settle his family in a rural seat once the necessary wealth has been acquired.[63] The phenomenon can be discerned to a greater or lesser extent in most industrial countries of Europe, as Arno J. Mayer's book on *The Persistence of the Old Regime* suggests. We should remember Lionel Trilling's axiom, perhaps, that 'money is terribly ashamed of itself.'[64]

How should we interpret this? Max Weber was surely right to see it as 'one of the characteristic products of capitalism'. Neither in Germany nor elsewhere should we view these events as a straightforward matter of bourgeois feudalization—as Arno Mayer is inclined to do. It signalled rather the formation of a newly extended dominant class, with a symbiotic relationship between the old and new parts of this class. In England the consolidation of a new ruling élite is well attested. In Germany it can be seen in the Stumm, Hoesch, and Haniel dynasties, as in the persons of those three indomitable champions of Germanization in Polish Prussia: Hansemann, the bourgeois who successfully aspired to become an estate owner, Kenne-

---

[62] Cited in A. Briggs, 'The Language of "Class" in Early Nineteenth-Century England', in Briggs and J. Saville (eds.), *Essays in Labour History* (London, 1960), p. 72, n. 4. I used this quotation in the German edition, and it was instructive to find exactly the same quotation being used by Martin Wiener in *English Culture*, p. 14.

[63] See n. 25, p. 171 for references.

[64] L. Trilling, *The Liberal Imagination* (London, 1970), p. 260.

mann the wealthy Junker in his own right, and Tiedemann the rich Junker who married into commercial capital.[65] This intermingling of the old and new was nothing out of the ordinary by European standards. Nor should we find it strange that bourgeois parvenus seized many of the symbols of the older class. What other symbols were there? As E. J. Hobsbawm has remarked, 'rising classes naturally tend to see the symbols of wealth and power in terms of what their former superior groups have established as the standards of luxury or pomp.'[66] In England the bourgeoisie was drawn to the institutions where it (or its children) could rub shoulders with landed society: Oxford and Cambridge, the local hunt, London clubland, the major sporting venues on the social calendar. Its country houses in 'Old English' and 'Queen Anne' made a similar point. The German bourgeoisie also marked its arrival by purchasing country estates, hunting, and educating its children for the learned professions and administrative élite. In just the same way, it rejected the simplicity of Biedermeier in its increasingly spacious houses and opted instead for gothic extravagance and armchairs with embossed leather covers depicting hunting scenes.

We should not confuse form and substance when we evaluate this. The terms on which the élite came together were at least as important as the 'traditions' with which it surrounded itself.[67] It would be misleading to interpret external symbols as a conclusive victory for the archaic values of a traditional caste. In many respects the Junkers actually demanded less of an accommodation on the part of the bourgeoisie. Unlike the more mellow and urbane English landed rentiers, the Junkers had fewer social pretensions and sensibilities which they could impose on newcomers. Probably

[65] Rosenberg, *Probleme*, p. 18.
[66] E. J. Hobsbawm, *The Age of Revolution* (London, 1977), p. 224. See also Riedel, 'Bürger, Staatsbürger, Bürgertum', p. 699: 'The emancipation of the bourgeoisie expressed itself in forms which allowed the style of life of the aristocracy, with which it constrasted its own, not only to remain intact but to form a model. Nevertheless, this ideal itself had, at root, something "bourgeois" about it.'
[67] Ringer (*Decline of the German Mandarins*, p. 7) has suggested that the particularly privileged status of the 'learned' in Germany can be partly explained by the intermediate phase in which neither landed nor mobile wealth had an undisputed hegemony. Wiener's discussion of the educated administrative élite in Victorian England runs along very similar lines.

more of them actually disliked newcomers; certainly there
was no equivalent of the English metropolitan season, and
the Junkers were more crassly agrarian and provincial than
their English counterparts. It was, inevitably, Max Weber who
complained in good bourgeois fashion that the Junkers' own
'parvenu physiognomy' prevented them from offering a social
model of the gentleman.[68] Against that, of course, the
Junkers did stand for a pervasively military ethos. Yet the
very narrowness of their coarsely militarized code of honour
can be seen, to some extent, as a limitation on their social
influence. Many identified with the reserve officer corps
despite, rather than because of, its 'Junker' qualities. Certainly there were powerful expressions of bourgeois nationalism and chauvinism which were hardly Prussian in the
understood sense, and which betrayed an impatience with
thick-headed Junker rigidity.[69] There are, in addition,
reasons for viewing the formation of a new élite as the sign
of bourgeois buoyancy as much as capitulation. It is worth
noting that during the crucial decades after the 1870s the
income of agrarian capitalists was hit much harder than the
income of those who disposed of industrial or commercial
capital. It was, after all, Junker indebtedness that allowed
the bourgeois purchase of estates and brought about so many
intermarriages. For all the economic compromise of 'iron and
rye', it is fair to say that the older wing of the new élite was
more on the defensive. There is confirmation of this in the
spread of titles and ennoblement. Even in Prussia, as that
sharp-eyed observer Robert Michels pointed out, the old
aristocracy was obliged to share its social prestige with the
'freshly-minted bureaucratic nobility, noble or non-noble
plutocrats, baptized or unbaptized Jews, yes, now and then
even with more or less hirsute scholars.'[70] Some returned
their titles when a Jewish stock-exchange dealer or similarly
'undesirable' bourgeois received his, and a nervous sense of
social flux was widespread in aristocratic circles. It was

[68] Weber, 'National Character and the Junkers', pp. 386–95.
[69] Stig Förster's recently completed dissertation on the 'two militarisms' of
Imperial Germany is highly pertinent here, and its publication will be very valuable.
The general point is put at greater length in the companion essay in this volume,
and in Eley, *Reshaping the German Right.*
[70] Cited in Rosenberg, *Probleme*, p. 8.

expressed with unusually playful clarity by Leo Poggenpuhl, son of an old Junker family, in Fontane's novel: 'Who today does *not* have a name? And what does a name really *mean*? Pears Soap, Blookers Cocoa, malt extract from Johann Hoff. Knights and heroes simply can't live up to that.'[71]

The new élite which was formed in Germany in the nineteenth century, especially in the last decades, continued to have a powerful aristocratic component, as in England and elsewhere. But the bourgeoisie which constituted the growing part of this élite did not simply succumb to the aristocratic embrace. The nature of the symbiosis of old and new wealth, the terms on which the new men intermarried, bought estates, and received titles, is a subject that deserves closer attention. What seems too easy, even when we consider the classic examples of 'feudalization', is to regard them as evidence of a simple one-way process. The process in question, like the growing bourgeois conservatism of which it formed a part, was altogether more ambiguous.

Scepticism about the feudalization argument is heightened when we examine one of the main reasons usually advanced to explain it. What we call feudalization is often—and rightly —seen as a product of the growing bourgeois distance from the classes below it. Its 'marriage' with the aristocracy was predicated on a 'divorce' from the lower classes. There is certainly plenty of evidence for the latter. If we look at the petty bourgeoisie, for example, there are numerous signs of such an estrangement in the last third of the nineteenth century. A gulf was opening up between the bourgeoisie proper and the petty bourgeoisie, whether we look at economic opportunities, social contact in associations, or styles of life—the ability to maintain servants, for instance.[72] More commonly noted, however, has been the growing bourgeois distance from the emerging working class. This has usually been dated from the 1860s and has been traced at a number of levels: the divide in the place of work between masters and men, the cleavage in associational life, changing patterns of marriage and mobility. Leo Kofler puts a standard case with particular force when he places bourgeois 'self-abasement' and

---

[71] Cf. *Piers Plowman*: 'Soap sellers and their sons for silver knights are made.'
[72] See Blackbourn, 'Between Resignation and Volatility'.

'leaning towards feudal Prussianism' against this background. 'Fear of the proletariat', he argues, 'led to a complete betrayal by the bourgeoisie of its own historical goals and ideals.'[73] Many historians with less explicit views about the historical goals of the bourgeoisie have come to a similar conclusion.

There can be little argument about this growing divide between the bourgeoisie and the popular classes: it has already been noted in this essay in a number of contexts. What is less clear is how far this encouraged a general feudalization, which can be held responsible in turn for further increasing the distance between the bourgeoisie and its social inferiors. It seems likely that this growing social distance, and the attitudes that accompanied it, were more widespread than the phenomenon of feudalization *tout court*. Especially where the working class was concerned, a sense of distance, often coupled with an anxiety that it must somehow be 'contained', became almost a defining characteristic of German bourgeois life. But it was by no means always accompanied by flight into the arms of the aristocracy; sometimes quite the reverse. This can be illustrated if we recall the case of Theodor Heuss. His experience with a student-duelling corporation may seem a routine example of feudalization. In fact, the episode clearly had little long-term significance for the young Heuss. It was marginal to the thoroughly bourgeois values he imbibed from family, friends, and *Gymnasium* in Heilbronn. And Heuss was soon to find himself in that bourgeois circle which included Weber and Friedrich Naumann, whose awareness of the social question, above all the 'problem of the working class', led them to criticize the social *mores* of the aristocracy. For this very important strand of bourgeois opinion, the example of the Junkers and the attitudes of a 'feudalized' magnate like Stumm, were not a solution to the social question, but were themselves part of the question.[74] To borrow from Karl Kraus on psychoanalysis, they were the symptom of what they claimed to be

---

[73] Kofler, *Zur Geschichte*, p. 561.

[74] The best approach in English to this circle is through W. Struve, *Elites against Democracy* (Princeton, 1973), chs. 2-4; W. O. Shanahan, 'Friedrich Naumann: A Mirror of Wilhelmian Germany', *Review of Politics*, 13 (1951),

the cure. This was a restatement of a characteristically mid-century bourgeois viewpoint: divorce from the aristocracy should precede marriage with a suitably civilized working class, not the other way about. A similar stance and similar conclusions can be found among the self-conscious Catholic bourgeoisie of Imperial Germany. Here one finds a determination to keep the working class within the fold under enlightened bourgeois leadership, coupled with an impatient rejection of Catholic aristocracy and Prussian Junkers alike. Realization of the 'social problem' posed by the working class actually sharpened hostility towards the aristocratic world of horse-racing and duelling. As the Catholic lawyer and politician Adolf Gröber argued, how could workers be weaned from their rough and dangerous ways if their 'betters' continued to butcher each other at twenty paces?[75]

We are not dealing here exclusively, or even primarily, with a narrowly liberal and marginal distaste for aristocratic values. The objections in question often reflected fundamentally conservative, but nevertheless thoroughly bourgeois, notions of social respectability and decency. That, in social terms, was what united Max Weber's critique of student duelling corporations with the critique of a (politically and ethically very different) Catholic contemporary like Gröber. Such a position often contained a strong sense of honour and duty, but these had little to do with any aristocratic model. An example is furnished by the establishment in one south-German town of an *Ehrenschutzverein*—a Society for the Protection of Honour—which explicitly rejected duelling as part of its code of honour.[76] In urban and small-town Germany, a bourgeois sense of propriety and social superiority produced its own exclusiveness and snobberies. There is little need to invoke the theory of feudalization. We are dealing rather with an essentially bourgeois sense of caste: it was this that determined the pecking order in the local philanthropic

278-82; and W. R. Ward, *Theology, Sociology and Politics* (Berne, 1979), esp. pp. 78-122. But see also Mommsen, *Max Weber und die deutsche Politik.*

[75] See the report in the *Deutsches Volksblatt*, 30 Jan. 1895. See also H. Cardauns, *Adolf Gröber* (M-Gladbach, 1921). More than 20,000 university-educated Catholics joined the Catholic anti-duelling movement in Germany: Rost, *Lage*, p. 6.

[76] Kaschuba and Lipp, 'Zur Organisation des bürgerlichen Optimismus', p. 82.

association or who dined at the Ratskeller.[77] This can be seen at its strongest in the Hanseatic towns, in the world of *Buddenbrooks* or Margarete Schneider's *Ilse Petersen*. It found expression in the tragicomic ballad composed by a budding laureate of the Bremen doctors' association, on the characteristic occasion of commemoration festivities:[78]

> Victor und Ottilie
> Liebten sich gar sehr;
> sie war aus 'Familie'
> er vielleicht noch mehr.

> (Victor and Ottilie
> loved each other dearly;
> he was of good family,
> she not quite so clearly.)

Such a sense of caste, socially exclusive, yet explicitly owing nothing to an aristocratic model, can be seen in the case of Alfred Krupp. An industrial patriarch in his own right, Krupp was scornful of those who truckled to the nobility and personally refused all titles and decorations. His lavish homes and social receptions were no more evidence of feudalization than the equivalent excesses of a Vanderbilt.[79]

The conclusion to be drawn from this is not only that we should note the ambiguities of the 'feudalization' process. We should also recognize that what we call feudalization was only one particular variant of a broader social conservatism, just as cultural despair was only one particular variant of a

[77] Cf. the account of Gottlob Egelhaaf, a *Gymnasium* teacher in the Württemberg town of Heilbronn: describing his childhood in Gerabronn during the 1850s and 1860s, he noted that 'through the position of my father as *Ortsvorsteher* [local official], as financial administrator of the district, and as a result of our 5-acre holding, our establishment of servants and our assets of all kinds, we belonged to what one would like to call the "local aristocracy" (*Ortsaristokratie*).' The Gerabronn notables in his father's circle met at the *Post* on Friday evenings and the *Lamm* on Mondays. Egelhaaf adds that in neighbouring Hall, 'Sunday evenings in the *Lamm* made up the general "Notable Society" (*Honoratioren-Gesellschaft*) of Hall'. G. Egelhaaf, *Lebenserinnerungen*, ed. A. Rapp (Stuttgart, 1960), pp. 7, 23, 29. The pattern was universal in German towns.
[78] H. Tjaden, *Bremen und die bremische Ärzteschaft seit dem Beginn des 19. Jahrhunderts* (Bremen, 1932), p. 110.
[79] Kitchen, *Political Economy,* p. 127.

broader social anxiety. There are reasons enough to account for the conservatism of the German bourgeoisie without placing an undue explanatory burden on the feudalization thesis. As the case of Krupp indicates, this could be true even in the upper echelons of the bourgeoisie, so often seen as the 'threshold to the aristocracy'. It was certainly true at a humbler and more local level, among the 'great mass of the bourgeoisie' whom Kofler indicts for aping the feudal aristocracy. Here the visible and invisible barriers of caste were altogether more prosaic. Men did not aspire to the nobility or a landed estate; they aspired to the title of sanitary councillor or councillor of justice. These were usually granted automatically after twenty years of service as a doctor or lawyer—provided, significantly, that the applicant was guilty neither of a criminal conviction nor of Social Democratic sympathies.[80] Aspirations of this kind, like membership of the reserve officer corps, are often conflated—at least implicitly—with the purchase of a Junker estate and a patent of nobility. It is probably more sensible to keep them separate in our minds, and to remember that the latter cases constituted only a tiny minority. They may be regarded as examples of feudalization, provided that we bear in mind the caveats already entered. In the much more numerous other cases, however, we are dealing with a set of attitudes towards 'authority' more generally. It is, of course, true that if one regards Prussia-Germany after 1871 as essentially an aristocratic-feudal state, then the distinction that has just been made disappears again. Genuflecting before the mighty state, with its military monarchy and aristocratic officer corps, can be read simply as another form of feudalization. It is to this crucial question about the nature of the state in Germany that I now want to turn.

[60] Lewinsohn, *Das Geld in der Politik*, p. 27.

IV
The State and Politics

1. *Discrepancies*

There may be readers who feel that the question of state power is already overdue. 'Certainly', they may say, 'a form of bourgeois society developed in nineteenth-century Germany, with the features you describe. But even if that is conceded, what does it add up to in political terms? Surely, when all is said and done, the bourgeoisie did compromise itself as a political force in the way so often suggested—in 1848, in its subsequent incapacity to dislodge the old élite of what became Prussia-Germany, in the failure to establish some genuinely parliamentary form of regime in the Reich?' Here we return to the idea noted at the outset, that there was a basic discrepancy in Germany between economic dynamism and social and political backwardness. On this reading, German peculiarity derived from the lack of synchronization between developments at the different levels of Hans Rosenberg's 'great triad'. My own view is that many historians of Germany have taken this immensely fruitful idea and applied it rather rigidly on the one hand, while on the other hand not exploring the full logic of its implications. The rigidity of its application is certainly something I have tried to address above. The links between economy and society, for instance, have been telescoped in many accounts. The bourgeoisie did not simply take·the money and run; the impact of a dynamic capitalism was not confined to an encapsulated sphere of the economy. My account of Germany's richly variegated and differentiated civil society has tried to establish this point.

At the same time there is undoubtedly more to be said about such discrepancies, and this provides a useful context for our consideration of the political sphere. Take, for example, the pedigree of the 'discrepancies' argument. One of the major channels through which the idea has passed into German historians' work is the writing of Ernst Bloch, a maverick German philosopher of the left who owed something to both German Romanticism and to Marx. In the present context, it is above all Bloch's concept of the 'Gleichzeitigkeit der Ungleichzeitigen' which has proved so seminal.[1] Bloch argued that because different aspects of a society's development move at different historical speeds, at any one time we encounter an uneven, and potentially explosive, juxtaposition of the old and the new, of what has been superseded and what is still in the process of taking shape. We can recognize how this idea has been put usefully to work by historians of modern Germany, and it would be wilful to deny the great usefulness of arguments like this. If we go a little further, though, the point that emerges is that Germany was not unique in this respect. It is the political implications of this point that I want to draw out below.

In his work as a whole, Ernst Bloch showed the powerful imprint of the Romantic legacy to the nineteenth century—a legacy whose political ambiguity has been sawn off by Nazi pedigree-hunters concerned to demonstrate that the shortest distance between Novalis and Hitler is a straight line.[2] Within this pattern of thought it was a stock idea to deplore the emergence of the 'economy' as a separate sphere of human activity, of the *homo oeconomicus* as a purely economic animal. The rise of the 'professional' in bourgeois society was similarly deplored, like the later emergence of the 'professional' politician. In the terms of Romantic and post-Romantic discourse, this sundering of the whole man and the organic society was not viewed as a German, but as a universal, problem. We have seen this in our discussion of cultural despair. We can also take this a stage further. This part of Bloch's intellectual patrimony also reveals his links to Max Weber, to whose circle he belonged in pre-1914 Heidelberg. Not only did Weber discuss this growing specialization as a universal problem; he also made the classic distinction (much

---

[1] See E. Bloch, *Erbschaft dieser Zeit* (Zurich, 1935), first published 1933. For a general introduction, see *Über Ernst Bloch* (Frankfurt/M., 1968).

[2] I have recently tried to discuss the broader problems presented by this approach in a review article on Hans-Jürgen Syberberg's 'Hitler' film. See 'The Big Show', *London Review of Books*, 3-17 Mar. 1983. Löwy, *Georg Lukács—from Romanticism to Bolshevism*, discusses both with commendable sensitivity.

borrowed by German historians) between economic power, social status, and political authority. These, for Weber, could be differently located in a given society, even over a considerable period of time. The German variant of the pattern was only one among others.

From the end of the eighteenth century, in fact, a familiar vocabulary existed to describe the moving apart of the economic, the social and the political. We encounter it in complaints that the economic had become an end in itself; we see it in the common distinction between the classic *societas civilis*, which included a political dimension, and the new civil society, which lacked such a dimension;[3] we see it more generally in contemporary discussion about the shifting line which divided 'public' and 'private' man.[4] From the middle of the nineteenth century, much of this discussion took the form of an engagement with the work of Marx, as the writings of both Weber and Bloch make clear. The idea of discrepancies between the economic, social, and political is, after all, central to Marx's thought. How could we otherwise make sense of his arguments on Bonapartism? More fundamentally, the marxist theory of historical change would lose its in-built dynamic without a sense of the tension between unevenly developing forces of production and the institutional shells in which they are encased. We should not, in other words, expect the two to be a perfect fit. Only vulgar marxists (and vulgar anti-marxists) still cling to the view that the social and political 'superstructure' should be a reflection of the economic 'base'.

In themselves, therefore, these discrepancies or non-correspondencies in the German case should occasion neither great surprise nor talk of peculiarity. It is not the existence of these non-correspondencies in Germany that provides a key, but the particular form they took. In attempting to place the German experience on a continuum I am certainly not trying to argue German *differentiae specifica* out of existence. I am trying, rather, to give full weight to them, but with an

[3] See U. Haltern, 'Bürgerliche Gesellschaft—Theorie und Geschichte', *Neue Politische Literatur*, 19 (1974), 472-88.
[4] A classic example is F. Tönnies, *Gemeinschaft und Gesellschaft* (1897), with its distinction between 'community' and 'society'.

emphasis rather different from the usual one. The discrepancies between the economic, the social, and the political in Germany were very considerable. But in this respect Germany constituted a heightened version of the typical as much as the exceptional. Not only the timing, but also the intensity of the emergence in Germany of a bourgeois economy and society actually helps to explain the distinctive character assumed by the political domain. That is one of the political implications which flows from what I have described in earlier chapters: the very success of a dynamic capitalist economy and a buoyant bourgeois society in Germany made political dominance, in one sense, less necessary. This is really to restate a familiar argument about bourgeois immersion in the non-political, but with the emphasis placed differently. There is, however, a further point. If non-political dominance made political power less necessary in one respect, it also made it less desirable in another. We have already seen that the form of bourgeois dominance which developed in Germany generated problems of its own. These problems bore a family resemblance to those found elsewhere, but arguably they assumed a particularly sharp form. Here we have a further reason for bourgeois satisfaction with a strong state which could act as a buffer or neutralizing force. It could undertake the task of resolving, at the level of state power or through less coercive forms of intervention, what had failed to resolve itself within the spheres of economy and society. That is what I want to explore in the section that follows.

2. 'The Magic Spear which Heals as well as Wounds'

Friedrich Dahlmann once described Prussia as a state which wielded 'the magic spear which heals as well as wounds'.[5] The metaphor captures the potential for both reform and repression, and this section will be concerned with that double-edged quality. It is the second of the two characteristics with which we are perhaps most familiar, and that may offer the best starting-point.

[5] Cited in Sheehan, *German Liberalism*, p. 39.

There are many grounds for talking of an unreformed and repressive Prussian state, both before unification and in the years after 1871, when Prussia formed the core of the new Reich. For contemporaries, as for later historians, Prussia and Prussia-Germany were regarded as textbook examples of the overmighty bureaucratic state. In the period before 1848 this was overt, its most obvious symbol being the army. In 1840 more than half of Prussia's 3.8 million urban civilian population lived in towns that were also garrisons. In Saarlouis there was one soldier to every 2.5 civilians.[6] More generally, however, censorship, the surveillance of citizens, restrictions on free association and the policing of many areas of everyday life made the bureaucratic state ubiquitous. Prussia epitomized the *Beamtenstaat* that prevailed in Germany before 1848, which in many respects enjoyed a new lease of life during the 'era of reaction' in the 1850s.

Many of these overtly repressive characteristics, it is true, did not survive into the last third of the nineteenth century. We have already seen how rights of association and assembly were largely confirmed by the 1860s, together with the legal accountability of the bureaucracy in the following decade. There were comparable moves in the non-Prussian states.[7] After 1890, especially, the new Reich also saw a broad trend towards the confirmation and even extension of civil rights, including the freedom of the press and even the right to picket on strike (although not for those employed by the state itself). It is noteworthy that successive tough measures against civil rights in the 1890s failed to enter the statute book: the Revolution Bill (*Umsturzvorlage*), the Lex von der Recke, the Hard Labour Bill (*Zuchthausvorlage*). Certain rights were clearly extended by abolition of the *Verbindungsverbot* in 1899, immediately before the implementation of the Civil Code, and by the new law of association in 1908.[8]

[6] A. Lüdtke, 'The role of state violence in the period of transition to industrial capitalism: the example of Prussia from 1815 to 1848', *Social History*, 4 (1979), 199.

[7] See, e.g., A. Weinmann, *Die Reform der württembergischen Innenpolitik in den Jahren der Reichsgründung 1866–1870* (Göppingen, 1971); and L. Gall, *Der Liberalismus als regierende Partei. Das Grossherzogtum Baden zwischen Restauration und Reichsgründung* (Wiesbaden, 1968).

[8] A. Hall, *Scandal, Sensation and Social Democracy* (Cambridge, 1977), pp. 55 ff.

The latter liberalized the law on women's rights of association and indirectly those of men as well, since meetings had often been closed on the grounds that women were illegally present.[9] All this lends some plausibility to the claims of Prussia-Germany to be, in formal terms, a legally based *Rechtsstaat.* The creeping legitimacy of the rule of law deserves to be taken seriously.

Yet we can hardly ignore the repressive interference of the state towards Catholics during the *Kulturkampf,* and towards Social Democrats and trade unionists during the period of the Anti-Socialist Law (1878-90). Even after 1890 administrative powers were used against both groups in the form of petty restrictions and harrassment. The laws of *lèse majesté* were employed frequently, for example, to stifle the press;[10] and the discriminatory pattern of recruitment to state service, with its perceptible bias against Social Democrats, Catholics, and Jews, constituted a form of repression in itself.[11] Historians may sometimes have exaggerated the degree of authoritarianism in the Prussian-German state—recent evidence on the frequently cited 'Puttkamer era' of the 1880s, for example, suggests that this cannot be regarded after all as a major purge of the bureaucracy in a reactionary direction.[12] But the weight of a bureaucratic authority which saw itself standing 'above' society can hardly be denied. The official ideology of the civil service itself, and the favouring of bureaucrats over businessmen and professionals in the awarding of titles and

[9] Evans, *The Feminist Movement,* pp. 72-3, 87, 93. Evans, it should be noted, brings out skilfully the conservative effect which this paradoxically had on the feminist movement: ibid., pp. 100-1, 107, 179-80, 245, 273-4.

[10] See, esp. Hall, *Scandal, Sensation and Social Democracy.*

[11] J. C. G. Röhl, 'Higher Civil Servants in Germany, 1890-1900', in J. J. Sheehan (ed.), *Imperial Germany* (New York, 1976), pp. 129-51. On discrimination against Catholics, see Blackbourn, *Class, Religion and Local Politics,* pp. 32-3.

[12] M. L. Anderson and K. Barkin, 'The Myth of the Puttkamer Purge and the Reality of the *Kulturkampf'*, *Journal of Modern History,* 54 (1982), 647-86. The standard view on this, as on so much else, originated with the writings of Eckart Kehr, a heterodox historian of the Weimar period whose work was exhumed in the 1960s, above all by Hans-Ulrich Wehler. His essays are now available in English. On the Puttkamer era, see 'The Social System of Reaction in Prussia under the Puttkamer Ministry', in E. Kehr, *Economic Interest, Militarism and Foreign Policy* (Berkeley, 1977), pp. 109-31.

honours, were both indicative of the bureaucracy's special status.[13] Above all, the army continued to occupy a powerful and privileged position within the new state, after the victories that had helped to bring· that state into existence. Shielded from constitutional checks by virtue of its special relationship to the Kaiser, meting out its own internal justice, it was an institution which jealously preserved its sense of independence from and superiority to mere civilians.[14] It was the power of the uniform that Carl Zuckmayer caricatured in *Der Hauptmann von Köpenick* and Heinrich Mann in *Der Untertan*. But the figure of the strutting officer was not just a caricature. Under legislation dating from 1851, the country was divided up into areas, each with a military commander, in the event of an 'emergency'. The military commanders had powers to declare martial law, suspend civil liberties, and arrest dissidents. Events in the Alsatian garrison town of Zabern in 1913 showed that an emergency could include minor disturbances sparked off when 'insolent' civilians presumed to laugh at a young lieutenant.[15]

If the Reich remained an unreformed state in these respects, the composition of its leading personnel was no less revealing. The stubborn persistence of the old élite in the higher echelons of state service has been so often cited that only a few examples are needed here. In 1914 the German foreign service boasted eight princes, twenty-nine counts, twenty barons, fifty-four untitled nobles, and only eleven commoners. In the Prussian domestic administration, 62 per cent of the *Landräte* were of noble birth in 1891. Of the appointments between 1888 and 1891, 62 per cent of the *Oberpräsidenten*, 75 per cent of the *Regierungspräsidenten*, and 83 per cent of the police directors were noble. Twenty years later, all but one of the *Oberpräsidenten* and twenty-three of the thirty-seven *Regierungspräsidenten* remained aristocratic.[16] In the

---

[13] For an excellent critical discussion of this issue, see J. Caplan, 'The imaginary universality of particular interests: the "tradition" of the civil service in German history', *Social History*, 4 (1979), 299–317.

[14] See the articles by Manfred Messerschmidt and Wilhelm Deist in M. Stürmer (ed.), *Das kaiserliche Deutschland* (Düsseldorf, 1977), pp. 89–118 and 312–39. In English, G. A. Craig, *The Politics of the Prussian Army* (Oxford, 1955).

[15] D. Schoenbaum, *Zabern 1913* (London, 1983).

[16] Röhl, 'Higher Civil Servants', pp. 134, 142.

army it was a similar story. On the eve of the First World War, 30 per cent of all Prussian officers were still noblemen. Among generals and colonels, nobles accounted for more than half.[17] It is evidence like this that has led Helmut Böhme to talk of the dominance within the state apparatus enjoyed by the 'bloc of the pre-industrial power system— landowners, military, Church, and bureaucracy'.[18] The point is one that has been made again and again.

Even at the level of personnel, however, it is easy to gain a misleading impression of the unreformed state. If we take the army, for example, there was a marked embourgeoisement of the Prussian officer corps in the period after unification. In 1860, 65 per cent of all Prussian officers were noblemen, only 35 per cent bourgeois; by 1913 these positions had been more than reversed. Even in the higher ranks there was a sharp contraction of noble officers in the same period. This was most striking in the infantry regiments, whose officers became almost as bourgeois as those in the artillery had always been. Noblemen actually dominated only in particular Prussian cavalry and guards regiments, as they did in other German states, and indeed, other European countries. Much the same pattern can be observed in Saxony; while the Bavarian and Württemberg armies had never had the kind of aristocratic officer corps associated with Prussia in the first two-thirds of the nineteenth century.[19] In the navy it is well known that the officer corps had a bourgeois stamp from the first.[20] Similar points could be made about civilian state service. Ambassadors may have been almost entirely noble, but the consular service was 'wholly middle class'.[21] In the regular civil service the noble Junker stereotype fits the Prussian field administration much better than it does the central Prussian administration in Berlin or the

[17] K. Demeter, *The German Officer-Corps* (London, 1965), p. 28; Deist, 'Die Armee in Staat und Gesellschaft 1890-1914', p. 322.

[18] H. Böhme, 'Thesen zur Beurteilung der gesellschaftlichen, wirtschaftlichen und politischen Ursachen des deutschen Imperialismus', in W. J. Mommsen (ed.), *Der moderne Imperialismus* (Stuttgart, 1971), p. 49.

[19] Demeter, *German Officer-Corps*, pp. 28-46.

[20] H. Herwig, *The German Naval Officer Corps* (Oxford, 1973).

[21] Röhl, 'Higher Civil Servants', p. 134.

Reich civil service. Of the eighty-six higher civil servants working in Reich offices other than the Foreign Office at the beginning of 1895, no more than twelve were of noble birth. An even smaller percentage of noble officials worked in the Prussian ministries in Berlin.[22] In the light of this, it is worth noting how difficult it sometimes is to distinguish which of two rather different points historians are trying to make about the 'old élite'. Was it supposedly dominant in army and bureaucracy? Or was it actually hanging on stubbornly by retreating into certain inner fastnesses of the foreign service, cavalry, and guards regiments and the Prussian local administration? Certainly the latter seems closer to the truth.

These remaining noble enclaves naturally gave them a key position which was out of proportion to their numbers. But we nevertheless have to set their rearguard action, however impressive, within the context of a state bureaucracy, both military and non-military, whose numbers swelled greatly in the decades before 1914. This was partly a matter of bourgeois consular officials and technical artillery specialists; it was much more a matter of engine drivers, factory inspectors, schoolteachers, and steamship booking clerks. It is for this reason that we necessarily have to consider measures as well as men: the functions of the state as much as the background of its leading servants. Leo Kofler has argued that the state 'tolerated the bourgeois economy only to the extent that it could be used as a tool of the feudal state order.'[23] But might it not make sense to complete the proposition by adding that the reverse is also true: that the feudal-state order was tolerated only to the extent that it guaranteed the bourgeois economy? This is the relevance of the 'magic spear that heals as well as wounds'. We have already noted the crucial part played by state power in laying the foundations of the new economic order. It is naturally true that the *dirigiste* role of German bureaucracies was designed, from the start, to serve *raison d'état*. But interests of state were not unchanging, and from the eighteenth century onwards they were defined in circumstances where capitalism was establishing itself

---

[22] Ibid., p. 143.
[23] Kofler, *Zur Geschichte,* p. 540.

elsewhere in Europe. The German states were under what one historian has called 'the compulsion of economic modernization',[24] and there is abundant evidence that activity in fields such as education was prompted by a strong awareness of relative German economic and institutional backwardness. By the middle decades of the century, the individual states inside and outside the Prussian-led *Zollverein* found themselves working within the tolerances of an economic system they themselves had helped to establish. The mutual dependence of state and economy had acquired a powerful momentum by the time of unification. The part played by the interventionist state during the era of organized capitalism marked a further qualitative change in the same direction. The growing role of the state apparatus did not run counter to the prevailing rationality of competition and profit, however other-worldly the training and ethos of many individual officials may have been. More advanced industrial training schemes, greatly expanded provision of higher technical and scientific education, the filling in of the transportation infrastructure, palliative social welfare, the aid given to commerce by naval expansion and the consular service: all these worked with the grain of the capitalist order.

There were many points at which the perceived interests of the state and dominant economic interests clearly coincided. One telling example was the question of 'preserving' the *Mittelstand* of craftsmen and small shopkeepers, an issue widely discussed in political and academic circles during the last years of the century. Ostensibly the Reich and state governments took a positive view of demands that the economic clock be turned back to 'save the *Mittelstand*', speaking fulsomely of their concern to preserve the small producer and retailer as a 'healthy bulwark' in society. This has not passed unnoticed by historians: the concern has often been traced to pre-modern, conservative traditions within the state. In fact, however, as they became increasingly dependent on taxation revenue from large-scale industry and commerce, the German states were unwilling to countenance measures with more than a cosmetic effect in protecting the small man from

[24] Gugel, *Industrieller Aufstieg*, p. 276.

'unfair competition'. The elaborate machinery of so-called *Mittelstandspolitik*—revived pseudo-guilds, department-store taxation, changes in the tender system—was largely ineffectual; it was tacitly disregarded when *raison d'état* came into play. The Prussian War Ministry, for example, rejected official guidelines that tenders for public contracts should be encouraged from craft producers. These, it argued, produced inferior work and failed to meet their delivery dates. Growing public bureaucracies, moreover, like large private concerns, required a growing supply of labour; and much of this was obtained from the marginal sectors of the economy—from the sons and daughters of the small family business, if not from craftsmen and shopkeepers themselves. The countervailing tendency towards a 'reinsurance of the *Mittelstand*', like agricultural protection, should certainly not be disregarded. But such measures remained a countervailing tendency; it was they that went against the grain.[25]

The intention here is not to resurrect the 'state-monopoly capitalism' argument put forward for so long by historians in the German Democratic Republic, in which the state apparatus simply 'reflected' the dominance of a particular interest or group of interests. There should be no suggestion that certain capitalist interests somehow suborned or captured the state for their own ends. Such an approach, often presented through arguments about the role played by interest groups, has too narrow and (sometimes) conspiratorial a perspective. The state retained a relative autonomy in this sphere and was capable of acting against particular interests—including major capitalist interests—where this was judged appropriate.[26] The crucial point, perhaps, is to recognize the overall reciprocity in the state–economy relationship. The state had its own criteria of prestige, economic strength, and public order, which naturally changed in detail over time. On the other side, as we have seen, the operation of the capitalist system benefited from the actions of the state in

---

[25] Details in Blackbourn, '*Mittelstand*', 'Between Resignation and Volatility' and 'La petite bourgeoisie allemande et l'état, 1871–1914', *Le Mouvement Social*, 127 (1984).

[26] As argued, e.g., by Jürgen Kocka in Winkler (ed.), *Organisierter Kapitalismus*, pp. 26–7. See also Eley, 'Capitalism and the Wilhelmine State'.

lending the imprimatur of its own authority to try and smooth out natural disharmonies 'from above'. Similarly, as the state came to rely on the advice and information of the chambers of commerce, so the latter came to rely on the vicarious authority bestowed on them by a semi-official status.[27] There were certainly circumstances in which the idea of the state 'above' society, and hence above social conflict, assumed a positive attractiveness. A characteristic remark of the Elberfeld-Barmen Chamber of Commerce makes the point well. The chamber not only claimed that 'industry is the driving force in the state'; it added that 'to attack it is to injure the well-being of the nation, to diminish the power of the state.'[28] The identification of industry with the state is as significant as the identification of the state with industry.

But the authority which the bourgeoisie looked for in the state should by no means be identified solely with the guaranteeing of profits and dividends. 'The spear which heals' was to guarantee the social order as a whole. At its most basic, this meant the defence of property—the 'principal task' of the state, according to the prominent liberal Schulze-Delitzsch.[29] But bourgeois desiderata also embraced a wide range of legal, educational, and other institutional adjustments, where the state was expected either to cut through the dead wood of 'backward' vested interests, or to protect the productive from lawless envy. In the earlier part of the nineteenth century the emphasis was on the former. The state, for example, received admiring bourgeois support for its offensive role in the connected spheres of education and secularization, just as the Prussian army did for its defeat of 'backward' Austria and southern 'clerical' particularism.[30] By the end of the century bourgeois aspirations were more defensive on the whole. As the belief in self-regulating harmony in society declined, so the willingness to turn to the neutralizing role of the state above society grew accordingly.

[27] Gugel, *Industrieller Aufstieg*, pp. 154-67, 175-9, 234 ff.
[28] Ibid., pp. 156-7.
[29] Ibid., p. 200.
[30] Sheehan, *German Liberalism*, pp. 35-50, 108-40; Gall, *Liberalismus*; Zang (ed.), *Provinzialisierung*.

Bourgeois attitudes towards the double-headed question of law and order give a good measure of this changing emphasis on social security rather than social transformation. The change was a real one. But state authority as such had never been viewed as undesirable in itself, as something which ought to be limited on principle. Freedom of movement (*Freizügigkeit*), freedom of association, and freedom from actions outside the law were certainly demands aimed at specific limitations on the arbitrary exercise of authority; but even many unambiguous bourgeois critics of the bureaucratic state were nevertheless concerned at the implications of appearing to weaken authority.[31] Events such as the Paris Commune, of course, served as a reminder of where this had threatened to lead in 1848. Similarly, voluntary associations demanded and largely obtained a public space free of state interference. But they customarily saw their role as supplementing or complementing that of the state. On the other side, authority often lent its name to particular social or charitable projects, while officials frequently sat *ex officio* on association committees. There was, as Thomas Nipperdey has put it, 'a broad zone of co-operation'.[32] And as many associations turned effectively into interest groups, rather than into bodies with broader social ambitions, so the co-operation (in suitable cases) was more likely to grow than to diminish.

The relative bourgeois modesty suggested here forms part of a pattern we have already noted. Retreat behind the 'magic spear' ran parallel to retreat into cartels, legal positivism, and a gelded civic activism. Social dominance backed by the reassuring presence of state authority, together with indirect influence on public affairs, seemed to offer many advantages; it was certainly not equated automatically with impotence. As Schulze-Delitzsch boasted of the bourgeoisie in the 1860s, it was 'a power which one has to respect if one wishes to govern'.[33] An element of satisfaction, as well as the more obvious air of resignation, can also be seen in the

[31] Sheehan, *German Liberalism*, pp. 115-6, 134; Gugel, *Industrieller Aufstieg*, pp. 195-202.
[32] Nipperdey, 'Verein als soziale Struktur', p. 198.
[33] Gugel, *Industrieller Aufstieg, p. 172, n. 85.*

celebrated self-criticism of German bourgeois liberalism
written by Hermann Baumgarten during the same decade.
'The middle class', argued Baumgarten, 'is little suited for
real political action'; the bourgeois 'is made for work, but not
for governing, and the essential task of the statesman is to
govern.' Yet there was considerable compensation; 'He will
invariably be a major factor in the life of the state, his insight, his activity, his resources will always be given primary
consideration by the state, his interests and inclinations will
have to be taken note of first by any sensible statesman.'[34]
This is not a heroic portrait; but it is one which many bourgeois in Bismarck's Germany found they could contemplate
with satisfaction.

3. *The Limits of Notable Politics*

To be a power which was 'respected', 'given primary consideration', 'taken note of first': was this the limit of bourgeois
political ambition? Clearly it was not. There also existed in
Germany, as elsewhere, a powerful complementary idea of
'open action' in public affairs: politics on the stage, political
life as drama. This idea was to be found above all in those
sections of the bourgeoisie, politically dominant in the middle
decades of the century, that were broadly liberal in per-
suasion and identified themselves with Progress of a more or
less ill-defined sort. France might seem to have been the *locus
classicus* of this stylishly choreographed form of bourgeois
politics. One thinks of a figure such as Lamartine and the
way in which he interpreted his 'role',[35] or of Marx's writings
on France, which are saturated with metaphors of the stage,
role-playing, tragedy, and (especially) farce.[36] But Germany
was hardly different. Political writers, the critics of the new

---

[34] Cited in Beutin, 'Das Bürgertum', pp. 297-8. Part of the passage is quoted
in English in Sheehan, *German Liberalism*, p. 176.
[35] See Sennett, *Fall of Public Man,* pp. 224-37, for an imaginative discussion
of this. Cobden, Bright, and Gladstone are the English figures who most strongly
suggest a parallel. They have been discussed with orginality in Vincent, *Formation of the Liberal Party*.
[36] See S. S. Prawer, *Karl Marx and World Literature* (Oxford, 1978), as well
as works such as 'The Eighteenth Brumaire of Louis Bonaparte'.

drama of bourgeois public life, frequently employed similar metaphors, and the liberals dramatized their own role with a comparable flourish.

In fact we face a paradox here. For in Germany in these years, much more than in England or France in their classic revolutionary periods, there actually was a numerous bourgeoisie which was not only socially buoyant, but also liberal-minded politically—and conscious of its 'role'. This was partly a matter of imitation; or rather, it was a case of history seeking to imitate myth. As a relative late-comer, the German liberal bourgeoisie aspired to what it imagined to be the strengths of its English and French counterparts. There are numerous examples of this: the Anglo-French borrowings of political encyclopedists such as Rotteck and Welcker, the political uses to which the French *feuilleton* was put, the demands for trial by jury in Prussia. But imitation is only one part of the story. Liberals did, after all, have perceived problems of their own in Germany. These included both the arbitrary state and the fragmented sovereignty of pre-unification Germany. The latter not only impeded trade and a common legal system; it also perpetuated a dispersed and provincial public life. More self-consciously even than in France, the German bourgeoisie put the creation of a truly national public life forward as a basic demand. This was regarded as a touchstone of success. National unity and the creation of a national public life, even through Prussian arms, was not a stick with which to beat the bourgeoisie: it was the goal of those who considered themselves politically conscious.[37] National and bourgeois-liberal aspirations seemed to go—publicly—hand in hand. As the National Association trumpeted in 1861: 'Prussia, in order to fulfil her German mission, must be free of all feudal fetters. Only

---

[37] The view that bourgeois liberalism 'capitulated' in the face of nationalism has a long pedigree. This is not really surprising, for it is essentially Treitschke's view with all the moral signs reversed. It can be seen at its relentless worst in F. C. Sell, *Die Tragödie des deutschen Liberalismus* (Stuttgart, 1953), with echoes in English-language works such as Hans Kohn's *The Mind of Germany.* In recent years the 'fateful lure' of economic interest has commonly been substituted for the 'fateful lure' of the nationalist siren song, with disconcertingly similar results in some cases.

a bourgeois state can win the German bourgeoisie.'[38] The rhetorical extravagance of the sentiment would have graced a Macaulay or a Michelet.

The question, of course, is how far the German state of 1871 met these expectations. The optimism was not, perhaps, quite as misplaced as some historians might lead one to suppose. By the 1870s a distinctively bourgeois mode of public life and politics had come into existence in Germany. Popular indifference and aristocratic dislike were both, in different ways, a testimony to its presence. The form of notable politics (*Honoratiorenpolitik*) which crystallized in the decades between 1850 and 1870 owed its existence to the establishment of a national communications network through the railway, telegraph, and press. It was also predicated on important changes we have already noted: equality before the law, rights of association, the creation, in short, of a public sphere where 'opinion' could be formed.[39] This form of notable politics shared the characteristics of the more socially exclusive associations; indeed the substantial propertied and university-educated men who dominated the branches of the National Association, the Progressive Party, and (after 1866) the National Liberal Party were often the same men who controlled the local museum club or choral society. This made notable politics narrow in one sense; but it was, at the same time, national rather than parochial in its orientation and its rhetoric. The events between 1866 and 1871 can be said to have created a permanent national stage on which this rather exclusive drama of notable politics could be acted out.

Notable politics had clear limits, and I should like to consider two of these in particular. It was limited, first, in the very modest increment of constitutional advance which its practioners registered in 1871. Imperial Germany was clearly not a limited parliamentary monarchy. There is little dispute among historians that the hybrid constitutional arrangements of unified Germany allowed for only a 'sham

[38] T. S. Hamerow, *The Social Foundations of German Unification 1858–1871: Ideas and Institutions* (Princeton, 1969), pp. 315-20. Quotation on p. 319.
[39] Habermas, *Strukturwandel.*

constitutionalism'.[40] Bismarck's artful draughtsmanship left the Kaiser responsible for the choice of chancellor and ministers, not the elected Reichstag; indeed, ministers could not be members of that assembly, thus excluding party leaders from consideration. The Kaiser's government, conversely, was not responsible to the Reichstag. The latter had negative blocking power over legislation, especially in financial matters, but even this was severely diminished in the case of the army budget (and later the navy budget).[41] Against the formidable power concentrated in the hands of the monarchical executive (effectively in Bismarck's hands until 1890), the Reichstag did not enjoy even legislative primacy. It was not the Reichstag that initiated legislation, but the Bundesrat, made up of members sent by the constituent states of the federal Reich; and it also possessed a veto on measures that passed the Reichstag. At every level, moreover, the institutions of the Reich were closely integrated with those of Prussia, the dominant state in the union. The German Kaiser was the King of Prussia, the Imperial Chancellor was the Prime Minister of Prussia, Prussia had effective control over voting in the Bundesrat. And in Prussia itself, of course, constitutionalism was more 'sham' than in the Reich as a whole or in some of the southern states. Notable politics coexisted rather modestly alongside this massing of executive powers. When local notables exchanged the Ratskeller for a Berlin hotel and became parliamentarians, they found they could talk at length and block bills; but they did not wield power, either as individuals or through their parties. .

The impressive consensus which liberal bourgeois notables mobilized among their own kind in the National Association, Progressive and National Liberal Parties thus counted for little in terms of wielding authority, as opposed to influence. And it is certainly true that there were many liberals who wanted more and pushed for further budget rights (especially over army appropriations), for ministers drawn from party

---

[40]   There is a useful summary of constitutional arrangements in Craig, *Germany 1866–1945*, pp. 38–55.
[41]   See V. R. Berghahn, *Der Tirpitz-Plan* (Düsseldorf, 1971).

leaders, and for curbs, first on Bismarck's 'dictatorial' procedures, later on a Kaiser who believed that he ruled 'as an
instrument of the Lord'.[42] While a sense of dissatisfaction
clearly existed, it is nevertheless difficult to argue that
bourgeois liberalism betrayed itself by failing to insist on a
more genuinely parliamentary form of government. We
should recognize, to take up a first point, that in liberal (as
indeed in non-liberal) notable politics there was a strong
component of what might be called apolitical politics. What
passed for notable politics was thought 'above' politics in the
destructive sense; and fomenting political conflict fell into
the latter category. This was very much in line with the
approach to political matters in the associations from which
notable national politics had grown, and it was most clearly
evident when it came to nationalism itself. Nationalism in the
1860s or 1870s signified the opposite of politics in the sense
of conflict: its value, in the National Liberal Party as in the
Choral Society, lay in the fact that it was thought to be
above vulgar political strife. That is why the achievements of
Bismarck and the Prussian army warranted respect even from
clear opponents of militarism and the Junker elements of
Prussianism. This was especially so when, from the liberal
perspective, it appeared during the 1870s that their own
healthy national convictions were now carrying the new
government in a crusade against clerical conservatism, particularism, and internationalism.

   In addition to this, however, we should consider the actual
constitutional aspirations of liberals during the Bismarckian
era. Much of what we might be tempted retrospectively to
label as thwarted liberal aspirations to parliamentary government was, in fact, a modestly satisfied acceptance of constitutionalism as such—of a constitutionalism, that is, which
fell short of full parliamentarism. The long tradition of
German Dualism—with its emphasis on the separate tasks of
government and parliament—undoubtedly helps to explain
much of this.[43] But we should also note the way in which,

---

[42] Wilhelm II, cited in V. R. Berghahn, *Germany and the Approach of War in
1914* (London, 1973), p. 86.
[43] L. Krieger, *The German Idea of Freedom* (Boston, 1957), remains an outstanding account in English of Dualism.

during the Prussian constitutional conflict of the 1860s, oppositional liberalism tended to couch its demands in legal rather than political-constitutional terms: it was the legal, rather than political, accountability of ministers that Bismarck's opponents in the Prussian Landtag called for.[44] All of this may seem reprehensible by Anglo-Saxon standards; but at least we should not be in error about the terms in which contemporary liberal demands were framed in Germany. Their expectations were partly coloured, of course, by constitutional realities (and perceptions of them) in contemporary France and England. And if German bourgeois liberals often seem to have retreated from what they saw there, this should not be attributed too readily to a complacent defence of the superior German *Sonderweg*. Rejection of the French or English model was generally neither so self-satisfied nor so innocent as that. Just as the liberal bourgeoisie in Germany aspired to what it saw as the strengths of its English and French counterparts, so it sought to avoid what it saw as their weaknesses. It made sense, in their terms, to entertain a considerable degree of scepticism about parliamentary government. The July Monarchy, for example, as an episode of imagined open class rule by the French bourgeoisie, was cited again and again in Germany as something to be avoided at almost any cost. The popular disturbances over a second instalment of parliamentary reform in England during the 1860s were noted with a similarly keen interest.[45]

The comparison with England brings us to a second major point. The German Reich not only differed from England in not possessing parliamentary government; it also differed in possessing universal male suffrage, at least to the Reichstag. By the standards of German liberalism during the 1860s and 1870s, the presence of the one was arguably more 'illiberal' than the absence of the other. This was, in fact, the second principal limitation of notable politics in general, and of its predominant liberal species in particular. Direct, equal, and universal suffrage for males aged twenty-five and over was

[44] Sheehan, *German Liberalism*, pp. 115-16; Gugel, *Industrieller Aufstieg*, pp. 81-91.
[45] Gugel, *Industrieller Aufstieg*, pp. 207-11.

introduced by Bismarck, first for the North German Confederation in 1866, then for the new Reich. One of its aims
was to dish the liberals. Some historians have detected a fully
Bonapartist and plebiscitary intention behind its introduction, a reading which has been backed up by references
to the subsequent use of 'national threats' at elections between 1871 and 1890.[46] It may be that this exaggerates the
'modernity' of Bismarck, by comparision with Napoleon III,
at the expense of his conservative fatalism: certainly Bismarck
saw himself very much as the sorcerer's apprentice in this
respect.[47] More important, perhaps, it might well be argued
that some writers on Bismarck's Bonapartism have also pre-
dated the advent of a truly popular politics in Imperial
Germany, and have also thereby exaggerated its manipulated
character. I shall return to this point below. What seems
certain, as even critics of the Bonapartist interpretation
agree, is a degree of calculation on Bismarck's part concerning liberal vulnerability to popular opinion. It seems
equally clear that this was indeed a source of weakness.

The problem of the people always troubled bourgeois
liberals, and this adds a further explanation for their seeming
complacency about a strong executive power. From the
early nineteenth century, liberals had suspected the lower
orders of lacking true independence, and thus constituting a
prey to reactionaries and revolutionaries alike. Liberal
notables also set their own lofty universal pretensions against
the sectional egoism they discerned lower down the social
scale. One prominent Rhenish liberal, Peter Heinrich Merkens,
objected in 1832 even to an extension of the franchise for
the Cologne Chamber of Commerce. This, he argued, would
compromise the deliberations of 'the most *excellent* merchants and wholesalers' by admitting petty restaurateurs,
craftsmen, and fruit peddlers.[48] David Hansemann, a noted
liberal in 1848, described popular sovereignty as a 'pernicious

---

[46] See the references in n. 33, p. 173 above.
[47] This is a central theme of Lothar Gall's *Bismarck. Der weisse Revolutionär*
(Frankfurt/M., Berlin, and Vienna, 1980). See esp. pp. 146, 325, 366, 459 ff.
('Der Zauberlehrling'). I have discussed these themes in a review article on Bismarck biographies in *Archiv für Sozialgeschichte*, 22 (1982), 756-60.
[48] Diefendorf, *Businessmen and Politics,* p. 299.

theory'.[49] The experience of 1848 itself undoubtedly cut deeply. Hansemann sat on the commission which introduced the three-class franchise to the Prussian Landtag—that much-cited 'bulwark of the aristocratic authoritarian state in Prussia', as Hans Rosenberg has called it.[50] In the 1860s and 1870s, as in 1848, liberalism was divided, uncertain and disturbed over popular suffrage. Some believed that it was necessary as a means of educating popular opinion; rather more thought that the appropriate level of education and wisdom should first be earned. (The parallel with arguments over Jewish emancipation is a compelling one).[51] All could see the dangers. It may be useful to rehearse some of their arguments during a decade—the 1860s—when the outlook of liberal notables was generally optimistic. Karl Twesten expressed his fears of the 'dilettantism and charlatanry' which would follow from truckling to the people. Treitschke, attacking the principle of democracy in the name of the state, rejected a situation in which 'the uneducated, immature, and unreliable man would have as much influence as someone who is wise, industrious and patriotic.' Even a supporter of universal suffrage such as Schulze-Delitzsch warned of stimulating the 'passions' of the lower orders. It was, he argued, all too easy 'to cross the dark borderline where the animal touches on the human'; and the 'unbound beast', once aroused, would 'tear everything apart with its lion claws'. Lion metaphors seem to have been very popular, for a colleague of Schulze's offered similar advice to let 'sleeping lions' lie. Bestial images also pervaded the anxious ruminations of a parliamentarian called Löwe (an unfortunate name, perhaps) on the subject of 'worker battalions'.[52] Attitudes of this kind were ubiquitous in the bourgeois liberalism of the 1860s, 1870s, and beyond. Hermann Baumgarten, author of the liberal self-critique and a political mentor of Max Weber, was to talk scathingly of 'the dominance of the

[49]   Ibid., p. 344.
[50]   Rosenberg, *Machteliten*, p. 96.
[51]   Rürup, *Emanzipation*, pp. 11–73.
[52]   Gugel, *Industrieller Aufstieg*, pp. 184–8; Sheehan, *German Liberalism*, pp. 104–7.

raw instincts of the masses in all things'. The young Weber himself described universal suffrage as the 'Danegeld'.[53]

The notable politics of the unification era was therefore limited, or limited itself, in two directions: above and below, in its relationship to state power and in its relationship to the people. The two were connected in complex ways, as contemporary discussion itself makes clear. Some, like Treitschke, defended the powerful state against the people. Others, like Baumgarten, made a more interesting connection between the 'raw instincts of the masses' on the one hand and the cynical calculation of the 'Caesarist' Bismarck on the other. The latter, on this reading, had unleashed the former. Here we have a contemporary account of Bonapartism. Weber, following in the line of Baumgarten, continued this double-track analysis of a bourgeois liberalism squeezed between state and people. But with Weber the critique comes full circle. For he identified the bourgeoisie itself, above all figures like Treitschke, as a foremost victim of Bismarck's political system. The bourgeoisie had, he argued, been too willing to embrace a strong man; and it had been burned by gazing for too long at the Bismarckian sun.[54]

What is common to these and other readings is a sense of the changed political landscape with the formal creation of a national politics in the 1860s. Bourgeois notables identified themselves strongly with unification, and their aspirations were met perhaps to a greater extent than is often allowed. But they were right to be anxious, after their different fashions, about the emergence of a national political stage with a potential cast of millions. I tried to show earlier in this essay that the silent bourgeois victories in the new economic order and in civil society were not without their problems. But none of them presented such a double-edged and ambiguous effect as changes in the political sphere. For, if a powerful state provided the means of trying to neutralize economic and social conflicts, the open arena of public life

---

[53] Mommsen, *Max Weber und die deutsche Politik*, pp. 6–8.

[54] Ibid., pp. 7–13, 47 ff. See also Weber, 'Economic Policy and the National Interest in Imperial Germany', pp. 264–8, and 'Parliament and Government in a Reconstructed Germany', in G. Roth and C. Wittich (eds.), *Economy and Society* (New York, 1968), appendix, pp. 1385–92 ('Bismarck's Legacy').

offered the possibility of political expression to economic and social grievances. It was at the political level, in short, that many of the problems of bourgeois society in Germany came to a head. If we therefore talk about bourgeois achievements, of a liberal-notable kind, at the political as well as socio-economic level, we have to be careful to make a distinction. These two sets of achievements—the stealthier ones in economy and society, the more open ones at the political level—were by no means equal. The former were extensive and durable, the latter limited and fragile. The former tended to unite the bourgeoisie, the latter to divide it. The former enabled the bourgeoisie to make its claim to represent a general interest, the latter provided a forum where such claims could be challenged. The former was a sphere where state institutions acknowledged the strength of the bourgeoisie, the latter was a sphere where the bourgeoisie accepted the need for strong state institutions. Bourgeois authority in Germany was thus least vulnerable where it was least visible; it was most vulnerable where it was most visible. That vulnerability was greatest in the domain of public life and politics, on that open stage which exposed the divisions and limitations of the bourgeoisie as a putative general class. It is to these sources of vulnerability that I now want to turn: to bourgeois political divisions, and to the problems faced by the bourgeois parties in their relations with subaltern social classes.

V
The Political Stage
and the Problem of Reform

1. *Bourgeois Divisions and the Rise of Mass Politics*

It is important to recognize that there were major divisions
within the bourgeoisie in Germany, as there were elsewhere.
These ran along economic, occupational, regional, and
religious lines; and they often overlapped. But these divisions
were more acute, were literally more visible, at the political
level than they were in everyday social life. It was relatively
easy to agree on property rights, the ordering of family life
and the importance of philanthropy. It was also possible to
agree on the importance of the rule of law in general, and on
certain basic rights of association and assembly in particular.
These were fundamental civic rights. They constituted un-
spoken bourgeois assumptions which largely united the
propertied and educated, the Badenese and Prussian, the
industrialist and merchant, the Protestant and Catholic, left-
and right-wing liberals. Associational life expressed this unity
of the bourgeoisie at the basic sociological level. Reflecting
both the local social power of the bourgeoisie, and its regional,
religious, and sectional diversity, voluntary associations were
apt symbols of where the real strength of the class lay. But
when the bourgeoisie acted on the larger, national political
stage, very real sectional, regional, and religious divisions became apparent and were magnified. These took on political
form; and political divisions proper came into the open. This
was evident in the splintering of political groupings at the
Frankfurt Parliament in 1848; it could be observed in state
parliaments through the 1850s and 1860s; and it became
more obvious still in the Reichstag after 1871.

The chief victim of political discord within the bourgeoisie
was undoubtedly that part of the class that thought of itself
as both liberal and national. Temporarily dominant in the

middle decades of the century, it had made the most extravagant claims to represent the general interest of the bourgeoisie as a whole. (It also claimed to represent the general interest of society as a whole; but that was less divisive, for as we have seen it was a claim which bourgeois generally were fond of making.) When the liberal-inclined National Association talked of the need for a 'bourgeois state' to 'win the German bourgeoisie', its rhetoric was just sufficiently vague to invite no more than suspicion from those to whom 'bourgeois' and 'national liberal' were not synonymous. When the National Liberal Party showed after 1871 what was meant in practice by such a phrase, its actions proved seriously divisive of bourgeois political unity. Nowhere was this more apparent than in the matter of religion. National Liberals and their left-liberal allies provoked massive Catholic opposition by supporting the *Kulturkampf*, for it became clear that the church and Catholic schools would be among the principal victims of this particular brand of bourgeois-liberal Progress. Substantial Catholic notables, who had often identified themselves with liberalism in a general way, and were natural National Liberals even after the 1870s in every respect except that they happened to be Catholic, found themselves driven into a pariah status if they allowed the claims of faith. And while many Catholic lawyers, merchants, and academics had doubts about infallibility, the Jesuits, and the effusions of popular piety, they nevertheless found that religious loyalties transcended class loyalties when it came to making a political choice. In social terms they still had more in common with their National Liberal peers than with the mariolatrous Catholic peasant; in political terms they sided with the peasant. Political Catholicism in Germany thus acquired an important and later crucial stratum of bourgeois leaders which it might otherwise have been denied.[1] Germany was not the only country where confessional issues assumed political form, nor the only one where bourgeois liberalism was seriously weakened as a result. A similar political landscape existed in

[1] Blackbourn, 'Die Zentrumspartei und die deutschen Katholiken', and 'The Centre Party and its Constituency'. See also Gall, *Liberalismus als regierende Partei*, and 'Die partei- und sozialgeschichtliche Problematik des badischen Kulturkampfes', *Zeitschrift für die Geschichte des Oberrheins*, 113 (1965), 151–96; and Zang (ed.), *Provinzialisierung*.

Belgium, Austria, and Switzerland, so often and unjustly neglected when comparisons are made with Germany.[2] The point is that Germany, once again, provided the heightened version of the norm. The circumstances of the dramatic bourgeois entry on to the political stage showed that the underlying unity of the class in the everyday material sphere was not matched by an equivalent unity on more public issues.

The confessional issue was not the only one to surface in the political arena. The liberal-nationalist consensus was fractured along other lines as well. National Liberalism was faced in the new Reich with bourgeois opponents on the left, who questioned the quality of its liberalism. It was also faced with bourgeois critics on the right, who questioned the quality of its nationalism. The changing meanings attached to nationalism after 1871 provide, in fact, a revealing commentary on bourgeois divisions. In the notable politics of mid-century, nationalism was more of a consensus than an issue: a label for a kind of apolitical politics on which men of education and substance could agree almost without discussion. The bourgeoisie of the Choral Society, the National Association, or the early National Liberal Party embodied the conviction that the national cause was above politics. When nationalism became an open political issue after 1871, this rather cosy unanimity disappeared. Catholics laid claim to their own version of German nationalism, attacking the arrogance with which National Liberals presumed to monopolize the sentiment. Left Liberals developed a parallel line of attack, criticizing National Liberalism for its complacent fixation on the Bismarckian settlement. Perhaps most important of all, the apolitical nationalism of earlier decades itself became a more strident political creed, disturbing the backwaters of liberal notable politics. Radical Nationalist organizations such as the Pan-German and Navy Leagues, manned to a considerable extent by disillusioned former National Liberals, challenged the élitist *insouciance* of the old National Liberal establishment. Like their predecessors of the earlier generation, they employed the language of a nationalism above political horse-trading. But they did so

[2] See U. Altermatt, *Der Weg der Schweizer Katholiken ins Ghetto* (Zurich, 1972), for a clear Swiss parallel.

with an energy and a cutting contempt which was strongly directed against the complacency of old notable politics. In reformulating the 'primacy of the national' as an explicit political objective, they achieved a politically disruptive effect which disclosed the disunity of bourgeois politics even on the national issue. By the 1890s nationalism itself was a source of political conflict.rather than apolitical consensus, and there were clear connections between this development and the creation of an open political stage. Certainly few political groups were more conscious of politics as a dramatic struggle against 'veiled influences' than the radical nationalists, whose style perfectly mirrored their convictions.[3]

Open political action not only exposed divisions within the bourgeoisie. It also revealed its vulnerability in political relations with subaltern social groups. The mode of notable politics which took shape in the middle decades of the century betrayed, in sharpened form, a problem we have already noted: the gap between bourgeois rhetoric and reality. Bourgeois-dominated political associations, whether the 'People's Associations' (*Volksvereine*) of the left liberals, the 'Casinos' of the Catholic urban bourgeoisie, or the National Association, claimed to speak for all classes; in fact they

---

[3] At the risk of overloading these notes with freight, it is necessary to indicate some of the principal works on the problem of liberalism. A pioneering enquiry is T. Schieder, 'Die Krise des bürgerlichen Liberalismus', *Staat und Gesellschaft im Wandel unserer Zeit* (Munich, 1974), pp. 58–88. On the period up to the 1870s, see the works by Langewiesche (n. 5, p. 177) and Gall (n. 7, p. 242). Also by Gall: 'Liberalismus und Nationalstaat. Der Deutsche Liberalismus und die Reichsgründung', in Berding *et al.* (eds.), *Vom Staat des Ancien Régime zum Modernen Parteienstaat*, pp. 287–300; and 'Liberalismus und "Bürgerliche Gesellschaft": zu Charakter und Entwicklung der liberalen Bewegung in Deutschland', *Historische Zeitschrift*, 220 (1975), 324–56. Also important on the period before unification is H. A. Winkler, *Preussischer Liberalismus und der Nationalstaat* (Tübingen, 1964). There is a growing number of works, especially by American historians, that treat both left- and right-wing liberalism after 1871 with sensitivity. See J. C. Hunt, *The People's Party in Württemberg and Southern Germany, 1890–1914* (Stuttgart, 1975) and D. White, *The Splintered Party. National Liberalism in Hessen and the Reich, 1867–1918* (Cambridge, Mass., 1976). Sheehan, *German Liberalism*, covers the whole of the nineteenth century and is indispensable. Recent debate on the nature of liberalism is joined in *Geschichte und Gesellschaft*, 4 (1978), in the contributions by Winkler, Sheehan, and Wolfgang J. Mommsen. Finally, the absence of a work that places the radical nationalist associations fully in the context of their soured National Liberalism has now been remedied by Eley, *Reshaping the German Right*.

intoned the language of universality, but were themselves lubricated by family, personal, and professional ties of a much narrower kind. In this they differed little from formally non-political associations. But the claims made by the political associations, and the parties that grew out of them, were more likely to invite dispute, precisely because they were made at an explicitly political level. The openness of bourgeois claims to natural leadership in the political realm provoked a response from other classes; and this potential challenge was amplified because other forms of anti-bourgeois hostility were, as we shall see, 'displaced' on to the political domain.[4] The result was a growing opposition in the closing decades of the century, sometimes inchoate, but often self-conscious, to the narrowly based notable politics of earlier years. Sharp economic and social antagonisms were coined into political currency; and the public sphere, accessible to all in more than just a formal sense, became the stage on which class and sectional struggles were fought out. As the stage became more densely peopled, however, so its procedures and performances were transformed. The definition of what constituted politics and public debate changed; the political nation was enlarged; and bourgeois claims to represent a general interest in society came under fire.

Class and sectional conflicts within a rapidly changing economy and society brought this challenge into existence. It was fuelled by the growth of education and the press, extended communications, and the possibilities of public association. The enormous increase in popular electoral participation then made it a fact of cardinal political importance. Attacks on the comfortable natural superiority assumed by notable politicians came from a variety of directions. They were mounted by special interests who insisted with a new stridency that their preoccupations were 'political', and by excluded or disaffected classes or groups who sought to become more than simply extras on the political stage.[5] A

---

[4] Habermas, *Strukturwandel*, pp. 176ff.

[5] The watershed was the period from the late 1880s to the late 1890s. This decade witnessed an explosion of new organizations which challenged the existing and limited mode of politics. These included the principal anti-semitic political parties, the Bavarian Peasant League and Hesse peasant movement, the earliest

measure of the problem was given by one south-German minister in the 1890s, who sourly catalogued the agitation of the 'homœopaths, the anti-inoculationists, the pro-cremationists, the agrarians, the publicans, etc.'.[6] Broadly speaking, though, we can distinguish a challenge to notable exclusiveness from three main directions: from the working class, the petty bourgeoisie, and the peasantry. Each, in its different way, attacked the comfortable and rather lofty notable politics which had established itself in mid-century; each resisted the bourgeois notion of itself as a general class. Their aggregate effect was to fracture, more effectively in some respects than government repression, the mould in which bourgeois public life had set. As a result that fragile mid-century form of politics gave way to a new kind of politics in the closing years of the century: a transitional mode of politics which was contradictory and unstable, less self-assured and more febrile than what had preceded it. The political idiom as a whole was altered in the process. Once again, however, liberalism was the main loser.

Let us turn first to the efforts of the German working class to emancipate itself from bourgeois political tutelage. The rise of the Social Democratic Party measured the failure of the bourgeois political parties. Both liberals and the Catholic Centre Party found it difficult to retain strong working-class support. The leadership of the Centre (increasingly bourgeois, rather than clerical or aristocratic, after the 1880s), recognized the danger and tried to meet it. This was an important motive in the founding of the People's Association of German Catholics in 1890, and in compelling recognition that Christian Trade Unions were a likelier vehicle for attracting Catholic

---

Mittelstand organizations, the major radical-nationalist associations, the German Peace Society, and the German feminist movement. There is insufficient space in this essay to deal in any detail with two important general components of this political leavening. The first was the emergence of a new kind of maverick political figure who, in Weberian terms, lived 'from' rather than 'for' politics. The second was the challenge to the notable mode of politics from what might be termed the revolt of the philistines (*Spiessbürger*) and parish-pump politicians: a reaction, in one sense, against the politics of Meinecke's 'cosmopolitan bourgeoisie' (*Weltbürgertum*). Both are subjects to which I hope to return on a future occasion.

[6] Hauptstaatsarchiv Stuttgart, E 41, Anhang II, Bü 4, 'Votum des Staatsministerium' on constitutional revision, 1897.

workers than the paternalistic workers' associations. In these attempts to hold on to a Catholic proletarian constituency the old language of class harmony was restated in a more strident form: popular acceptance of the idea could no longer be taken for granted. Despite these efforts, the movement of Catholic workers away from the Centre Party gathered pace. 1912 saw its pre-war electoral high-point.[7]

The effect of working-class defection on the liberal parties was more severe. The inability of German liberals to place themselves politically at the head of the working-class movement was evident as early as the 1860s. In a celebrated phrase of Gustav Mayer, that decade saw the crucial 'separation of proletarian and bourgeois democracy'.[8] German liberals did not benefit from the restricted franchise that was the reality behind the Gladstonian coalition; they lacked the rhetoric of a common revolutionary heritage which their Radical counterparts in France put to conservative use; and they lacked any support from the Catholic Church, whose parish priests at least lent the Centre Party the appearance of the common touch at local level. Bourgeois liberalism was unable, and often unwilling, to take this problem as seriously as it might have done. The gap between universal rhetoric and notable style was revealed in the failure of workers' education associations in the 1860s, and the decline of working-class support was visibly more serious by the close of the century. The liberal form of political organization was too exclusive, too dominated by conceptions of natural social superiority, for the circumstances in which it was placed in Germany by universal suffrage. As the separate working-class political presence grew up to and during the 1890s, this source of vulnerability became more apparent. The left wing of liberalism worked hard to retain, or regain, a base among the working class, revitalized to some extent (as in England at the same period) by a patent threat to its position. Both Friedrich Naumann's social-liberal initiative and the broader regrouping

---

[7] Detailed arguments on these points in Blackbourn, *Class, Religion and Local Politics*, esp. ch. 1.

[8] G. Mayer, 'Die Trennung der proletarischen von der bürgerlichen Demokratie in Deutschland, 1863–1870', now in H.-U. Wehler (ed.), *Radikalismus, Sozialismus und bürgerliche Demokratie* (Frankfurt/M., 1969), pp. 108–78.

of the German New Liberalism around the turn of the century were, like parallel Catholic initiatives from the Rhenish and Westphalian bourgeoisie, an attempt to restate the language of class harmony in a more aggressive and, it was hoped, more appealing form. The distance from the workers' education association of the 1860s to Naumann's National-Social Association was as great as the distance on the Catholic side from the Casinos of the 1860s to the People's Association of German Catholics.[9]

Efforts to revitalize bourgeois politics in this way failed to prevent a very significant part of the working class from moving towards Social Democracy. And for all the differences between the bourgeois parties, there was one crucial impediment common to all of them when they faced this problem: the developing structure of German capitalism before 1914. German capitalism was the most dynamic in Europe and arguably the most successful in restricting working-class demands at the point of production. Restrictions on trade-union organization at plant level, black lists, yellow company unions, and tied housing all helped to shackle organized labour at the factory. One result was the displacement of class hostility on to the political level. Metal workers, for example, were particularly hedged about by large firms when they sought to organize industrially; but they constituted a vital part of the SPD's membership and voting strength.[10] Universal male suffrage to the Reichstag, and increasingly democratic franchises in many of the individual states (Prussia being the important exception) provided German workers with a weapon they could use in the political arena directly, and one they were commonly denied at other levels. The rising fortunes of the SPD were a measure of working-class resort to this weapon.

The pace and nature of German economic development therefore contributed materially to undermining the allegiance

    [9] On Naumann, see Struve, *Elites against Democracy*, pp. 78-113, and on the National-Social Association, D. Düding, *Der Nationalsoziale Verein, 1896–1903* (Munich, 1972).

    [10] Eley, 'Capitalism and the Wilhelmine State', pp. 742-4; D. Geary, 'The German Labour Movement 1848-1919', *European Studies Review*, 6 (1976), 297–330.

of workers to the non-socialist parties. Changes in the structure of the capitalist economy during the last decades of the century also had an impact, but a more ambiguous one, on the politics of the petty bourgeoisie, or *Mittelstand*.[11] Until around the middle of the nineteenth century, the term *Mittelstand* included members of what were to become the bourgeoisie and the petty bourgeoisie. It corresponded to a society whose middling ranks were less socially differentiated than they were to become. It was still possible for the butcher and the merchant to think of themselves as having a good deal in common—not least that both might be members of the same philanthropic or cultural association. Business concentration in both manufacturing and commerce drove a wedge between the two. But growing class differentiation between bourgeoisie and petty bourgeoisie did not occur only at the level of production or distribution, fundamental though that was. It was also revealed by relative degrees of access to education, the ability to maintain servants, and levels of participation in associational life. There was widespread demoralization in the petty bourgeoisie in the closing decades of the century. Sometimes this produced resignation, but sometimes volatility. Certainly there were many manifestations of discontent with the seemingly false promises of bourgeois society. The formation of protection organizations against 'unfair competition', among craftsmen from the 1870s and shopkeepers from the 1890s, provided evidence of one kind about the exploded nostrums of competition.[12] The new interest groups of the petty bourgeoisie were also a rejection of the long-standing and bourgeois-dominated trade associations (*Gewerbevereine*), in which the needs of both large and small business were notionally represented. Like the trade unions of the working class, however, petty-bourgeois interest organizations were at a disadvantage in the market place. In its frustration the *Mittelstand* sometimes resorted to illegal direct action—organizing attacks on

[11] References for the following in Blackbourn, '*Mittelstand*', and 'Between Resignation and Volatility'.

[12] See, respectively, S. Volkov, *The Rise of Popular Antimodernism*, and Gellately, *Politics of Economic Despair*. See also the opening chapter of Winkler, *Mittelstand, Demokratie und Nationalsozialismus*.

department stores, for example. The attitudes towards the rule of law revealed by such actions are significant in themselves. To an increasing extent, however, faced with the difficulty of defending itself through interest groups of a purely material kind, the petty bourgeoisie followed the same path as the working class: it organized itself at the political level. It demanded a wide range of measures from governments and parties: subventions, a revived guild system, special taxes, laws against 'unfair competition', changes in the tender system. And it channelled these demands through increasingly broad-based organizations which ultimately sought to encompass the *Mittelstand* as a whole. Nowhere in German society was there a greater belief that the state, once apprised of the true facts, would intervene as a just paterfamilias to restore justice. This expectation was not dented by frequent disappointment; it may even have grown. Faith in party leaders, however, was strained rather more seriously.[13]

Historians have often presented resentments and demands of this kind as a species of anti-modernism. They have viewed these articulations of petty-bourgeois rancour as something that signalled a defeat for liberalism and served to provide political support for Prussian Conservatism.[14] While the element of truth in this interpretation cannot be denied, it nevertheless tends to undervalue the full meaning of what was happening. Liberalism was indeed the principal target of *Mittelstand* resentment: it was liberalism in its various forms that was most tainted with 'Manchesterism' and 'Jewish capital'; and it was liberal-political claims to represent a general interest that were most obviously undermined by economic and social change.[15] But it was the larger bourgeois claim to stand above sectional egoism and represent a general interest that was, however inchoately, under attack. And it was in the political arena, the soft

[13] Blackbourn, 'Between Resignation and Volatility'.
[14] Volkov and Winkler (n. 12 above) both illustrate this common approach. The former, it should be said, is considerably more alive to the ambiguity of petty-bourgeois political reactions.
[15] On this, see A. Leppert-Fögen, *Die deklassierte Klasse* (Frankfurt/M., 1974), ch. 2.

under-belly of the bourgeois world, that the truculent sectional demands and the general distemper of the *Mittelstand* proved generally most subversive. Their demands, both in substance and tone, were inherently distasteful to the run of established politicians of every colour: to leaders of the Centre Party such as Lieber, Hertling, and Gröber, who claimed to stand above vulgar interests, as well as to their left-liberal and National Liberal counterparts. Centre and liberal leaders alike nevertheless found themselves obliged to descend from their Olympian preoccupation with the universal and attend to the everyday complaints of butchers and bakers. They attempted to meet this challenge, as they tried to meet the challenge posed by the working class, by restating the precept of class harmony in more strident terms. The common interests of bourgeoisie and petty bourgeoisie had visibly moved apart in market place and society; they had to be re-emphasized at the political level. The rhetorical excess and dishonesty of so-called *Mittelstandspolitik* was the result.[16]

The Prussian Junkers certainly made political capital out of this embarrassment, especially in the liberal camp. Or, more precisely, professional functionaries of the Agrarian League such as Hahn and Oertel skilfully deployed the selectively anti-capitalist rhetoric of *Mittelstandspolitik* as a means of securing popular support for landowning Conservatives.[17] This was of great party-political importance, for it confirmed the liberals' narrowing base of support. It also indicated the extent to which a part of the Junker class was prepared to modernize its political style in order to survive as a political force. These points have often been made by historians to buttress their arguments about the persistence of pre-industrial, pre-modern forces in Germany. But the point of overriding significance, perhaps, is not that the landowners, via the Conservative Party and the Agrarian League, were prepared to use such methods, but that all the non-socialist parties were to some extent driven to do the

---

[16] I argue this point at length in *Class, Religion and Local Politics*, where references can be found.

[17] H.-J. Puhle, *Agrarische Interessenpolitik und preussischer Konservatismus im wilhelminischen Kaisereich, 1893–1914* (Hanover, 1966), pp. 98 ff.

same. Leaders of the National Liberals and of the Centre Party, even the left liberals, were often startlingly demagogic in their espousal of *Mittelstandspolitik*. They offered panaceas which they often knew to be bogus; indeed, had the measures they affected to support been effective, they would have undermined the basis of Germany's advanced capitalist order. Politically, more than at other levels, the grievances of the petty bourgeoisie thus exposed contradictions in the general bourgeois position and injected a new measure of mendacity into political debate.

A similar pattern holds true for the peasantry and politics. Both the speed and unevenness of economic growth in Germany gave rise to major peasant discontent in the last decades of the nineteenth century. As Germany became breathlessly industrialized and urbanized, while simultaneously becoming part of a world market in primary produce, the peasantry faced problems of uncertain income, rising costs of many kinds, and indebtedness.[18] None of these problems was entirely new; nor was the tendency to blame them on 'outsiders'. But the perception of exploitation became more sharply focused as the self-sufficiency of the peasant economy was eroded, and the peasant locked more firmly into a market economy in which the countryside was patently dominated by the town. This transformation helped to cast old grievances in new form. The traditional figures who had served the peasant as symbols of the parasitic and exploitative outsider changed; they were up-dated in line with the advancing bourgeois social order. The lawyer remained as a symbol of oppression by city men—although there were no 'peasant advocates' in the 1890s. But the money-lender was overshadowed by the banker, the grain-dealer by the grain speculator on the commodity exchange,

---

[18] The best introduction to these problems remains the work of Hans Rosenberg and Hans-Jürgen Puhle. Kitchen makes the main arguments available in English. See also Puhle, 'Conservatism in Modern German History', *Journal of Contemporary History*, 13 (1978), 701–7. But there is a growing (and I believe more convincing) view that both Rosenberg and Puhle attribute too large a role to the malign Junkers. This latter view, it is perhaps worth adding, has nothing in common with the recent nostalgia for the Junkers, or *Preussenwelle*, in the Federal Republic. Sentimentalists about the old Prussia seldom address these questions at all.

the landlord's agent by the agricultural inspector, the hawker by the fertilizer ring.[19]

Like the working class and petty bourgeoisie, the peasantry tried to organize itself at the point of production or distribution, most obviously through co-operatives. But these were difficult to sustain except in certain branches such as dairy farming.[20] Peasant discontent was also displaced, therefore, on to the political level. Historians have tended, once again, to see this as an essentially anti-modern phenomenon which undermined liberalism and gave the Junkers a new lease of political life. The Agrarian League has been portrayed as the vehicle of a popularized Prussian Conservatism, offering blandishments to secure peasant support. The reality was more complex and contradictory. In the first place, the tenor of peasant resentment was broadly anti-notable, rather than specifically anti-liberal or anti-modern. The objects of peasant grievance included landowning grandees, Junker and non-Junker, as well as obvious targets of the capitalist system such as the stock-exchange dealer, the lawyer, and the veterinary surgeon 'with top hat and kid gloves'.[21] There was some significance in the way the Bavarian Peasant League bracketed the priest and the aristocrat together with the doctor and the professor in its rogues' gallery of those whose political tutelage the peasant should reject. A similar strain, anti-notable in the sense of being anti-bourgeois and anti-aristocratic, ran through the rhetoric of peasant tribunes such as Hermann Ahlwardt, Otto Böckel, and Philipp Köhler.[22]

---

[19] Details and references in Blackbourn, 'Peasants and Politics in Germany, 1871-1914', *European History Quarterly*, 14 (1984), 47–75.

[20] In 1890 dairy co-operative accounted for 639 out of a total of around 3,000 co-operatives. U. Teichmann, *Die Politik der Agrarpreisstützing* (Cologne, 1955), pp. 543 ff.

[21] The reported phrase of a Swabian peasant, rather disingenuously quoted by the deputy leader of the Centre Party in Württemberg during the course of a parliamentary debate: *Verhandlungen der Württ. Kammer der Abgeordneten auf dem 36. Landtag. Prot.-Band IV*, p. 2483, 100 Sitting, 14 June 1905.

[22] The anti-semitic and populist agrarian movements are dealt with in English by P. W. Massing, *Rehearsal for Destruction* (New York, 1949), P. G. J. Pulzer, *The Rise of Political Anti-Semitism in Germany and Austria* (New York, 1964) and R. S. Levy, *The Downfall of the Anti-Semitic Political Parties in Imperial Germany* (New Haven, 1975). For a good recent account of the Böckel move-

It was not just liberalism that was threatened by peasant rumblings. The liberal parties did, of course, prove to be the most obvious victims of peasant anger; and the Agrarian League, for its part, did succeed in containing and canalizing a good deal of this rural upthrust in the interest of the large landowners. No one, I think, would wish to deny the importance of this in party-political terms, or to deny its significance as a measure of the political staying-power and adaptability of the Imperial German Junkers. The success of the Agrarian League, however, was achieved by means which some old Junkers such as Mirbach and Limburg-Stirum considered 'alien and unaristocratic'.[23] They were right, by patrician standards. By the same token, the political acrobatics of the other non-socialist parties when faced with peasant discontent could be termed 'alien and unbourgeois'— alien and unbourgeois, that is, by the standards of notable politics in an earlier period when the political stage was more bare. From the 1890s, Centre, National Liberal, and (to a lesser extent) left-liberal leaders sought, with varying degrees of success, to persuade their respective and unruly peasant constituencies of their impeccable agrarian credentials. They finessed this trick in different ways: by support for measures that held out the hope of protecting the peasantry from market forces, and by often rather forced genuflections to 'peasant virtues'. The central point is this: in the case of the peasant, as in that of the worker and petty bourgeois, the mid-century language of class harmony had worn thin. The gap between universal claims and the reality of German capitalism had widened and become an issue in the political arena. Challenged in this arena, bourgeois politicians responded by restating the precept of class harmony with a studied demagogy which would have outraged their notable predecessors. In this

ment, see White, *Splintered Party*, pp. 136 ff.; and on the Bavarian *Bauernbund*, I. Farr, 'Populism in the Countryside: the Peasant Leagues in Bavaria in the 1890s', in Evans (ed.), *Society and Politics in Wilhelmine Germany*, pp. 136-59. See also Blackbourn, 'Peasants and Politics'.

[23] The phrase is Hans-Jürgen Puhle's: *Agrarische Interessenpolitik*, p. 275. Cf. Philipp Eulenburg's view of the Agrarian League as demagogic and 'democratic': I. Hull, *The Entourage of Kaiser Wilhelm II* (Cambridge, 1982), p. 114.

respect, it is the distance travelled by German political life as a whole between the 1860s and 1914, not the particular success of the Agrarian League and the weakness of liberalism, that deserves our closest attention.

The bourgeois mode of politics which crystallized in the middle of the century was based on main-line railways, the growth of the urban press, and the mobilization of the notables. The rise of opposition to it at the end of the century was based on the expansion of local and suburban railway lines, the growth of the local press, and the mobilization of the masses. In a very real sense, therefore, the system of politics that had come into being during the years of relatively self-conscious bourgeois dominance in the middle of the century was attacked with its own weapons: communications, association, the mobilizing of 'opinion'. More than that, the very speed of economic and social transformation in Germany contributed to undermining bourgeois claims to represent a general interest in society. It was the thoroughness of bourgeois transformation in economy and society that generated the multiple discontents that were carried in to the political domain. There, these discontents were painfully contained in the years before 1914. The words 'painfully' and 'contained' require equal stress; for the way in which pressure from out of doors was contained explains a good deal about the unstable and febrile nature of politics in Imperial Germany.

To borrow a phrase from Carl Schorske which he applied to contemporary Austria, we are entitled to talk of a 'politics in a new key'[24] in Germany from the 1890s. This new politics had three principal sources. First, economic and social conficts were displaced on to the political level with a greater intensity than elsewhere. Secondly, universal suffrage along with rights of association provided considerable scope for the public expression of these conflicts. We should remember that the Reichstag elections of 1907 and 1912 saw a turn-out of 84 per cent. Elections to the parliament of one southern state registered even higher figures, and there were by-elections where the turn-out reached 93 and 94 per

---

[24] C. E. Schorske, *Fin-de-Siècle Vienna* (New York, 1981), pp. 116–80.

cent.[25] The sale of black-market tickets to the Reichstag gallery gives a further small indication of the degree to which national politics had become a truly popular drama. And yet, of course, this seething popular politics found no outlet in the ministerial responsibility of party leaders. That is the third major reason why the 'new politics' acquired the form it did. There were no true German parallels to Gladstone's Midlothian campaign or Gambetta's great Republican sweep through France in the winter of 1871-2. However much party leaders cultivated a popular, and even populist, style out of doors, in parliament itself they remained brokers, lacking ultimate political responsibility. In fact, their dual activities as parliamentary brokers and out-of-doors demagogues were really two aspects of the same role. It was not, as contemporary patricians complained, parliament that 'heated the passions' of the people; it was universal suffrage, coupled with the lack of parliamentary government. We have already considered the original constitutional settlement of 1871 in the light of these twin characteristics. It is necessary to consider finally the question of reform in the years down to 1914.

2. *What Kind of Reform?*

Historians have sometimes talked rather misleadingly about political rigidity and stasis in Imperial Germany. The formal constitutional arrangements of 1871 did indeed remain unchanged until the war; but the political content of the system changed considerably. The complex and contradictory nature of Bismarck's handiwork, far from suggesting some kind of historical straitjacket which confined the form of the Imperial polity, should alert us rather to its plasticity. Two changes in the political reality of Imperial Germany have already been noted: the creeping legitimacy of the rule of law, and the emergence of a vigorous popular politics. There were other, no less significant shifts in the political and constitutional status quo. The Reich, for example, took on an increasingly

---

[25] See the appendices in Blackbourn, *Class, Religion and Local Politics*, pp. 246-8.

unitary rather than federal character. Connected with this in a number of ways was a marked change in the stuff of political debate and decision-making, from the formal constitutional issues of the 1870s (the role of the individual states, State–Church relations) to the predominantly economic and social issues of the 1890s and beyond. The place of the Reichstag in political life reflected and in turn reinforced these changes. The years from the 1870s to the First World War witnessed the growing legitimacy of parliamentary politics. This was aptly symbolized by the opening of a new Reichstag building in the 1890s, and by the granting of allowances to Reichstag deputies, a step which Bismarck had always resisted. The Reichstag enjoyed an increasing *de facto* authority *vis-à-vis* the Bundesrat. Evidence of this can be seen in the mounting volume of Reichstag business, especially in committee, the growing importance of major party leaders and committee experts in influencing political decision-making, and the increasing readiness of successive chancellors to take such figures into account. These changes all pointed in the same direction and they had a cumulative significance.[26]

The intention here is not to resurrect the theory of silent parliamentarization once favoured by conservative historians and recently revived by Manfred Rauh. The Kaiser clearly did not become a limited constitutional monarch and the chancellor did not become a party leader drawn from a majority grouping in the Reichstag. The Kaiser's constitutional prerogatives and his wilfully unpredictable use of them hardly need to be rehearsed at great length. The constraints imposed on successive chancellors by the need to tack between this impossible master and his entourage on the one hand, and an often intractable Reichstag on the other, were evident in different ways in the careers of Hohenlohe, Bülow, and

---

[26] See M. Rauh, *Föderalismus und Parlamentarismus im Wilhelminischen Reich* (Düsseldorf, 1972) and *Die Parlamentarisierung des Deutschen Reiches* (Düsseldorf, 1977), on these changes. I should add that I cannot share Rauh's conclusions about the 'parliamentarization' of the Reich. More important, Rauh's books are disfigured by highly polemical attacks on the 'Critical School' of historians in the Federal Republic. J. C. G. Röhl, *Germany Without Bismarck* (London, 1967), and P. Molt, *Der Reichstag vor der improvisierten Revolution* (Cologne and Opladen, 1963), also give a valuable sense of the changing status and composition of the Reichstag, and of its workings.

Bethmann Hollweg. The Zabern affair of 1913 suggests the limits to the Reichstag's authority as well as the gain in importance which had accrued to it in the preceding decades. It was undoubtedly significant that Zabern did actually become a cause celebre: press, opinion, and parliamentary parties were outraged, and the latter formed a temporary united front in the Reichstag debates of December 1913. Yet, in the end, the army refused to admit any error and the Minister of War blamed everything on 'screaming mobs and yellow journalism'.[27] When the Kaiser characteristically set his face against any concessions to the ruffled feelings of Reichstag parliamentarians, both the liberal-minded governor of Alsace-Lorraine and the nice-minded Chancellor Bethmann were left politically in the lurch. The political parties, for their part, were left with no further recourse: their united front predictably collapsed. More even than the issue of control over army and navy budgets, the political outcome of the Zabern episode revealed the everyday impotence of parliament when it came to enforcing its will on the Kaiser and 'his' government.

There is no easy explanation for this 'failure'. Given that parliamentary politics did in many respects acquire a new importance in Wilhelmine Germany, the problem nevertheless needs to be addressed. In tackling it, an initial point follows from the arguments made earlier in this essay: parliamentarism and ministerial responsibility were by no means the natural focus even of reformist aspirations. Even for many who did aim at this target—one thinks again of Max Weber—the means of parliamentary government were secondary to the ends of strengthening and stabilizing the power of the executive.[28] More commonly, especially in bourgeois circles where historians expect reformist urges to originate, the growing public face of national politics prompted a retreat off the political stage. This was perhaps most obviously the case among large businessmen, who preferred to air their affairs in a less public forum. But it was also true of many whose celebration of the non-political virtues was directly proportionate to the mounting volume of noise made by the

[27] Schoenbaum, *Zabern*, p. 122.
[28] Struve, *Elites against Democracy*, pp. 114–48; Mommsen, *Max Weber und die deutsche Politik*, pp. 115 ff.

Reichstag and many state parliaments.[29] Abstinence from
national politics was no less evident among many publicly
active figures whose political as well as social power base
remained in individual towns and cities. Both old-fashioned
notables and new-style technocrats found a greater scope for
administrative reform in the municipality, as councillors and
especially as mayors, than they could expect in Berlin. There
were many before 1914 who shared Konrad Adenauer's
feelings during the 1920s, when he preferred to remain as
mayor of Cologne rather than stoop to becoming chancellor
of the Weimar Republic. In Frankfurt, Stuttgart, and elsewhere there were Wilhelmine mayors who saw themselves as
politically enlightened and progressive, but whose reformism
was conceived in local and often apolitical terms.[30] This
ethos of enlightened administration as a substitute for the
politics of conflict clearly had affinities with one strand of
opinion within the Prussian bureaucracy (and other state
bureaucracies); but it had more in common with 'advanced'
opinion in the Berlin ministries than it did with backwoods
Junker *Landräte* of the Imperial era. Similar attitudes can be
found in the radical nationalist associations. Their impatience
with parliamentary 'talking shops' articulated a broad sentiment not to be confused with habitual patrician disdain,
which betrayed many 'modern' features.[31] In earlier chapters
I have tried to show the specific social context of attitudes
like this, and the reasons why they enjoyed such a wide
currency.

The advent of a popular dimension to German political life
clearly played a part in determining the options for reform.
It may be said to have had, in fact, a curious double effect.
On the one hand it alienated many older notables and newer
technocrats. Where they retained public as well as private
ambitions, these were usually channelled into municipal

[29] Gottlob Egelhaaf, a local National Liberal notable of the old sort in
Württemberg, registered with distaste the 'agitation against the "gentlemen"' in
the late 1880s. From he 1890s he was increasingly disenchanted with the more
vulgar tone of hustings and parliamentary proceedings in the state. See Egelhaaf,
Lebenserinnerungen, pp. 58, 84–5, 125–6.

[30] Sheehan, *German Liberalism*, esp. pp. 235–8; and 'Liberalism and the City
in Nineteenth-Century Germany', *Past and Present*, 51 (1971), 116–37.

[31] Eley, *Reshaping the German Right*.

reform or some other, frequently single-issue cause. The changes in associational life already noted were a pointer to this trend. On the other hand, the rise of a mass politics encouraged many—radical nationalists and Agrarian League strategists among them—to conceive of a direct form of popular, even populist politics which would, so they hoped, make parliaments irrelevant. This latter view, with all its Bonapartist overtones, owed more to the political climacteric of the 1890s than it did to Bismarckian Caesarism; and its initial impulse came from below, even if subsequent governments such as Bülow's sought with ambiguous results to orchestrate it. It was the authentic outcrop of bourgeois, post-liberal contempt for the notable politics of the past, the horse-trading politics of the present, and the imagined parliamentary politics of the future. The soured emancipatory impulse it embodied was not the handy weapon of the old guard it is sometimes represented as: it was much more a challenge to constituted authority. Equally clearly, though, parliamentary government of the English kind was not at all what it understood by reform.[32]

Reform in the broadest sense, then, did not necessarily mean reform in the direction of parliamentary government; it might mean quite the opposite. Moreover, even if we examine parliaments and parties themselves, there are a number of good reasons why a major instalment of constitutional reform remained elusive. Some general impediments have been rightly noted by historians: the bias in the Reichstag electoral boundaries which, like the Prussian three-class suffrage, favoured the parties of resistance rather than movement; the party leaders' fears that if they pushed too hard they might invite a *coup d'état* from above, or *Staatsstreich*; the sheer difficulty for the parties in breaking out of the subsidiary role to which they were formally assigned. This last clearly developed a powerful momentum; and it helps to explain the importance of horse-trading and interest-broking which came to characterize the Wilhelmine political parties. In considering the failure of a powerful reformist thrust in parliament, it is nevertheless difficult to escape the impression that

[32] Ibid.

a 'manipulative' interpretation has been pushed too far. Not all the weaknesses of the parties can be attributed to their emasculation by Bismarck and his successors. There were, after all, numerous sources of authentic division between the parties and these also acquired a notable momentum. They arguably deserve as much attention as the sticks and carrots wielded by the executive. The outstanding German historians of the Imperial period have actually written curiously little about the character of party politics in the broad sense. A more detailed picture is only now emerging, and it seems to confirm the importance of chronic party divisions for the opening and closing of political (and potentially constitutional) options. It also suggests that the origins and ramifications of these divisions were more complex than is often implied. I have written on this elsewhere at considerable length.[33] In the present essay I have tried to show how economic, social, religious, and other conflicts not only were displaced on to the political stage, but were also magnified in the process. The struggle of interest groups, which seriously divided the bourgeois parties among themselves (as well as dividing all from the SPD), serves as an obvious example. But there are other instances of divisions which, in Germany, acquired a particularly shrill inflection in the political domain.

The fact that the non-socialist parties each filled the idea of political advance with its own distinctive content certainly worked against the possibility of a united front in a body such as the Reichstag. It is, for example, revealing to see how the Centre Party and the liberal parties were willing to support, and even to demand, politically repressive measures against the supporters of the other, the former in the name of public morality, the latter in the name of Progress. The Centre was hostile to the Revolution Bill of the 1890s, but happy to see it become a legislative cudgel against 'freethinking professors'.[34] It was also the Centre that made the running in trying to turn the Lex Heinze, originally concerned with

[33] Blackbourn, *Class, Religion and Local Politics*.
[34] A detailed account in English can be found in J. K. Zeender, *The German Center Party, 1890–1906* (Philadelphia, 1976), pp. 50–5.

organized crime and prostitution, into a sharply illiberal package of anti-immorality legislation, an aim which was frankly embarrassing to the Imperial government itself.[35] It was, on the other hand, a left liberal who coined the phrase *Kulturkampf* to describe what liberals generally viewed as a justified use of state power to crush 'clerical reaction'. It was the same strain of arrogance, already noted in this essay, that enabled National Liberals to disregard Centre Party objections to the anti-Polish language paragraphs of the 1908 law of association.[36] It is worth remembering here that a liberal critic of Kaiserdom like Max Weber actually left the Pan-German League because he considered its policy too soft on the Poles.[37] On matters Catholic or Polish, and above all on matters Catholic and Polish, German liberals showed a marked tendency to be *plus royaliste que le roi*. These divisions, as we have seen, grew out of fierce conflicts within society. They naturally owed a good deal to government repression of varying kinds, whether continuing or in the past; and ministers were not above encouraging them on the principle of 'divide and rule'. Here too, however, the metaphor of the sorcerer's apprentice is appropriate. Inter-party divisions took on a vigorous life of their own; they also had a profound effect on the behaviour of the political parties. The conduct of the parties after the first angry unanimity over the Zabern affair, for instance, cannot be fully appreciated without taking the depth of these divisions into account.

We should therefore consider carefully just what we mean by the idea of thwarted constitutional reform in Imperial Germany. At least since Arthur Rosenberg half a century ago posed the question of why there had been no 'Gladstonian coalition'[38] in Germany during this period, there have been historians who have looked hypothetically at the potential reformist blocs whose non-realization constituted a 'missed opportunity'. The most recent example is Beverly Heckart's

[35] See R. J. V. Lenman, 'Art, Society and the Law in Wilhelmine Germany: the Lex Heinze', *Oxford German Studies*, 8 (1973–4), 86–113.

[36] Cf. Hall, *Scandal, Sensation and Social Democracy*, pp. 55 ff.

[37] See his letter of resignation, printed in Marianne Weber, *Max Weber, A Biography*, ed. H. Zohn (New York, 1973), pp. 224–5.

[38] A. Rosenberg, *Imperial Germany* (London, 1931), p. 18.

study *From Bassermann to Bebel*, which has the subtitle 'The Grand Bloc's Quest for Reform in the Kaiserreich, 1900–1914'.[39] Such studies have often been valuable and I am aware of having tried to make my own contribution to the problem.[40] But the tendency of such an approach is necessarily to ask questions about what did not happen rather than what did. It should perhaps be emphasized, therefore, that the lack of a unified reformist drive in Imperial Germany is not really very surprising. It was the result of authentic political divisions within the non-socialist parties, and between them and the SPD; these were only exacerbated by the problematical relationship of all parties and parliaments to German governments.

There is a final point which also follows from the arguments made earlier in this essay. Divisions between the parties also proceeded from the varying kinds and degrees of difficulty they experienced in dealing with their own popular constituencies at a time when the political nation was expanding. The issue of electoral reform brings this out. Attitudes towards electoral reform were partly, of course, a reflection of regional party variations and the narrow calculation of local party advantage. Thus, to take one example, the Centre Party supported a system of proportional representation in Württemberg but opposed it in Alsace; the National Liberals supported it in Alsace but opposed it in Württemberg.[41] A similar set of rival political opportunisms contributed materially to the failure of Prussian electoral reform.[42] But there was certainly more than tactical advantage at stake in these cases. It is noteworthy that the Centre Party, whose demagogy worked better with rural and small-town Catholics than with workers, should generally have been hostile to electoral reforms which threatened to redraw constituency boundaries in favour of urban areas. There are many examples of this reluctance, and the sentiment can be found more strongly

[39] B. Heckart, *From Bassermann to Bebel* (New Haven, 1974).

[40] In Blackbourn, *Class, Religion and Local Politics*, and in earlier articles which appeared in the *Historical Journal* (1975) and *Central European History* (1976).

[41] On Alsace, see Heckart, *From Bassermann to Bebel*, pp. 162-6; on Württemberg, Blackbourn, *Class, Religion and Local Politics*, pp. 129-31.

[42] Heckart, *From Bassermann to Bebel*, pp. 55-6, 154-60.

still in political Conservatism. The liberals had more wide-ranging problems in this respect, for their universal claims had left them with universal difficulties. National Liberals were responsible for legislation which introduced a more restrictive franchise in Bremen, Lübeck, and a number of Saxon cities in order to minimize the electoral impact of the SPD. Left liberals in many cities were similarly opposed to electoral reform which would benefit Social Democracy. Nor did these problems exist only in urban areas: National Liberals supported the introduction in 1896 of a three-class franchise for state elections in Saxony, and consistently opposed the introduction of electoral reform which included the direct vote in Baden and Bavaria.[43]

This was only partly a matter of party advantage. Or, rather, the recognition of party advantage in the narrow sense was in itself only a recognition that the people, or sections of it, should be kept out of the political arena. The detailed arguments over proposals to reform the Prussian Landtag in 1910 reveal the degree of apprehension on this score. At one level, the failure of reform seems to fit a familiar pattern: the Junker-based Conservatives dug their heels in and argued that even the government's modest proposal had gone too far. But the Conservatives did not, in fact, possess a majority in the Prussian lower house. The three-class franchise certainly protected them electorally, as often noted; but it also produced a regular aggregate of rather more than 200 seats for the Centre Party, National Liberals, and left liberals. This bloc of seats would not have remained intact had the SPD achieved a return of seats which fairly reflected its share of the total vote. And that was the crucial point. None of these three parties wholeheartedly favoured the introduction of equal, direct, and secret voting for the Prussian Landtag. The Centre and National Liberals each favoured a different kind of compromise reform which would balance hoped-for gains against anticipated losses. The left liberals were theoretically committed to equal, direct, and secret suffrage, but in practice they also saw grounds for concern.[44]

[43] Sheehan, *German Liberalism*, pp. 221 ff.
[44] W. Gagel, *Die Wahlrechtsfrage in der Geschichte der deutschen liberalen Parteien 1848-1918* (Düsseldorf, 1958), pp. 113-25, 163-7, on the general problems of the liberal parties and democracy.

When we talk about the failure of reform, we should therefore be quite clear what sort of reform we are talking about. Even if we focus our attention on the political parties, it may be misleading simply to pose the question why they failed to reform a sham-constitutional system. These parties reflected very real divisions over political matters; each filled the idea of constitutional, political, and electoral reform with its own content. It deserves note that when, after 1912, a form of *de facto* parliamentary government came into effect in Bavaria, the political content it was given by the dominant Centre Party was highly illiberal. Indeed, liberals in the state had regularly opposed electoral reform which they feared would lead to this. These political divisions in turn had an important popular component. We cannot really keep the various conceptions of reform among the political parties separate from the overall (and changing) relationship between the parties and the populace. Even though party leaders would have defined rather differently their apprehensions about the threat from 'below', all would have agreed that it had to be contained. The importance of this is obvious enough on occasions such as 1848-9 and 1918-19; these were political dramas when clearly more was at stake than different variants of modest constitutional reform. But we should not lose sight of this dimension of politics in the years between 1848 and 1918. As this essay has tried to show, the very success of the bourgeois economic and social order in these years stored up problems at the political level. Everyday material and social grievances were transmuted into political discontent. The closing years of the last century, in particular, marked a period when the set-piece and rather comfortable drama of notable politics was rudely interrupted from offstage as new voices demanded to be heard. The process whereby these demands were met and contained, both before and after the First World War, was to be of crucial importance for the future of German politics.

VI
Conclusion

All national histories are peculiar, but some appear to be more peculiar than others. Few historians of modern Germany, whether native or non-native, can escape awareness of that. Historians of other countries are also engaged in some manner with examining national myths: 1688 and the English genius for gradualism, 1789 and the French revolutionary tradition, Easter 1916 and the Irish nationalist mystique. The work of revisionism, in each of these cases, has frequently been a matter of debunking, questioning the pieties of the myth, and pointing up its paralysing as well as emancipating features. But post-war historians of Germany have seen themselves presented with a still more daunting task. They have been concerned not just with residual elements of a myth, but with explaining why the course of German history led to 1933. This explanation has taken different forms. After 1945, an influential generation of British historians concerned itself especially, although by no means exclusively, with the combination of militarism and political 'immaturity' which had seemed to mark out modern German history. Their views (and the vulgarized versions of them) continue to have considerable resonance among the academic and lay publics, certainly in Britain and the United States. Since the beginning of the 1960s, however, German history has been approached in different ways. But its peculiarity—the sense of it as an aberration—has remained very much on the agenda, even though the idioms in which it is described have changed. One such approach has been the identification of the peculiar German Mind, distinguished by its lack of civic sense and a disposition towards a sinister irrationalism. Another has been the diagnosis of an authoritarian misdevelopment of German political life, dating back at least to unification and leaving a legacy of pre-industrial and traditional institutions and values which were not successfully modernized. Each of these related ways of looking at the German past also has a powerful purchase. In the latter case, indeed, the approach in question has become a formidable set of organizing assumptions as a result of monographs, general accounts, historiographical interventions, and the purposive rediscovery of works by formerly neglected historians.

What can be said about these ways of looking at the German past? First, of course, their questions and answers have produced much of the most illuminating work on modern German history during the last decades. In no way has the present essay sought to belittle these achievements. Secondly, these perspectives on the past are clearly not identical with each other. They emerged from different milieus and betray different casts of mind and temperament. In many points of detail and interpretation they would make odd, even incompatible, bedfellows. But there are certain basic questions and answers which they share. They view 1933 as the final outcome of a particular historical continuity; they see that continuity as the product of German peculiarity; and they see a crucial element of that peculiarity in the aberrant behaviour of the German bourgeoisie. While these approaches are therefore neither identical with each other, nor of course the only ones in which modern German history has been discussed, they nevertheless have sufficient common threads and sufficient stature to be worthy of critical attention. If there is a figure in the carpet it is German peculiarity, of which in turn the failure of the bourgeoisie to conduct itself like a 'proper' bourgeoisie is a central motif. It is dissatisfaction with this way of looking at things that has prompted the present essay.

The concept of historical peculiarity is clearly a useful tool of comparative history; but in the German case it seems often to have been applied more as a standard against which one particular national history has been measured and found wanting. I have tried to suggest why this seems to me unsatisfactory, and above all to raise the question of what we mean by a 'failed' bourgeois revolution in Germany. A basic problem here is that historians have often adopted, at least implicitly, a rather restricted idea of what constituted a successful bourgeois programme. In this scheme of things an economically buoyant and socially self-conscious class asserts itself against traditional forces, with representative institutions and modern values emerging as the outcome of its successful struggle. By these standards, of course, the German bourgeoisie was a failure: it received what it wanted in material terms 'from above', while leaving a dominant role in political life and the setting of social values to pre-industrial elements. But this picture is changed if one takes a less restricted view. I have used the concept of bourgeois revolution to denote a broader pattern of material, institutional, legal, and intellectual changes whose cumulative effect was all the more powerful for coming to seem 'natural'. The key here is civil society. My emphasis has been to recover the texture and meaning of that civil society as it unfolded in nineteenth-century Germany, by looking at changes in property relations, the market economy, and the way they were perceived, in the rule of law and what it signified, in ideas about progress, in associational life, in patronage, taste, and concepts of respectability. It is in this context that the vexing phenomena of bourgeois cultural despair, civic quietism, and social 'feudalization' have been located.

In stressing the importance of civil society, however, I have not tried simply to redefine bourgeois revolution with the politics left out. I have tried, instead, to look critically at the place politics actually occupied within German bourgeois society. Changes in civil society had far-reaching political implications. They were a prerequisite for the creation of a public sphere, and this in turn provided the model for a form of bourgeois notable politics on a national scale which crystallized in the 1860s. This is not, of course, to substitute an unmitigated bourgeois success story for a story of unmitigated bourgeois failure. This essay has emphatically not been about 'rising middle classes'. The point, rather, is that what I have called a silent revolution was most impressive precisely where it was most silent—where its dispensations came to seem 'natural'. By the same token, bourgeois dominance was most open to attack in the most overtly public domain—politics itself. On the political stage, more than in everyday material life, the world of associations, or the sphere of law, the bourgeoisie was exposed: its divisions were more apparent, its claims to social leadership more open to challenge. This was not just true 'above', in relations with crown, army, and bureaucracy; it was also true 'below'. As I have tried to show, the working class, peasantry, and petty bourgeoisie felt able to challenge bourgeois claims to leadership in the political sphere in ways which they seldom could in the market-place or the lawcourts. This challenge was variously resisted and deflected and exploited in ways which had a decisive effect on both the direction and the style of German political life.

To the extent that this challenge was resisted, two important consequences should be noted. First, the major brokers of bourgeois interests tended to retreat off the political stage into pressure groups, away from public scrutiny. Parliaments and public sphere were thus short-circuited. As Charles Maier has recently reminded us, this process was by no means confined to Germany. But as with many of the other developments discussed above, Germany may be considered the paradigm case. Secondly, the vulnerability of public life to the challenge of vulgar interlopers placed a premium on a strong state. This set certain limits to bourgeois enthusiasm for democracy and even parliamentarization. When combined with the very real political divisions between the bourgeois parties, this undermined certain kinds of reformist thrust in Imperial Germany. I have tried here to explore some of the implications for our understanding of 'reform'. Where there were attempts to harness pressure from below the consequences were no less important. Social and economic grievances, 'displaced' on to the political level, were contained and orchestrated only as a result of significant changes in political life. One of these was a major stepping up of mass party organization; another was the tendency of the parties to restate the language of class harmony, taken for granted earlier, in increasingly strident terms. This was not the exclusive preoccupation of Conservatives: it was evident also in the bourgeois parties of the centre. The result was to impart an intensified and recklessly demagogic tone to German politics on the eve of the First World War.

It is perhaps worth underlining that this approach offers little encouragement to historians of an apologist bent. It should be clear that my interpretation does not depict a modern German history innocent of class interest and social conflict; it does try to specify what was at stake in that conflict. I have tried to loosen the strait jacket of interpretation which arguably lays undue stress on the political role played by the 'bloc of the pre-industrial power system'. That role has not been disregarded; but emphasis has also been placed on the fracturing of a mode of 'notable politics' inherited from the middle of the nineteenth century, and its replacement by a more uncertain, transitional kind of politics in the years before 1914. In stressing the challenge which helped to precipitate this change, I have also questioned the idea of 'manipulation' with which historians have commonly described the cynical preservation of class interests (particularly those of a 'pre-industrial élite'). This, once again, does not entail denying the elements of political dishonesty which characterized Imperial Germany; but it is easy to misidentify the range of would-be manipulators, and to approach the question of political manipulation itself one-sidedly. I am sceptical of accounts that depict the political process, in Gramsci's words, as 'a continuous *marche de dupes*, a competition in conjuring and sleight of hand'. It does greater justice to a complex historical process to recognize that if we are to talk of manipulation at all—and I prefer the term demagogy—we should at least recognize that it was a two-way process which was politically unpredictable and potentially dangerous. This approach need be neither ingenuous nor 'populist'. The purpose of questioning the idea of manipulation by a particular élite is not to substitute a view that everything happened 'from below' (which might be called the populist heresy), or that it happened because of the entry of 'the masses' into politics (the older conservative orthodoxy). The intention here has been to try to add the missing dimension to accounts that habitually present the sound of only one hand clapping. Similarly, I have not sought to deny the elements of continuity that link the history of Imperial Germany with the Weimar Republic and the Third Reich. It would hardly be necessary to make such a disclaimer, perhaps, had apologist historians not insisted on portraying the Third Reich as an 'accident'. The real question about continuity is not 'whether' but 'in which ways?' I have offered an implicit answer to the second of these questions by suggesting that we examine nineteenth-century Germany itself from a rather different perspective. This arises partly, of course, from a desire that Imperial Germany especially be treated less as a mere prelude to what followed. In terms of continuity, however, this could be put in more positive terms. To return to the opening remarks of the essay, the real strands of continuity across the divide of the First World War can best be followed if we look at what did happen in Imperial Germany rather than at what did not.

Perhaps a final observation is called for on the dangers of complacency, moral as well as historical, if we insist too much on a certain kind of German peculiarity. While he was preparing *Doctor Faustus*, Thomas Mann warned of creating 'a new German myth, flattering the Germans with their own "demonism"'. Nearly forty years on, we see this problem at its most acute in the ephemera which has helped to establish the Third Reich as a macabre, but chic, chamber of horrors. That is what Hans-Jürgen Syberberg meant by referring to the Third Reich as 'our Disneyland'. Historians cannot dismiss this problem with an impatient gesture, for it raises moral implications for their own work. The charge of 'trivializing' the Third Reich has been raised in recent acrimonious exchanges between historians of the 1930s, and the general issue is clearly present beneath the surface of the *Sonderweg* debate. My own view is that serious historians are perhaps most likely to 'trivialize' modern German history in an involuntary manner: by exaggerated emphasis on the absoluteness of German peculiarity, which indirectly bolsters the morbid mystique of German history. There is a pedagogic, as well as a historical, argument for denting that mystique, just as there is a parallel case for not placing swastikas routinely on the covers of books dealing with twentieth-century Germany. That does not mean that we should write the history of Germany as if it were like the history of everywhere else; only that we should not write it as if it were quite unlike the history of anywhere else. The distinctiveness of German history is probably best recognized if we do not see it (before 1945) as a permanent falling-away from the 'normal'. In many respects, as I have tried to show, the German experience constituted a heightened version of what occurred elsewhere. This is true of Germany's dynamic capitalism, and of the social and political consequences it generated. It is true of the complex mesh of private and public virtues and vices which were characteristic of German bourgeois society. It is true of a widespread sentiment like cultural despair, and of the crass materialism which unwittingly reinforced it. It is true, I believe—although not all will want to accept this— of the way in which these and other phenomena discussed above combined to produce Germany's exceptionally radical form of fascism. What stamps the German case as distinctive is, of course, the particular, uneven combination of these elements. This is not an attempt to smuggle peculiarity in again through the back door. As we have also seen, this unevenness of economic, social, and political developments was not in itself peculiarly German: Germany was much more the intensified version of the norm than the exception. That it so often appears exceptional probably owes a good deal to the distorting focus of a more acceptable myth—that of a benign and painless 'western modernization'. There is much to be said for shifting our emphasis away from the *Sonderweg* and viewing the course of German history as distinctive but not *sui generis*: the particular might then help to illuminate the general, rather than remaining stubbornly (and sometimes morbidly) peculiar. That would be less likely to encourage apologetics than to disarm them. It might also enlarge rather than diminish our sense of modern Germany as a metaphor of our times. We recognize the richness of allusion when Walter Benjamin called Paris the 'capital of the nineteenth century'. We should be similarly open to the full meaning of Germany as the 'tragic land' of the twentieth century. Our historical and moral sense of that tragedy is sharpened, not blunted, if we decline to view it solely as the final culmination of German peculiarity.

Bibliographical Note

The purpose of this brief note is to indicate a few salient works in English for the guidance of the non-specialist reader. Given the wide-ranging nature of the two essays, a full listing of all the works cited in the footnotes would provide an extremely unwieldy guide to the relevant literature. A sense of the latter is best gained, perhaps, by scanning the footnotes themselves. The listing that follows is by contrast an extremely selective one. Unless otherwise stated, the place of publication is London.

For good statements of the views we have been discussing, a number of general works may be consulted, some of them extensively cited in our two essays. The most important are Ralf Dahrendorf, *Society and Democracy in Germany* (1968), and Barrington Moore Jr., *Social Origins of Dictatorship and Democracy* (1967), esp. chs. VII and VIII. Thorstein Veblen's idiosyncratic *Imperial Germany and the Industrial Revolution* (Ann Arbor, 1966, originally published in 1915) may still be read with profit, as on a more limited topic may Alexander Gerschenkron's *Bread and Democracy in Germany* (Berkeley, 1943), and Leonard Krieger's extraordinarily fertile *The German Idea of Freedom. History of a Political Tradition* (Chicago, 1957). For a general account which reflects many of the common conceptions of the German past, see John R. Gillis, 'Germany', in Raymond Grew (ed.), *Crises of Political Development in Europe and the United States* (Princeton, 1978), pp. 313–45. Other useful essays are those by Theodor Schieder, *The State and Society in Our Times* (1962), and Ernst Fraenkel, 'Historical Handicaps of German Parliamentarism', in Theodor Eschenburg (ed.), *The Road to Dictatorship. Germany 1918–1933* (1964), pp. 25–38.

Most of the key literature on Imperial Germany is unfortunately still in German, particularly the important works of Hans Rosenberg and Hans-Ulrich Wehler. However, the key works of Eckart Kehr (originally published in the late 1920s and early 1930s), which have exercised a considerable influence on recent historical studies of Imperial Germany, are now available in translation: *Battleship Building and Party Politics in Germany, 1894–1901* (Chicago, 1975), and *Economic Interest, Militarism, and Foreign Policy. Essays on German History* (Berkeley, 1977). James J. Sheehan (ed.), *Imperial Germany* (New York, 1976), is a valuable collection, which includes amongst others essays by Hans Rosenberg, Hans-Ulrich Wehler and Wolfgang J. Mommsen. Many of the established interpretations of nineteenth-century German economic and political history are expounded straight-forwardly in Martin Kitchen's *The Political Economy of Germany 1815–1914* (1978). The detailed literature on German liberalism may now be approached through James Sheehan's excellent synthesis,

German Liberalism in the Nineteenth Century (Chicago, 1978). Hans-
Ulrich Wehler's views are stated with particular clarity in 'Industrial
Growth and Early German Imperialism', in Roger Owen and Bob
Sutcliffe (eds.), *Studies in the Theory of Imperialism* (1972), pp.
71–92. Two helpful general accounts, which incorporate the findings
of recent research into the Imperial period, are Volker R. Berghahn's
Germany and the Approach of War in 1914 (1973), and *Modern
Germany. Society, Economy and Politics in the Twentieth Century*
(Cambridge, 1982).

The general context of historical writing on Germany during the
twentieth century and in the post-1945 period in particular may be
approached through two books by Georg Iggers, *The German Conception of History: The National Tradition of Historical Thought
from Herder to the Present* (Middletown, 1968), and *New Directions
in European Historiography* (Middletown, 1975, shortly to be published in a new edition). John Moses, *The Politics of Illusion* (1975),
which deals with the Fischer Controversy, is also useful. Though rather
selective in its treatment of more recent research, Pierre Ayçoberry,
*The Nazi Question. An Essay on the Interpretations of National
Socialism (1922-1975)* (New York, 1981), may also be consulted.

Our own previous work may be encountered in David Blackbourn,
Class, Religion and Local Politics in Wilhelmine Germany (1980), and
Geoff Eley, *Reshaping the German Right. Radical Nationalism and
Political Change after Bismarck* (1980), and in a collection of essays,
Richard J. Evans (ed.), *Society and Politics in Wilhelmine Germany*
(1978), to which we both contributed.

Index